Student-Centered Classroom Management

Student-Centered Classroom Management

BEATRICE S. FENNIMORE

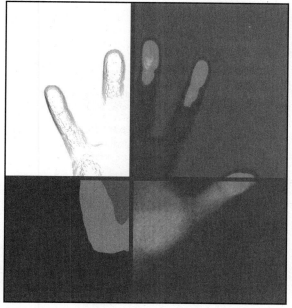

Delmar Publishers

I(T)P™

An International Thomson Publishing Company

Albany • Bonn • Boston • Cincinnati • Detroit • London •Madrid • Melbourne • Mexico City
New York • Pacific Grove • Paris • San Francisco • Singapore • Tokyo • Toronto • Washington

NOTICE TO THE READER

Cover Design: Katie Hayden

Delmar Staff

Publisher: Diane McOscar
Associate Editor: Erin O'Connor Traylor
Production Coordinator: Barbara A. Bullock
Editorial Assistant: Glenna Stanfield

COPYRIGHT©1995
By Delmar Publishers
a division of International Thomson Publishing Inc.

The ITP logo is a trademark under license.

Printed in the United States of America

For more information, contact:

Delmar Publishers
3 Columbia Circle, Box 15015
Albany, New York 12212-5015

International Thomson Publishing Europe
Berkshire House 168-173
High Holborn
London, WC1V 7AA
England

Thomas Nelson Australia
102 Dodds Street
South Melbourne, 3205
Victoria, Australia

Nelson Canada
1120 Birchmont Road
Scarborough, Ontario
Canada, M1K 5G4

International Thomson Editores
Campos Eliseos 385, Piso 7
Col Polanco
11560 Mexico D F Mexico

International Thomson Publishing GmbH
Konigswinterer Strasse 418
53227 Bonn
Germany

International Thomson Publishing Asia
221 Henderson Road
#05-10 Henderson Building
Singapore 0315

International Thomson Publishing—Japan
Hirakawacho Kyowa Building, 3F
2-2-1 Hirakawacho
Chiyoda-ku, Tokyo 102
Japan

1 2 3 4 5 6 7 8 9 10 XXX 02 01 00 99 98 97 96 95   12-8-99

Library of Congress Cataloging-in-Publication Data

Fennimore, Beatrice Schneller.
   Student-centered classroom management / Beatrice S. Fennimore.
      p.   cm.
   Includes bibliographical references and index.
   ISBN 0-8273-6692-2
      1. Student-centered classroom management—United States.   2. School discipline—United States.
3. Teaching—United States.   4. Teacher-student relationships—United States.   I. Title.
LB3013.F46   1995
371.1'024—dc20   95-42817
                                                                                         CIP

For my brother Jimmy with love

C O N T E N T S

P R E F A C E

Why write a book about classroom management when so much
has already been written on this topic? Some educational challenges
are so demanding and central to the mission of schools that they
must be approached and reapproached from a variety of perspectives. No challenge is greater to American teachers than that of
student behavior. Teachers cannot face that challenge simply by
learning general management skills or techniques. The problem of
discipline in schools is complex because it reflects the quality of
institutional relationships. The relationships between teachers and
children today are strained by social and economic changes that
have made all their lives more difficult. Teachers who seek to
"manage" and "discipline" will need to do so with patience, kindness, and genuine caring about their students and the world in
which they live.

Many students (whether they live in rural, suburban, or urban
areas) come to school with problems serious enough to undermine
their chances for educational success. These problems may be
related to poverty, unemployment, crime, family disruption, addiction, abuse, or a host of other factors. Teachers should expect to
experience some ramifications of these problems in their classrooms
and should also strive to develop the insight and compassion necessary to help children rise above them. Dedicated educators must
embrace the difficult realities of children and yet retain their determination to teach effectively.

This text is designed to balance acknowledgment of current
school realities with idealistic goals for the finest classroom practice
possible. Every school, no matter its quality or the resources available,
exists to promote the growth of the children it serves. Some schools

in America do have excellent resources and do provide many fine opportunities for the students who attend them. Teachers in those schools still face behavior and management challenges and still need to balance the needs of adults and institutions with the central focus on children. Other schools in America are overcrowded and overburdened. Teachers in those schools are stressed, and children may be overmanaged or overdisciplined simply to compensate for institutional inadequacy. Students may have to wait in long lines for bathrooms or buses, crowd into small lunchrooms, or sit quietly in classrooms that lack basic resources and learning materials. Schools characterized by stress and frustration are at risk for negative climates that further damage the educational opportunities of children.

Knowing the many challenges ahead, teachers can do a great deal to prepare intellectually and emotionally for the management of student-centered classrooms. This text is designed to help readers develop management skills as well as concepts and perspectives that will help them link management and discipline to relevant teaching and learning in classrooms. The focus on student-centered classroom management in this book is structured around three basic premises:

- Schools exist for children, and therefore the needs and interests of the students should be the central focus of all educational discourse about classroom management and discipline.

- Student-centered classroom management cannot exist without developmentally appropriate practice, which provides intrinsic motivation for relevant learning activities.

- Student-centered classroom management cannot exist without respect for human diversity and a multicultural commitment to equal educational opportunities for all children.

It is the focus on student centeredness, developmentally appropriate practice, multicultural education, and equity that may distinguish this book from some others on classroom management. Readers are continually encouraged to focus on the curriculum (and the activities and projects it generates) as the major component of classroom management. Students whose assigned tasks reflect their developmental needs and interests have greater opportunities to develop the intrinsic motivation that supports real and lasting self-discipline. Developmentally appropriate tasks and activities also help students to develop the habit of making appropriate choices in school and ultimately in life. Curriculum centered on the real lives of children can reflect multicultural respect for all the diversities found in modern American classrooms. Teachers with a personal commitment to multiculturalism can continually reflect on ways in which bias, or social and educational inequity, could affect their relationships with their students.

The organization of the chapters reflects my intention to build a comprehensive framework for professional thinking about the behavior of students. Chapter 1 introduces the contextual basis of issues in management and discipline. At the outset the reader is encouraged to perceive the relationship between student behavior and the presence or absence of sensitivity and relevance of instructional design. Chapter 2 explores important perspectives on the current challenges in the lives of American children. Emphasis is placed on the relationship of serious discipline problems in American schools to risks that can be created by negative institutional responses to many forms of student diversity. The reader is encouraged to build and maintain an approach to children that embodies multicultural respect, high expectation, and accountability for equitable classroom experiences. In Chapter 3, perspectives on schools, teachers, and curriculum place student-centered management in the context of schools' responsibility to children and current trends in school practice and reform.

The text shifts in Chapter 4 to examine the relationship between theories of development and motivation to appropriate behavioral expectations in classrooms. Teachers, who are ultimately responsible for shaping the behavior of children, need a foundation of theoretical information upon which to base their professional assumptions and decisions. Although almost all teacher preparation programs require some study of human development, teachers do not always have the opportunity to make specific connections between what they believe about the ways in which children develop and how they should interpret the actions of children in real classrooms. Chapter 5 moves the reader from reflection on theory to discussion of the philosophy of developmentally appropriate practice. Teachers who provide learning opportunities that allow children to develop personal competence and to acquire knowledge and invest it with meaning have a far greater opportunity to promote positive behavioral skills in students.

In Chapter 6 the text shifts to a closer look at management and discipline as separate educational concerns. The reader has the opportunity to compare the concepts of management and discipline and to conceptualize a total framework for analyzing and responding to behavioral challenges in the classroom. Chapter 7 provides general guidelines for management and describes five different models constructed to help teachers maintain positive discipline in the classroom. Teachers are encouraged to teach behavioral skills on a continual basis and to observe and analyze misbehaviors in the context of classroom life. The benefits and drawbacks of both punishment and reward are examined; teachers are urged to continue to focus on their design of curriculum and their positive relationships with their students as the most powerful forces in student-centered classroom management.

Finally, Chapter 8 encourages the reader to develop a vision of empowerment in education. Educators enter their field not only to participate in it but to change and improve it. Empowerment of administrators, families, schools, teachers, and students is described as a creative force in educational environments. Children who sense the determination of the adults around them to care about them and help them to solve problems can become more hopeful and thus better able to cope with the demands of school and society.

When they enter the actual classroom, all students of education find that at least some theoretical ideas they have studied in college are difficult to implement. This is often the case when idealistic theories of "child-centered" or "student-centered" education have been presented without realistic suggestions for practical application. It is far easier to be sensitive to the needs of children in theory than it is in practice. The college student who thinks, "Of course I would never do anything to discourage or hurt a child" may have little idea of what it is like to be confronted by a child who is disruptive, rude, or difficult to manage. Likewise, college students who embrace theories of multiculturalism may later be shocked and upset by children who are neglected, abused, poor, or living in circumstances very different from those with which they are familiar. Many college students are genuinely unaware of their ingrained biases toward children of diverse race, culture, or socioeconomic status—biases that will only emerge in the actual context of the less-than-perfect classroom. Future teachers may also be unprepared for the challenge of holding on to their ideals in schools where colleagues are biased, burnt out, or downright negative about the children, their families, and their communities. All future teachers are going to need a strong student-centered philosophy to support their sense of accountability as professional educators.

This text is designed to provide opportunities for applying theoretical concepts to real situations. The purpose of this design is twofold: to provide the reader with practice in applying theoretical information to practical situations, and to help develop a sense of confidence in readers' ability to relate the ideal in practice to less-than-perfect (or downright troublesome) classroom situations. Those preparing for teaching careers may be tempted to think that they can avoid problems with management and discipline by staying away from certain school placements or positions (such as those in disadvantaged rural or urban schools). Such thoughts are unrealistic and interfere with an ethic of commitment to all children. Furthermore, problems affecting children and families in America are so pervasive that no teacher can avoid them. America has an urgent need for excellent teachers who have the courage to embrace the realities of children and strive for the ideal in their schools. This book encourages the development of confidence and commitment in the reader in several ways:

1. Exhibits throughout the book provide brief descriptions of realistic situations in which hypothetical teachers try to apply theory to practice.

2. Questions to Consider are dispersed throughout the text to encourage readers to stop and think about ways in which the information being discussed relates to their lives and experiences or how it might apply to specific challenging situations.

3. Activity and Discussion ideas are dispersed in each chapter to describe realistic situations and to allow for individual thought and small group discussion. These are provided to give readers the opportunity to reflect on diverse personal interpretations of information and situations and to better choose and express opinions on best educational practice.

4. Make a Professional Decision activities are included in each chapter to encourage readers to take a more comprehensive position on an issue or problem using information from that chapter. These are included to help readers become better prepared to make and defend the kind of independent decisions so often required of classroom teachers.

5. Try These Ideas are included in Chapter 8 to provide some realistic and empowering ideas for the everyday life of schools and classrooms. Readers are encouraged to add their own ideas throughout their teaching careers.

Management of schools must be firmly centered on the best interests of the students. This is a difficult challenge in a nation in which so many interests of children are not well met by society at large. Yet educators must embrace accountability for having a positive influence on students. Teachers who provide developmentally appropriate learning experiences, and who develop caring and nurturing relationships with their students, do much more than manage their students well. They enable their students to grow from competent children into adults able and willing to make a strong contribution to our democratic society. This is a goal that should be cherished by all who teach today.

A C K N O W L E D G M E N T S

I extend sincere thanks to all the people who helped and supported me as I wrote this book. I am grateful to Delmar Publishers for expressing interest in a publication of this nature and for encouraging me to write it. Sincere thanks to Erin O'Connor and all at Delmar whose talent and support made the completion of this work possible. I am most appreciative of the excellent editorial support I received from Barbara Bullock at Delmar and Karen Thomas at Editorial Services of New England, Inc. The insightful comments and suggestions I received from my reviewers were of great assistance as I prepared the final version of this book.

The beliefs and ideas in this book developed in great part through my experiences in teaching a variety of graduate and undergraduate courses and supervising student teachers at Indiana University of Pennsylvania (IUP). Through my work with our students in rural, urban, and suburban public schools, I have gained invaluable insights into the vast dimensions of what it means to try to teach and learn in institutional settings. I am grateful to my students at IUP for teaching me so much and only hope I have returned the favor as they set out for the classrooms of America. Many ideas in this book also developed through enjoyable collaboration with colleagues at IUP as we sought to create supervisory excellence and ethics that are multicultural in practice.

Thanks also to my faithful mentor Leslie R. Williams at Teachers College, Columbia University, who has continued to support my work in so many meaningful ways. Her friendship over they years, and her companionship as I taught summer courses at Teachers College, have sustained my efforts to grow as a teacher and scholar. Thanks also to my students at Teachers College, whose lively discussions in class helped me to test and develop many ideas in this book. I have appreciated the company of many colleagues at Teachers College, particularly the generous friendship and professional support of A. Lin Goodwin.

This book spanned an important transition in my personal life, and I wrote it with better insights into some of the struggles faced by families and children in America. I have enjoyed the middle school, high school, and college-aged people in my life with a new appreciation for their courage in tackling the complicated world in which they live. Some of these wonderful young people are Dan Nocera, Rachel Cherry (faithful caretakers of our menagerie of pets), Dan Eger, Alex Robinson, Robbie Fein, Jenny Fein, and the many members of our early morning carpools to Reizenstein Middle School and Allderdice High School.

My daughter Maryann has been delightful company with her brilliant art, shining drama, constant enthusiasm for academic endeavor, and special gift for listening to others. My daughter Sharon has continued to be an adventuresome and articulate enthusiast for life and learning. She has made us proud of her courageous individuality and strong intelligence as she approached her undergraduate career at the University of Pennsylvania, which has included a long period of study in China. Marvin Fein listened and responded to most ideas in this book (more than once), mostly as we ran together in the early morning hours on Beechwood Boulevard. His loyal support and genuine enthusiasm for my work are lovingly appreciated.

I dedicate this book to my brother James David Schneller and in his honor to the children all over America who await the determined love and advocacy of committed adults who really and truly care about them.

The author and Delmar Publishers would like to extend their thanks to those who provided detailed reviews of the manuscript. The contributions and suggestions of the following individuals are greatly appreciated.

Suzanne E. Cobb, Ed.D.
West Georgia College
Carrollton, GA

Jan L. Hintz, Ph.D.
St. Cloud State University
St. Cloud, MN

Julia Saunders, Emerita
Johnson C. Smith University
Charlotte, NC

Melba Spooner, Ed.D.
University of North Carolina
Charlotte, NC

Dr. Theresa S. Stewart
Sangamon State University
Springfield, IL

M. Kay Stickle, Ph.D.
Ball State University
Muncie, IL

Chapter

1 | INTRODUCTION

Your decision to become a teacher will have an important influence on the lives of many children. The need for talented, dedicated, and enthusiastic teachers in American elementary schools has never been greater. However, great demands are going to be placed on all those who choose to teach. You probably have some concern about the many things you read and hear about American children and discipline problems in the classroom. It is important for you to learn to use appropriate techniques in student-centered classroom management. Your attitude toward discipline, and your philosophy of classroom management, will affect your entire career as a teacher. What is classroom management? What is behavior? What is misbehavior? What can a teacher do to establish control in a meaningful learning environment with as many as thirty-five or more young children in a single classroom? To create a context within which to answer these important questions and many others, let us first consider a hypothetical situation:

> You are a brand new elementary school teacher. It is September, and your principal has arranged for the entire faculty to take part in a folk-dancing workshop on a school in-service day. You are a little nervous because you have never been good at dancing and can still recall several embarrassing moments at social events in high school and college.
>
> At the beginning of the workshop the stern and unsmiling workshop coordinator leads the group in an exercise designed to assess basic dance ability. She looks right at you, shakes her head, and says in front of everyone, "You are going to have some real problems with these dances. Just try to pay attention and do your best." You are beginning to feel more self-conscious and a little upset. Then, although you are trying to concentrate, you make several directional

errors as the group practices the first steps. To relieve your anxiety you lean over to joke and laugh for a moment with the teacher next to you. Suddenly, you hear the workshop leader say, "Maybe if some people would pay attention, they wouldn't make so many mistakes."

You grow angry and distracted and begin to lose interest in trying to learn the steps. You whisper to the teacher next to you that you should have called in sick and throw an angry look at the workshop leader, who is watching you with annoyance on her face. She stops the music, looks at you, and says, "Anyone who does not want to learn this dance can just leave right now so those of us who are willing to work hard can do so." To your own surprise you pick up your coat and march from the room.

Once in the hallway, you burst into tears. Embarrassed and hurt, you worry about what your colleagues and principal will think of you. What began as an educational opportunity has ended as a threatening and potentially damaging event. You don't know what to do next.

Although you are unlikely to find yourself in such a situation as a professional educator, American elementary schoolchildren do find themselves in such situations every day. Children may come to school with a real interest in learning but then somehow become entangled in a web of failure that leads to negative emotions and inappropriate behaviors that cause problems for them, their teachers, their families, and their schools. These problems occur for many reasons. Sometimes the children are to blame, sometimes their families or communities are deficient or uncaring, and other times teachers or schools are at fault. But blaming people, whomever they might be, is seldom conducive to a positive learning environment. Far more productive is analyzing problems to understand not only what went wrong but what can be changed and improved so children can learn in a well-managed classroom environment.

This book places classroom management and discipline in the context of change and human growth. The underlying assumption is that educators are responsible for designing and managing learning environments that allow diverse learners to pay attention, to try even though the work may be difficult, to make errors and experience the emotions that come with failure, to try again, and to develop the confidence and competencies that will serve them well throughout their lives.

Let us return for a moment to the hypothetical story of the folk-dance workshop:

> You have been asked to explain to the principal why you left the room before the in-service workshop ended. What will you say? Most likely, you try to convince your principal that you were interested in the session and really did want to learn the dance but that you were intimidated by the assessment and had some initial difficulty in learning the steps. Instead of receiving encouragement and the opportunity to learn at your own pace, you felt singled out and embarrassed. You thought the workshop leader did not like you. Maybe you should not have laughed or whispered or walked out of the room, but you felt so confused and hurt that you really were not thinking clearly. You apologize, promise that it will not happen again, and say you will ask your colleagues to teach you the dances you missed. With any luck your principal is sensitive and understanding and forgets about the whole incident.

But what if you were a child who had behaved in the same way in a classroom? What if the principal had admonished you, called your mother or father at work to tell them that you were difficult and uncooperative, and suspended you for a day for insubordination? What if you had already been in trouble several times that week, or did not understand English well, or had serious problems at home that were distracting you? Do you think that your principal's reaction would have increased your ability and willingness to behave well in school? Or would it have increased your hurt, your anger, and your tendency to lose control of your emotions in classroom situations in which you feel like a failure?

ACTIVITY AND DISCUSSION

1. Can you recall any childhood experiences that embarrassed or confused you like the teacher was during the folk-dancing workshop? How did those experiences mirror this situation?

2. If the workshop leader asked for your advice about how to avoid confrontations or difficulties in the future, what specific suggestions would you give?

3. Discuss your ideas in a small group.

If you analyze what happened during the folk-dancing workshop, you will see that dancing had little to do with the negativity of that learning experience. It should have been possible for you to master the steps and even enjoy the session. Instead, attitudes and the quality of human interaction made that impossible for you. And the attitudes and quality of human interactions were further bound by the way in which the instruction was designed. The whole group was expected to learn in the same way at the same time, with little leeway for individual feelings, social interaction, learning styles, group dynamics, or individual pace in learning the dance. It would hardly be fair to label you a behavior problem or dismiss you as a "remedial dancer." Far more professional, logical, and fair would be to improve the method of instruction and to focus on attitudes and interactions that help participants feel comfortable and learn successfully.

How would you feel if you had to attend a second folk-dance workshop with your colleagues? You might be apprehensive, but you would be likely to find it easier to approach the challenge a second time because of your principal's willingness to listen, understand, and forgive what might have been viewed as insubordinate or professionally unacceptable behavior. All learners of every age need a real chance to thrive in educational settings that are well designed, allow for human feelings and human differences, forgive errors, and allow for continual opportunities to grow, develop, and experience success.

Human behavior never occurs in a vacuum. Unspoken and perhaps subconscious motivations underlie what people believe about each other, what they feel toward each other, and how they treat each other. This text considers classroom management and student discipline within the context of attitudes, feelings, human interactions, and instructional design in the classroom. You as a teacher will be continually encouraged to analyze situations and to create solutions to classroom problems. Structure and control are important but not for "making children behave." Rather, structure and control are an integral part of professional accountability in creating developmentally appropriate, interesting, and equitable classroom environments.

Teachers often must accommodate children whose earlier experiences of failure have made them anxious or angry, much like the teacher in the workshop. These children—and they are many throughout America—have a special need for student-centered environments that reinforce self-control, self-esteem, and willingness to keep trying to reach success. All children, regardless of background or experience, must have a comfortable and rewarding classroom environment in order to thrive. Teachers' understanding of what is happening to children in society today is a critical first step in understanding behavior, management, and discipline. Chapter 2 focuses on building a perspective on the lives of American children that will be helpful in developing student-centered classroom management.

2 PERSPECTIVES ON THE LIVES OF AMERICAN CHILDREN

Teachers must develop a perspective on the lives of American children in order to form a realistic and humane philosophy of classroom management and discipline. This chapter discusses the following topics:

- Discipline
- Risks in the lives of American children
- Multiculturalism and teachers' expectations
- Multicultural approaches to "children at risk"
- Deficit terminology and school accountability
- Equality and democracy in the classroom

DISCIPLINE

Teachers must know how to manage classrooms in order to promote positive and productive student behavior. However, teachers encounter some of their most difficult and frustrating challenges in the areas of classroom management and discipline. Beginning teachers are often amazed at how much time they spend on management-based activities and at how challenging classroom discipline actually can be. They frequently find that school administrators value management and discipline over all other professional competencies in teachers (Bellon, Bellon, and Blank 1992). For many, if not most, teachers confronting a behavior problem—anything from simple rule violations to disrespect, cheating, or open hostility—is a daily occurrence (Borich 1992). The illusion that "caring about children" is enough to create an orderly and productive classroom fades quickly. Unfortunately, undergraduate studies in education may fail to sufficiently prepare teachers for the realities of behavioral challenges in the classroom (Wong and Wong 1991).

ACTIVITY AND DISCUSSION

The introduction to this chapter gives a serious warning about behavior problems facing teachers in classrooms. As you continue to read this book, you should be forming a teaching philosophy that incorporates the reality that managing the behavior of your students will test you as a teacher. Discuss in a group your thoughts on the following points of view:

1. You need to 'crack down' on students today. They will not behave unless you convince them that they have to.

2. You need to find a job in a community that respects education and expects children to behave themselves. Unless you work in a 'good school,' you will spend your whole career dealing with serious behavior problems.

3. You need to build positive rapport with the children, and let them know you respect their feelings. Once they know they will be treated kindly, and that they can be successful at at least some tasks in your room, they will relax and start to cooperate with you.

Since 1969 a Phi Delta Kappa Society survey performed by the Gallup Organization has usually indicated that discipline is the foremost concern of the American public in regard to the public school system. Teachers experience stress, often severe, because of discipline problems encountered in their schools and classrooms (Charles 1992). More serious is that violence in and around schools has emerged as a persistent problem. Every day, ten Americans younger than 19 are killed in gun accidents, commit suicide, or are homicide victims. One in 7 children is affected by bullying, 1 in 12 stays home from school out of fear of being hurt, and 1 in 11 is a crime victim at school; 15 percent of schoolchildren report gangs in their schools. In addition, 3 million thefts and violent crimes occur on or near schools every year. Twenty percent of all public school teachers report verbal abuse, 8 percent report physical threats, and 2 percent report physical attacks (Association for Childhood Education International Exchange 1993–1994).

Concerns about discipline become even more serious when an estimated 40 percent of new teachers leave the profession in the first three to seven years of their service as educators (Charles 1992; Wong and Wong 1991).

Discipline problems are not confined to behavioral difficulties with individuals or groups of children. Equally elusive is developing children's curiosity and enthusiasm for learning (Bellon, Bellon, and Blank 1992). New teachers are often hired to take charge of a group of children who may be disinterested, apathetic, or unruly and told to influence them to become well-behaved, interested, and productive learners (Wong and Wong 1991). Teachers may be required to attempt this difficult feat in schools with limited funds, a shortage of materials, and some or many students who are experiencing social problems that range from poverty to serious family disruption to violence in their homes or communities (Kozol 1991). Teachers may encounter problems they never studied, children whose difficulties seem overwhelming, or colleagues whose enthusiasm has begun to fade. Even the most dedicated teachers must summon a great deal of energy and determination to establish student-centered classroom management that promotes real learning as well as positive attitudes and self-esteem.

QUESTIONS TO CONSIDER

1. What connections would you make between the existence of many serious discipline problems in schools and students who are apathetic and unenthusiastic about learning? As a future teacher, how do you think you should plan to face similar problems?

2. Why do you think that 40 percent of educators leave the profession in the first three to seven years of teaching? How do you think you will handle the initial frustrations and disappointments of teaching? Why do you believe you will stay committed to teaching despite the problems you will face?

Teachers do experience negative thoughts and emotions when they encounter serious discipline problems. Teaching is difficult under any circumstances, but students' behavioral difficulties greatly increase the demands on teachers. How should teachers frame their responses to the management and discipline problems they encounter? First and foremost, they must remember throughout their careers that they have opted to enter a helping and caring profession designed to provide a critical public service that enhances the quality of human lives (Wong and Wong, 1991). Even as children test teachers' patience—sometimes to the point that teachers question their own competencies within their chosen profession—children's need for self-esteem and positive guidance has never been greater. Many children across America are growing up in environments far more stressful than those experienced by their parents and teachers. Communities and homes may not be safe places in which children can develop a feeling of security. Indeed, among many other serious problems, some children are homeless or living in foster homes (Bredekamp 1994). Stressed and troubled children may be defensive, apathetic, hopeless, or anxious. They may seem inattentive or unable to pursue an activity. They may have many failure-avoiding behaviors as a result of negative or unproductive school experiences (Bellon, Bellon, and Blank 1992). These children need strong and determined teachers who are not only their mentors but also their advocates in the schools they attend.

It is a difficult time to be a child and a challenging time to be a teacher. A sense of journey and adventure will serve teachers well as they set about the serious and demanding business of education. On the one hand, a great deal remains to be learned about successful promotion of positive behavior through effective management of classrooms. On the other hand, many established skills and techniques, particularly those associated with the approach of developmentally appropriate education, can assist teachers in creating productive classrooms. One thing is certain—mastery of classroom management and student discipline, or the lack thereof, will determine the quality of life for teachers and students in every classroom.

PROFESSIONAL DECISION

Rules and Routines

You are going to begin a new teaching position in two weeks and are setting up your classroom. Many teachers are working in other classrooms, and you become aware of different activities taking place. Some of these are

- A teacher who is creating a learning center in her classroom that will include several live pets

- A teacher who is arranging her classroom library
- A teacher who is making a chart of class rules and consequences for infractions
- A teacher who is reviewing the math and reading programs for the year to formulate a series of individual projects for the students
- A teacher who is setting up his grade book with a series of pages of check lists to help him observe and monitor behavior
- A teacher who is moving desks into small groups and planning activities
- Two teachers who are talking about how they will establish rules and routines in their classrooms

Which of these activities do you think are most closely related to your priorities as a new teacher? What do you think your most important focus should be as you plan your classroom? What would you add to this list as an activity that you would most likely be doing? Discuss your ideas with a partner.

RISKS IN THE LIVES OF AMERICAN CHILDREN

Why is concern about the behavior and management of children in school so widespread? Why is violence emerging as a school problem? Why do many children pose behavioral challenges to their teachers? One important reason is that many children are not receiving the benefits of a comfortable and well-protected life in their homes and communities. As a teacher, you must develop a philosophy of discipline that integrates that reality.

Almost all Americans have become familiar with the expression "child at risk." This terminology arose from the growing awareness that many children in the United States are not experiencing optimal social and economic conditions. When are children at risk? Most important, children are at risk when they have problems serious enough to threaten their potential to become competent, healthy, and productive adults. Who are these children? They are children of all ages who come from poor families. They are racially diverse and immigrant children who often face discrimination. They are girls and young women who do not receive the educational opportunities often offered to males. And they are children from diverse backgrounds whose special needs are underserved or categorized in ways that expose them to inadequate educational opportunities (National Coalition of Advocates for Students 1988). A child at risk is any child who faces barriers to becoming all he or she can be in school or society.

The at-risk label, like all labels with the power to affect the lives of children, must never be applied casually. It was originally designed to connote a future orientation, referring to children who *might* fail in school, drop out of school, or fall short of becoming productive adults. Although the risk label was intended to mean that students *could* be susceptible to adverse environmental conditions in community, home, or school, it appears now to be routinely applied to students who have certain characteristics but who may or may not be succumbing to adverse conditions. A particular concern is that socioeconomic, racial, or cultural characteristics might now be routinely used to designate children as at risk without justification, thus continuing harmful stereotypes (Natriello, McDill, and Pallas 1990). Nieto (1992) points out that at risk may have become a code phrase for children of color or children who are economically disadvantaged, when in fact estimates indicate that a significant number of *all* American children fall into risk categories.

QUESTIONS TO CONSIDER

1. When you have heard the term *at risk* applied to children in the past, how have you interpreted it?

2. How would you describe an elementary school student who is at risk?

It is important that teachers understand *why* so many children are suffering from risks to their well-being in our society. Child and family experts around the United States are voicing concern that the current generation of children is the first to be demonstrably less well off than their parents. For example, the Council of Families in America, a group of seventeen scholars and family experts who represent diverse points of view, recently reported that one-fifth of the nation's children are poor, as are one-quarter of its preschoolers and one-half of its African American children (Steinfels 1992). One in 4 American children is now born to an unmarried mother. Reports of child abuse and neglect have increased by 40 percent since 1985. Juvenile crime has more than doubled. Rates of teenage death by homicide and suicide have almost tripled (Steinfels 1992). Many of the risks faced by children are economic. The gap between rich and poor in the United States has reached its widest point in forty years (Rosewater 1989). Some see this gap as threatening national unity and say it is characterized by deepening racial and social class schisms throughout America (Banks 1994).

Sweeping changes in the demographics of American society have given a greater urgency to the problem of the many risks to children. Fewer children are being born in the United States. Children comprised 36 percent of the population in 1960 and only 26 percent of the population in 1989 (Rosewater 1989). Although the overall number of American children has decreased, the number of children traditionally described as disadvantaged has increased, and some researchers anticipate a 37 percent increase in the number of children living in poverty in America by the turn of the century (Natriello, McDill, and Pallas 1990). By the year 2020 they believe, nearly one-half of all American students will be children of color— children who are more likely to be experiencing poverty and discrimination in their lives (Banks 1994). More than half of the nation's largest urban centers, for example, now have school populations that are predominantly African American or Hispanic American and are likely to be poor and from single-parent homes (Research and Policy Committee 1991).

Family lifestyles are a concern to many educators. Parents play an important role in the scholastic success of their children, but families of young children in America are facing enormous social and economic struggles that absorb their time and energy (Children's Defense Fund 1992). The single-parent home, once considered unusual, is now commonplace. Almost half of all marriages end in divorce, and the rate of marriage has declined across socioeconomic lines. In 1955, 60 percent of American households had a working father, a homemaker mother, and two or more schoolchildren. Those statistics now apply to fewer than 10 percent of American families. More than 60 percent of married women with children younger than six are now in the labor force (Children's Defense Fund, 1995). Child care of good quality and reasonable price is not available to many families. Maintaining jobs and family life can be so demanding that many parents are too distracted or even overwhelmed to give time to the school concerns of their children (National Commission on Children 1991).

The risks to children that permeate American society are going to have serious repercussions. The U.S. work force, for example, now faces major problems. As we enter the twenty-first century, many older workers will be retiring with far fewer younger workers to replace them. In the 1950s seventeen workers supported every retiree. The ratio is today 3 to 1. Added to the demographic imperative is the increasing concern of American executives that the available work force has not been well prepared. In fact, businesses have spent a great deal of money to educate high school graduates in basic work skills and are urgently telling public schools that they need a more competent work force (Banks 1994). However, concerns about children at risk go well beyond any problems anticipated by business. The very future of America depends on generations of citizens competent enough to support our democratic government and to maintain families strong enough to sustain social structures. On the level of humane concern the risks discussed in this section involve personal sufferings for a great many children. All professionals concerned with children must view these difficult childhood struggles with sensitivity and concern. Educators and all who work with children can be advocates for social improvements that alleviate many of the risks that unfortunately undermine the school performance of so many children (Fennimore 1989). As the Research and Policy Committee of the Committee for Academic Development states,

> *If we can ensure that all children are born healthy and develop the skills and knowledge they need to be productive, self-supporting adults, whatever is spent on their development and education will be returned many times over in higher productivity, incomes, taxes and in lower costs for welfare, health care, crime, and myriad other economic and social problems.* (1991: 15)

In summary, two important situations have emerged simultaneously. At a time when America needs every child to grow up to be a productive citizen and worker, all too many children are experiencing social and economic disadvantages. Educational opportunities are at a make-it-or-break-it point in the struggle to help all children overcome barriers to the development of basic school skills and life competencies. Often, a direct link between social and economic disadvantages and "educational disadvantages" interrupts the learning process. American children who do not fare well outside of school are likely to experience problems inside school as well. Research has identified five indicators of educational disadvantage (factors that may negatively influence educational outcomes for children): race and ethnicity, poverty, single-parent families, poorly educated mothers, and limited English proficiency. Note that the five indicators of educational disadvantage are also common indicators in research on lowered teacher expectations for student success (Fennimore 1989). Schools are at risk for treating students differently and expecting less from them just because they do have risk factors in their lives. Therefore, when considering effects of risks and discrimination on the lives of children, teachers must always examine the role of the institution as well as the roles of families and society. A conservative estimate is that at least 40 percent of all American children younger than eighteen are at risk for school failure because of one or more of these factors (see Exhibit 2-1). When so many children clearly need strong support to do well in school, all teachers must be prepared work with understanding and optimism within the existing constraints in the lives of children. Educational opportunities must be sustained with multicultural skills and attitudes, high teacher expectations, respect for the resilience of children, and commitment to equity.

EXHIBIT 2-1   **Examples of Risks in the Lives of Children**

Social and Economic Risks

Sheila was born to an unmarried teenage mother. Her father was killed a few years later in a car accident. Sheila and her mother live in a community that has a great deal of drug use and a high homicide rate.

John lives in a two-parent family in a rural community with a high unemployment rate because the factories have closed. His family has no health insurance. His father is an alcoholic, and his mother has worked six or seven days a week as a housekeeper since his birth.

Educational Risks

Sheila did not pass the kindergarten admissions test and was placed in a "transitional" program. Most teachers and administrators refer to the children in the program as at risk, and almost all the children in the "transitional kindergarten" are automatically placed in the remedial first grade.

John takes an hour bus ride to a small rural school that cannot afford to hire support staff such as psychologists or guidance counselors. Because he rubs his eyes constantly during reading and refuses to try to read aloud, he has been placed in the "slow" reading group. John mainly looks around the room and daydreams during reading activities of any kind.

ACTIVITY AND DISCUSSION

You are reading about social, economic, and educational risks that are undoubtedly going to affect some or many children you teach during your career.

1. List the problems and risks in our society that you think are most serious in terms of the health, education, and general welfare of children.

2. List the ways in which you can become more prepared to teach these children with optimism and sensitivity (for example, courses you might take, volunteer experiences that might be instructive, or books you might read).

MULTICULTURALISM AND TEACHERS' EXPECTATION

Almost every teacher will be responsible for the instruction of at least some children whose lives are disadvantaged by poverty, violence, or other serious difficulties in their families and communities. These children are often described as at risk, because we know that their energies and intellects can be distracted by the problems they face. While educators do need to be realistic about problems and risks in children's lives, they must not lose sight of the abilities of all children to respond in a positive way to meaningful and equitable opportunities in school.

Placing the Risks in Perspective

Some educators question the use of the at-risk label for children for several reasons. Although recognizing and being sensitive to the problems faced by American children are important, all too often identifying these problems leads to self-fulfilling prophesies of school failure (Natriello, McDill, and Pallas 1990). Truly, many children who are educationally disadvantaged do not succeed in school, but it is important not to anticipate failure. Many children who do have risks in their lives also have strengths and resources that make it more than possible for them to do well in school and in life (see Exhibit 2-2). Also, appropriate and optimistic school efforts can do a great deal to reduce the risks.

EXHIBIT 2-2

Finding Promise in Children at Risk

Think about Sheila and John, the two children described in Exhibit 2-1. If you were their teacher, how might you think about the positive as well as the negative aspects of their lives and abilities?

Sheila's Risks

Sheila's mother did not graduate from high school and has been on public assistance since Sheila was born ten years ago. They live in publicly funded housing and worry a great deal about violence because of the drug activity that permeates their community. Sheila has not had the experiences and opportunities that would have helped her score higher on her kindergarten assessment, and she already is aware of the fact that her class is "different." In fact, she has told her mother that most children in her class come from the "projects," just as she does.

Sheila's Promise

Sheila has a close relationship with her paternal grandmother, who is forty-five and willing to spend a great deal of time with her. If contacted by the school, she would be quite willing to take Sheila to the library once a week and to read to her more frequently. Sheila's mother is musically talented and has taught her daughter the words to many religious and cultural songs. Sheila is talkative and good at engaging adults in conversation. She responds well to verbal encouragement and is willing to work hard at any task if she gets frequent feedback and reinforcement from adults. Her behavior at school is excellent.

John's Risks

John experiences a great deal of social isolation in his rural community. His father drinks heavily at night, and his mother is at work six or seven days a week from 5:00 A.M. until 8:00 P.M. Because his parents do not have health insurance or a car, John rarely gets medical attention. No one has noticed that his eyesight is poor and that he needs glasses. John already knows that he is disappointing to his teacher and would rather avoid reading than cause any trouble or have negative experiences at school.

John's Promise

John's mother completed two years of college before her marriage and is thinking of returning in the future. She is a housekeeper for two college professors who are concerned about her and John and who might be able to find students willing to tutor John a few days a week. John's father, although not in control of his alcohol problem in the evening, is attentive and kind to him during the day. If the teacher contacts the school administrative office, John may be eligible for free vision testing. John loves animals and shows great responsibility and perseverance at home by caring for a horse, two dogs, chickens, and a cat every day. John enjoys working with his hands and is cooperative with other children.

It is neither fair nor appropriate to focus the at-risk label on students characteristics and deficits. After all, many policies and institutions in America are implicated in the problems of child poverty, family instability, and class or racial discrimination. The inadequacy of society, more than innate qualities of the child, has often created the risks in the first place (Natriello, McDill, and Pallas 1990). When an estimated 40 percent of children are at risk, negative labels and lower school expectations have the worrisome potential to reduce opportunities for a significant number of American students. For teachers to routinely apply the at-risk label to children, no matter how serious their disadvantages may be, is simply not productive.

How then can educators view in a positive and productive way the current national situation facing children? Shirley Brice Heath and Leslie Mangiola, in their book *Children of Promise: Literate Activity in Linguistically and Culturally Diverse Classrooms* (1991), make the point that children at risk, despite the labeling, are like all other students—children of promise. If all children are viewed as promising, the habit of recognizing the risks in their lives can be helpful rather than harmful. Instead of anticipating problems or failure, knowledge of the risks can be used to alter institutions that serve children so that educators can intervene more realistically and effectively. In addition, *all* children are likely to benefit from institutional changes that result in greater respect for individual lifestyles, difficulties, and challenges. (Natriello, McDill, and Pallas 1990). It is the function of schools to envision for children freedom from the past and change for the better (Putnam and Burke 1992). Teachers who try to fulfill this function may find it easier to design classroom management and discipline programs that truly build confidence and competence in all their students.

PROFESSIONAL DECISION | *Children at Risk*

You are seeking a new position as a public elementary school teacher. A nearby urban public school district has an opening, but many of your friends have discouraged you from applying for it. They cite the problems of poverty and family disruption faced by the students and seem to assume that you will not be able to teach effectively in that climate. You go to the interview and are asked the following question:

Many of our students receive public assistance and live in projects. Most of them are considered at risk. What difficulties do you anticipate with their behavior?

Think about the following answers:

1. "I do not plan to base my behavioral expectations on the socioeconomic status of my students. Rather, I plan to implement the basic strategies for class management I learned during my teacher education program."

2. "I will observe my students to see if they are experiencing stress in their lives. I may have to be sensitive to their individual needs in the ways in which I implement a discipline program in my classroom."

3. "I will make it clear to my students from the first day of school that they are expected to behave, and I will be consistent in indicating that misbehavior of any kind will not be tolerated and will have negative consequences."

What assumptions about children at risk are implied in each answer? If you were to create your own answer to the question, what would it be? Write it down, and exchange it with a peer for comparison and discussion.

MULTICULTURAL APPROACHES TO "CHILDREN AT RISK"

It is no longer enough for teachers to be committed to providing their classes with excellent educational opportunities. Confronted with a classroom filled with children of diverse backgrounds, experiences, and needs, teachers must have a multicultural perspective. *Multiculturalism* has several meanings and interpretations. Its essential focus is fairness and equal treatment of human beings. Educators who take a multicultural approach actively seek ways to recognize, respect, and incorporate *on an equal basis* the cultures and experiences of all their students (Fennimore 1989). Today's approach to multiculturalism differs from the past focus on America as a "melting pot" in which everyone was expected to abandon old cultural experiences for a single new national identity. Applied to a school setting, children were expected to conform in dress, language, lifestyle, and behavior. The melting pot in practice was neither fair nor humane, because family custom and cultural identity are central to self-perception and self-esteem. Furthermore, prejudice and discrimination have continued to pose significant barriers to the full acceptance and economic participation of many Americans (Banks 1994; Nieto 1992).

ACTIVITY AND DISCUSSION

1. Like almost every American, you were probably exposed to overt or subtle expressions of prejudice and discrimination—expressed either toward you or in regard to those who were different from you.

    Think back to your childhood and adolescence, and list some forms of prejudice and discrimination to which you were exposed or of which you were aware.

2. Reflect on some beliefs of people in your family that you may have retained at least in part as an adult. (Do you think many who receive public assistance don't really want to be employed? Do you believe that some racial groups have not worked hard enough to be successful? Do you think women should not compete for traditionally male jobs?)

3. Discuss ways in which personal beliefs can be a positive or negative force in viewing students whose parents are experiencing social and economic difficulties.

Some educators have suggested that the notion of a salad, in which a lively and productive society is created by individuals and groups that retain cultural differences, is a more humane and sensible approach than the melting pot (Baruth and Manning 1992). The salad approach is supported by multiculturalism, a term that describes the policies and practices in institutions such as schools that recognize, accept, and affirm human similarities and differences related to race, age, class, disability, and gender (Sleeter and Grant 1994). Applied to a classroom setting, multiculturalism means that children are accepted and valued for their individual characteristics and lifestyles and are encouraged to be tolerant and accepting of all their peers. Rather than deny differences ("I don't see color, I just see children"), teachers who have multicultural skills affirm and accept differences ("I see color in my students, and I make sure they know that I accept and value it") (Fennimore 1994).

Multiculturalism is a positive educational practice in its effort to create affirming, positive learning environments for children, but multiculturalism is also politicized and controversial. A multifaceted national debate concerns appropriate school curriculum, acceptance of different lifestyles, ongoing problems of prejudice and discrimination, and other areas of human difference. However, because equal educational opportunity remains an American mandate, teachers should value multiculturalism as part of the continuing effort to help all children function equally well as valued individuals in school settings. Banks (1994) states that multiculturalism provides freedom to be yourself and to understand others in an increasingly troubled and polarized world.

How does the concept of multiculturalism relate to classroom management and discipline? The same stereotypes that may cause the at-risk label to actually hinder the progress of children can affect the expectations of teachers in regard to the potential behavior and learning potential of all children. Banks (1991) refers to the "hidden curriculum" of institutional norms, attitudes, and expectations that have a strong influence on human beliefs and interactions.

QUESTIONS TO CONSIDER

1. Think back to the hypothetical case of the new teacher who experiences difficulty at the in-service training session in folk dancing. At what point do you think the issue of teacher expectation created or aggravated the problems that occurred?

2. In what ways might teachers "expect" behavior and learning problems from children who are stereotyped and exposed to prejudice in our society? How might those expectations be communicated in "hidden" ways that nonetheless strongly affect the feelings and attitudes of students?

3. Can you recall a time in your own childhood when you were strongly affected by the expectation of an adult?

Teachers' Expectations Are Important

Teachers today may often feel unfairly blamed for problems of children that are outside their control. In all fairness, teachers and schools cannot function on an optimal level without the support of families, communities, and social agencies. Teachers may also feel discouraged when they sense a lack of opportunity to influence the programs and policies of the schools in which they teach (Banks 1994). These and other professional difficulties have a serious effect on teachers' morale and retention and are discussed in more detail in Chapter 3. Although teachers do face real barriers, they have the power to influence their students in substantial ways on a daily basis.

Educational research gathered over more than twenty years consistently indicates that what teachers expect from children in terms of behavior and academic performance has a strong effect on how children behave and perform in school (Good and Brophy 1987). Regardless of detrimental conditions outside the school, teachers influence the progress and development of all children through their expectations as well as the professional behaviors generated from those expectations. This places the risks children face in a more hopeful school context, but it also places serious responsibility on teachers.

It is not easy to overcome stereotypes that may be a part of a teacher's own background and life experiences. Nor is it a simple task to help children successfully rise above what test scores indicate about their ability. In reality, clashes of norms and values may cause teachers to feel disapproval of the lifestyles of their students' families or communities. The concept of *cultural relativism,* or the ability to understand other cultural systems on their own terms rather than on the terms of your personal beliefs, can assist teachers in their efforts to support their students (Gollnick and Chin 1990). Teachers, who have chosen a public service profession, must continually struggle to be fair and equitable in a climate of diversity.

What does the term *teacher expectations* mean? Teacher expectations are the inferences that teachers make about the future behavior or academic achievement of students based on what they know now about those students (Good and Brophy 1987). These assumptions about students lead to *teacher expectation effects,* which are student outcomes that result from the actions teachers take in response to their own expectations (Good and Brophy 1987). Two forms of teacher expectation effects that affect children in classrooms have been identified. The first is called *self-fulfilling prophecy.* In this kind of expectation effect an originally incorrect or poorly based expectation ("His sister dropped out, so he probably will too") leads to behavior that causes the expectation to become true ("I'm going to place him alone in back of the room facing the wall so he can't get into any trouble and interrupt the other students as they work"). The second identified form of teacher expectation effect is the *sustaining expectation effect* (see Exhibit 2-3). In this form teachers expect students to maintain and sustain previous academic or behavioral patterns ("She could never pay attention to mathematics in September and failed the first two tests") and fail to observe and capitalize on real changes—the teacher does not notice that Susan has been choosing the math center for two weeks to work consistently on a difficult mathematics puzzle, and Susan remains in the slow math group although her work has improved.

Teachers do have a daily opportunity to observe students and to form correct perceptions of the current level of their students'

EXHIBIT 2-3   ***Teacher Expectation Effects***

Examples of Self-Fulfilling Prophecy

Jamaal has two older sisters who were outstanding students in elementary school. He is not very interested in reading and does not readily participate in class activities. His first-grade teacher, who also taught both of his sisters, gives him constant encouragement and affirmation. When he fails his first reading test, she takes extra time to carefully go over it with him and to reteach the material. By the end of first grade he is reading with enthusiasm and scores well on the end-of-year assessment.

Lydia's parents have an interracial marriage and are receiving public assistance. She often comes to school without bathing and is quiet and withdrawn. Lydia's seat is in the back of the classroom, and her teacher has told her twice that she does not know if she will be able to keep up with the rest of the students in the advanced fifth grade. When Lydia does raise her hand, she is rarely recognized. Her third written assignment falls considerably below the level of the first two, but her teacher does not speak to her about her work. At the end of the year Lydia's final assessment is not high, and she is moved to a different group of students.

Examples of Sustaining Expectation Effect

Jamaal does not like to go to the library with his class. His teacher is concerned, because she believes his reading will improve if he can find books he is interested in. For five weeks he is not attentive in the library and does not take out any books. The next week, however, he finds a book about trains and reads it for the whole period. His teacher notices his interest and encourages him to take the book out. He does and reads it at home.

Lydia is upset about her third assignment. She knows she did not spend much time on it. Too shy to talk to her teacher, she decides to make an extra effort in the classroom. Lydia concentrates on improving her handwriting, raises her hand more, and completes all her classwork on time. By the end of the week her teacher still has not called on her or noticed the improvement in her work.

competence and ability (Good and Brophy 1987). Low teacher expectations, and the problems they may create, are related to the inability of teachers to believe in children's capacity to develop and thus to change their level of educational ability. Children cannot change unless they receive continual opportunities for growth that are accompanied by support and indications from teachers that growth is attainable and expected. Researchers have connected race and culture, economic status, primary language, test scores, parental educational level and status, and family formation to low expectations of teachers (Fennimore 1989). Teachers must continually reflect on their classroom thoughts and behaviors to be sure that they do not stereotype less advantaged or culturally diverse students. It is the stereotyping that places teachers in danger of forming inflexible and unfair expectations of students who exhibit poor behavior and lower achievement levels.

Teachers can feel comfortable about acknowledging the current limitations in the achievements of their students and the barriers to school performance that exist in their family or community lives. High teacher expectation does not require denial of real problems. Teacher expectation is important in the attempt to envision and create positive change in every student and to reflect on the possibility of prejudice and stereotyping in forming initial impressions of students.

How can teachers observe and evaluate their expectations? Expectations are often reflected in *classroom climate*, or the mood and atmosphere within which interpersonal interactions of students and teachers take place (Good and Brophy 1987). Defining or measuring classroom climate is never easy, because beliefs, attitudes, and institutional practices are deeply rooted in school professionals. The ways in which perceptions of students influence or change behaviors and that form the climate of the classroom are often subtle (Mongon and Hart 1989). Oakes (1985) describes classroom climate as the relationships of all classroom participants, the quality of goal orientation toward personal development, and the maintenance of a classroom organizational system. A teacher whose classroom climate reflects multicultural considerations would exhibit a sense of advocacy for the students, a commitment to human equality, and dedication to high expectations for the accomplishments of all students in the class (Fennimore 1992). Specific interactions between students and teacher that reflect a positive climate might be evident in the way the teacher exercises authority in the classroom, expresses warmth and support, focuses on either competition or cooperation between students and encourages independent judgment and choice on the part of students (Borich 1992) (see Exhibit 2-4).

DEFICIT TERMINOLOGY AND SCHOOL ACCOUNTABILITY

Teachers who are committed to doing everything they can to reduce the educational risks in their students' lives by maintaining appropriately high expectations must be aware of the potential problems created by deficit theories and deficit terminology. The field of education has a legacy of language that focuses on the identification of disabilities or limitations in children ("children at risk," "disadvantaged children," "language-delayed children," "learning-disabled children," "crack babies"). This deficit terminology, often intended to help children by

EXHIBIT 2-4	*Examples of Positive and Negative Classroom Climate*
Problem:	John is a third grader who is continually late in completing his written work in class. Today, as he completes a math exercise, his teacher approaches his desk and speaks to him.
Positive Climate:	"You are working hard, John, and I think you'll be able to have your exercise done on time. Great!"
Negative Climate:	"Let's hurry, John. For once, it would be nice if you could finish your work with the rest of the class."
	(The positive climate anticipates progress without unnecessary reference to former problems or difficulties.)
Problem:	Thelma Greene's kindergarten class returns from library hour with a note from the librarian complaining about their "bad behavior" while listening to a story.
Positive Climate:	Ms. Greene says to her class "I know you all will do better next time. We will read a story later today and practice some good ways of looking at pictures and listening quietly. I'm going to ask Ms. Greene what her favorite story is this year, ask her for suggestions of how we could be better listeners. We'll surprise the librarian next time you visit!"
Negative Climate:	Ms. Greene says to her class "Just like class K-3, making trouble for other people because they don't pay attention. Maybe staying in from recess will help you remember how to behave next time."
	(The positive climate anticipates improvement through skill building and does not label or stereotype the class with an identity of poor behavior.)

targeting them for special programs and services, frequently has tended to isolate, label, or stereotype them.

ACTIVITY AND DISCUSSION

1. How many labels and classifications do you know that have been applied to children? Take a few minutes to list all that come to mind (examples: At risk, learning disabled).

2. Next to each label, classification, or term you have listed, note specific ways in which classroom teachers can remediate or circumvent the problem.

3. Have you found that you know many terms that connote negative meanings concerning children but are unsure about how to address many of the problems? Do you agree or disagree with the idea that children should never be classified or labeled unless doing so will create a specific and positive opportunity for help and remediation?

What is the *deficit theory* about children? This term refers to assumptions that some children, because of genetic, cultural, or experiential differences, are inferior to other children (Nieto 1992). Many such theories stem from the first compensatory programs created in the 1960s, which were based on the theory that some children were "culturally deficient." Although explicit theories of cultural or genetic deficits of children are not generally used today, the new terms of *deprived, disadvantaged*, and *at risk* can connote deficiencies in children themselves. This is unfair when children have not had the resources, opportunities, and expectations to help them develop to their full potential (Natriello, McDill and Pallas 1990). Deficit theories can also place full blame for the shortcomings of children on the home and family, thereby ignoring school and social responsibility as potential solutions. It is important to avoid blaming the victims because they have not received adequate opportunities to thrive (Nieto 1992).

School Accountability and Child Resilience

The school is accountable to the public for helping every child develop full potential. Problems and challenges exist, but they cannot be used to absolve the school of its basic purposes and responsibilities. Teachers cannot be blamed when children face struggles so severe that they cannot thrive as they otherwise might. However, teachers should always be able to articulate what they hope and intend to accomplish to the best of their abilities despite the barriers they may face (Fennimore 1992). Teachers' statements of responsibility and intention to succeed with children indicate a strong sense of professionalism and actually do influence school as well as classroom climate.

PROFESSIONAL DECISION

The Teachers' Room

You are sitting in the teachers' room of an elementary school. Some comments you hear about the students are quite negative. Work with a partner to analyze the comments listed here, and rewrite them to reflect the real problems they describe as well as a positive sense of teacher accountability:

> *Every year it seems as though we have more children who have been in early intervention programs because of exposure to drugs and alcohol during pregnancies. This year I have three children who I know were born addicted to crack, and I am suspicious of several others. It is getting harder and harder to cover the curriculum, and these kids just fall further and further behind.*
>
> *Most of these kids come from the projects, and you would not believe the lives they lead. I had one child last year whose father and uncle were both murdered. It's getting to the point in this school where we just get through the day.*

What does teacher accountability have to do with management and discipline? Student-centered management based on developmentally appropriate practice, which forms the basis of this text, must be built on a foundation of the expectation of success for teachers as well as students. Teachers do not control out-of-school influences but do play a significant role in maintaining positive attitudes toward school success (Bellon, Bellon, and Blank 1992). It is important that teachers facing daily challenges in the classroom believe that their work is important, particularly when they are in charge of specific children or groups of children for only a relatively limited amount of time. How can they remain optimistic when so many children have behaviors and attitudes that reflect their problems outside school? A very important emphasis can be placed on the concept of *resilience*, or the "self-righting nature of human development," which enables children to "bounce back successfully despite exposure to severe risks." (Bernard 1993: 44). Educators who move beyond the concept of risk (which is often futuristic and loosely defined) can have a comprehensive plan to create as many classroom conditions as possible that foster healthy human development. The profile of a resilient child is one who can work, play, and love well and expects life to be essentially positive. Resilient children have problem-solving skills and a sense of autonomy, purpose, and future (Bernard 1993). Researchers have provided evidence that children can use school activities to support personal growth in these areas when schools are sensitive to them and to the burdens the children carry (Garbarino, Dubrow, Kostelny, and Pardo 1992).

Classroom teachers can and do grow discouraged when they see serious problems affecting so many children in their classrooms. Although it may be difficult at times, teachers must focus on multiculturalism, high expectation, and hope in the resilience of the child. Teachers must also remain focused on the ongoing American commitment to equal educational opportunity and on the future of our democracy (see Exhibit 2-5).

EXHIBIT 2-5   **A Multicultural Classroom Model for Teachers**

Teachers *accept* the diversities in their classrooms in a nondeficit approach to the realities of children.

Teachers *value* the diversities as a challenge to the successful preparation of all children for life in a multicultural world, and are determined to find the valuable skills and attributes of all children.

Teachers *identify* and articulate exactly what they can accomplish for their students regardless of their diversities (such as learning disabilities, unemployed parents, or family abuse situations) that might be perceived as discouraging negatives.

Teachers willingly *model* excellence, acting as school leaders in terms of their positive and productive approach to diversity.

Teachers *advocate* for children through design of classroom interaction, professional peer interaction, and social interaction that might impact on the acceptance and positive valuing of their students.

Source: Beatrice S. Fennimore. (1992). The multicultural classroom climate. In E. B. Vold (Ed.), *Multicultural education in early childhood classrooms*. Washington, D.C.: National Education Association.

QUESTIONS TO CONSIDER

1. Think of a difficult struggle you have faced in your life. List the people and events that helped you to recover emotionally and to regain a sense of optimism and hope for the future.

2. Think of a time in your life when you persevered in a task at which you were not competent, because an adult encouraged you and gave you the impression you would ultimately be able to succeed. List the qualities in that adult that you found comforting and encouraging.

3. Are there ways that you can prepare to develop those qualities and to display them on a consistent basis in your classroom?

EQUALITY AND DEMOCRACY IN THE CLASSROOM

This chapter focuses on the real problems and issues teachers and children face in America. Preparation for the development of student-centered management must include recognizing these critical social challenges. As teachers make the decisions that form the management of their classrooms, they need to put the information in this chapter into perspective. What are the lives of students really like outside school? What is it that students should experience in the social lives of classrooms? For what are students ultimately being prepared?

Nieto (1992) states that no educational philosophy or program is worthwhile unless it focuses on two central concerns: how we can raise the achievement of all students and thus provide them with an equal and equitable education, how we can give students the opportunity to become critical and productive members of a democratic society. To keep outdated themes of deficits and student inferiority from continuing to permeate educational practice in subtle but powerful ways, teachers must focus on the democratic ideal of equality. What is equality? Edmonds (1979) describes it as the "simple sense of fairness," which he feels should be the bias of all educators. Fairness means that all students have equal resources and equal opportunities to develop their abilities to the fullest extent possible. Nieto (1992) says that, although equality of resources and opportunities would be a crucial step, equality also means all the skills and talents possessed by each student should be considered a valid starting point for education. Coleman (1990) suggests that educators focus less on equality of resources and emphasize instead the reduction of obvious inequalities that lead to unequal outcomes.

PROFESSIONAL DECISION | *The Other Side of the Track*

Henry is a teacher in a suburban public school district. Several communities are served by the district, including a wealthy community and another that is characterized by unemployment and economic hardship. Henry has observed that the tracking, or grouping, system in the school has resulted in almost all the places in the "gifted track" being held by children from the most advantaged community. A student in his class, who is exhibiting strong abilities in mathematics, has been unable to gain access to the gifted math program because of lack of space. This student is not financially advantaged and has a single mother who does not have a telephone. Do you think Henry can reduce the chance that his gifted math student will have an unequal outcome because of his educational situation? If so, how? Do you think Henry should try to address this situation? Why or why not?

Capper and Jamison (1993) state that public schools may well be failing the basic educational mandate of a democracy, which is to provide for equal preparation for and equal opportunity in society. They suggest that the system is most likely to fail those students who must struggle to reach success. Nieto (1992) reminds educators that, although American schools still subscribe to the values of equal access mandated by the 1954 Supreme Court decision in *Brown v. Board of Education*, real equality still involves a continual struggle.

The challenge for American educators is twofold. On one hand, they must continually express their own commitment to democracy and equality through equitable classroom strategies. On the other hand, they must create a system of classroom management that fosters the democratic ideal and assists students in their own preparation for productive citizenry in a society still characterized by inequalities. Teachers who are forming a philosophy and strategy of classroom management and discipline need to focus on ways in which the American ideals of equality and democracy can be incorporated.

CHAPTER SUMMARY

This chapter was designed to help teachers form a perspective on the life experiences of the children who fill American classrooms today. The chapter emphasizes behavior and management as critical problems for teachers. The discussion of the many American children who are experiencing risks in their social, economic, or educational lives was placed in a context of multiculturalism, high teacher expectation, and teacher accountability. The resilience of children, which characterizes their frequent ability to rise above difficult circumstances, was stressed. The overriding concepts of equal opportunity and preparation for life in a democracy were discussed as a basis for further conceptualization of strategies for student-centered classroom management.

CHAPTER REFERENCES

Association for Childhood Education International Exchange (1993–1994, Winter). Safe schools would send funds directly to districts. *Childhood Education, 70*(2), 96D.

Banks, J. A. (1991). *Teaching strategies for ethnic studies* (5 ed.), Boston: Allyn & Bacon.

————. (1994). *An introduction to multicultural education*. Boston: Allyn & Bacon.

Baruth, L. G., & Manning, M. L. (1992). *Multicultural education of children and adolescents*. Boston: Allyn & Bacon.

Bellon, J. J., Bellon, E. C., & Blank, M. A. (1992). *Teaching from a research knowledge base: A development and renewal process*. New York: Merrill.

Bernard, B. (1993, November). Fostering resiliency in kids. *Educational Leadership, 51*(3), 44–48.

Borich, G. D. (1992). *Effective teaching methods* (2nd ed.). New York: Merrill.

Bredekamp, S. (1994). Foreword. In D. Gartrell, *A guidance approach to discipline*. Albany, NY: Delmar.

Capper, C. A., & Jamison, M. T. (1993, November). Let the buyer beware: Total quality management and educational research and practice. *Educational Researcher, 22*(8), 15–30.

Charles, C. M. (1992). *Building classroom discipline*. New York: Longman.

Children's Defense Fund. (1992). *The state of America's children 1992.* Washington, DC: Author.

————. (1995). *The state of America's Children Yearbook 1995.* Washington, DC: Author.

Coleman, J. S. (1990). *Equality and achievement in Education.* Boulder, CO: Westview.

Edmonds, R. (1979). Effective schools for the urban poor. *Education Leadership, 31*(1), 15–23.

Fennimore, B. S. (1989). *Child advocacy for early childhood educators.* New York: Teachers College Press.

————. (1992). The multicultural classroom climate. In E. B. Vold (Ed.), *Multicultural education in early childhood classrooms* (pp. 66–77). Washington, DC: National Education Association.

————. (1994). Constructing a multicultural framework for coordinated children's services. In R. Levin (Ed.), (*Greater than the sum: Professionals in a comprehensive services model*) Washington, DC: American Association of Colleges for Teacher Education.

Garbarino, J., Dubrow, K., Kostelny, K., & C. Pardo (1992). *Children in danger: Coping with the consequences of community violence.* San Francisco: Jossey-Bass.

Gollnick, D. M., & Chinn, P. C. (1990). *Multicultural education in a pluralistic society.* Columbus, OH: Merrill.

Gollnick, D. M., & Chinn, P. C. (1983). *Multicultural education in a pluralistic society.* St. Louis: C. V. Mosby.

Good, T. L., & Brophy, J. E. (1987). *Looking in classrooms.* New York: Harper & Row.

Heath, S. B., & Mangiola, L. (1991). *Children of promise: Literate activity in linguistically and culturally diverse classrooms.* Washington, DC: National Education Association.

Kozol, J. (1991). *Savage inequalities.* New York: Harper Perennial.

Mongon, D., & Hart, S. (With Chris Ace and Anne Rawlings). (1989). *Improving classroom behavior: New directions for teachers and pupils.* New York: Teachers College Press.

National Coalition of Advocates for Students. (1988). *Barriers to excellence: Our children at risk.* Boston: Author.

National Commission on Children. (1991). *Beyond rhetoric: A new American agenda for children and families.* Washington, DC: Author.

Natriello, G., McDill, E. L., & Pallas, A. M. (1990). *Schooling disadvantaged children: Racing against catastrophe.* New York: Teachers College Press.

Nieto, S. (1992). *Affirming diversity: The sociopolitical context of multicultural education.* New York: Longman.

Oakes, J. (1985). *Keeping track: How schools structure inequality.* New Haven, CT: Yale University Press.

Putnam, J., & Burke, J. B. (1992). *Organizing and managing classroom learning communities.* New York: McGraw-Hill.

Research and Policy Committee of the Committee for Economic Development. (1991). *The unfinished agenda: A new vision for child development and education.* Washington, DC: Committee for Economic Development.

Rosewater, A. (1989). Child and family trends: Beyond the numbers. In F. J. Macchiarola & A. Gartner (Eds.), *Caring for America's children.* (4–19). New York: Academy for Political Science.

Sleeter, C. E., & Grant, C. A. (1994). *Making choices for multicultural education* (2nd ed.). New York: Merrill.

Steinfels, P. (1992, December 27). *Seen, heard, even worried about.* New York Times, p. 1, Week in Review section.

Wong, H. K., & Wong, R. T. (1991). *The first days of school.* Sunnyvale, CA: Harry K. Wong Publications.

3 PERSPECTIVES ON SCHOOLS, TEACHERS, AND CURRICULUM

Teachers who are forming a philosophy of student-centered classroom management must develop a perspective on the responsibilities of schools and the problems facing American teachers. They also need to understand current trends in curriculum and reform in American education. This chapter discusses the following topics:

- Challenges facing American schools
- Responsibilities of schools to children
- Problems facing educational professionals
- Current trends in school practice and reform
- Ethical considerations for teachers

CHALLENGES FACING AMERICAN SCHOOLS

Chapter 2 established that American teachers are facing the challenge of successfully educating children whose lives may be challenged by poverty, discrimination, racism, or a wide variety of other social and economic difficulties. These are times that call for courage and commitment on the part of anyone who chooses to enter a classroom. Negative teacher attitudes about the lives, abilities, or behavioral skills of children can only serve to exacerbate the problems. Difficult as the task may be, teachers today are in a position to alleviate the sad ramifications of the great social neglect of children. Heartfelt dedication to that challenge will create the groundwork for a better future for all who live in our country. How can teachers build a conceptual framework for the tasks ahead? Consider this scenario:

You have an appointment with a physician to discuss a health problem. You travel some distance to the office, wait with considerable anxiety, and finally have the opportunity to be examined and to consult with the doctor. To your surprise and dismay the doctor says, "You know, there really is not much doctors can do these days for many people. They don't eat correctly and fail to exercise; they are addicted to chemical substances. There is so much economic uncertainty, divorce, and disruption in families, and so many individuals are facing potentially devastating problems in their lives. People expect too much of doctors. Although we continue to see patients, the fact is that many, including you, will get sick and remain sick, and there is nothing we can do about it."

What would you say to this physician? Probably, you would point out that the doctor has a professional responsibility to assess the health situation of each patient and to recommend the most effective course of intervention. You would ask why anyone should pay a professional fee to someone who does not view herself or himself as competent to help them in any way. Next, you would wisely find another doctor. This time you would try to make sure that the doctor listens to you, assesses your situation, applies the most current research to your needs, and recommends the best intervention possible. No matter how serious your problems are, you want your physician to offer the best solutions to help you live your life to the fullest extent possible.

The example of the doctor raises the question of professional accountability. How do professionals in all fields articulate what they can do and what they hold themselves responsible for doing, no matter what the challenges and setbacks may be? The main principles here apply as well to the field of education. What do schools, which receive public trust and funding, fully intend to accomplish in most or almost all circumstances? This book defines teacher accountability as a self-assumed professional responsibility for creating a positive and respectful learning climate, for designing educational interventions based on multiple fair assessments and the best available knowledge in the field, and implementing educational strategies that seek to develop the highest potential of all students. All professionals sometimes fail despite their best efforts or meet circumstances beyond their control. This should not prevent them from consistently articulating the generally positive outcomes that clients (the public as well as students in terms of education) can routinely expect from their services. Unquestionably, teaching is difficult, and many children are facing social, economic, and family stresses beyond the control of teachers. However, teachers who are serious about successfully planning and implementing student-centered class management and discipline must have a clear idea of what they are determined to accomplish on a daily basis.

RESPONSIBILITIES OF SCHOOLS TO CHILDREN

Schools are institutions affected by social, educational, and political forces. Children and teachers are central to the process of education, but schools involve superintendents, district personnel, principals and other administrators, subject specialists, school boards, state and federal legislators, policy makers, and taxpayers. Thus discussing school responsibility requires striking a careful balance. Blaming teachers for problems created by society as a whole is unrealistic. How much does society value education? How much funding is available? How committed are administrators and policy makers to the real needs of children in the schools? How much professional support do teachers receive? How many services are available to help children with special needs and abilities? How much support are children receiving from their families and communities? How much overall social concern exists for the next generation, and how willing are most adults to sacrifice for the needs of children other than their own? Teachers cannot work miracles in a general atmosphere of neglect or discouragement. On the other hand, teachers have a great deal of power that must be identified and used to its full potential. The purpose of this section is to establish the responsibility of teachers, and the school, in meeting the needs of all children.

ACTIVITY AND DISCUSSION

This book provides you with the opportunity to think about the challenges facing children, teachers, and schools in America. Take a moment now to identify and list what you believe are the five greatest problems facing schools today. Be sure to include the "big picture"— social and political as well as community, family, and school forces.

Analyze each of the five problems on your list. Under each one, make two lists. One list, the Cannot Do list, is for all aspects of the particular problem that are beyond the control of teachers and schools. The other list, the Can Do list, is for all aspects of the particular problem that teachers and schools can affect. Compare and discuss your list with a peer. Be sure to examine areas of disagreement as well as agreement on your lists.

What Schools and Teachers Can Do

Schools and teachers can accomplish reasonable goals based on a full understanding of the mission of educators and the developmental possibilities of children. Nothing is accomplished that is not attempted, and educational attempts of any kind are ultimately centered on positive or negative attitudes of teachers (Postman and Weingartner 1969). Educators must be willing to try, must believe that their efforts have a good chance of being successful, and must have the skills to accomplish the task at hand. Their goals must be based on real developmental abilities of children and must incorporate the fact that a trial-and-error process is almost invariably part of the success of all long-term plans.

QUESTIONS TO CONSIDER

1. Emily is a new teacher who has won several Excellence in Mathematics awards for her brilliance in that subject. Most students in her fifth-grade classroom are scoring below the national norm in mathematics. Emily still loves teaching, but she really does not know how to approach students who cannot understand ideas that have come so easily to her. Make three practical suggestions for ways in which Emily can retain high standards but also meet the students at their current levels of achievements.

2. Emily has volunteered at a staff meeting to run a mathematics club after school that offers more advanced activities to any interested student. Another teacher said, "Are you kidding? They are not even on grade level, Emily!" What do you think Emily should say?

Interactions of Children, Teachers, and Schools

Behavior is responsive as well as innate. Children and adults do have distinct personalities as well as ingrained habits and dispositions that affect their interactions with all others. But children and adults also respond in different ways to different people and different social circumstances. Students and teachers alike can have well-established habits of behavior and attitude that create either difficult or positive circumstances in the classroom. Educators, who are professionally responsible to their students, need to develop something of a mental sorting mechanism that continually differentiates between characteristics that appear to be innate and responses that can be strongly influenced by teachers' behavior in the context of the classroom environment. It is the potential responses of children to encouragement and positive intervention to which educators must hold themselves most accountable.

Another way to look at the issue of schools and child behavior is to consider the importance of the interaction of children, adults, and circumstances. No matter how seriously a child may be disabled by circumstances, ability, or behavior, the interaction between that child and adults often remains much more in the control of the adults. One example of this can be found in the case of economically impoverished children. There is substantial empirical evidence that these children are more likely to fail in school, but there is little empirical evidence that living in a poor neighborhood has any real affect on the cognitive growth of a child. (Natriello, McDill, and Pallas 1990). Thus the existence of impoverished circumstances affects many of the child's interactions with people, circumstances, and events. Some of these interactions are not under the control of educators, but some are. Therefore the critical task of all educators is to identify which interactions with economically disadvantaged students they can influence and control in positive ways and then take appropriate action.

These ideas are supported by the efforts of educational researchers to distinguish between behaviors of children, effects of family and community life, and effects of schools. Wayson and Pinnell (1982) note that the discipline problems of children can often be traced to dysfunctions in the school's climate and organizational patterns rather than malfunctions in the individual. He points out that schools embody a system of roles and relationships that actually teaches children behavior and thus has the potential to teach them new behaviors. Mongon and Hart (1989) also point to a "school ethos" as creating a climate with a major influence on school behaviors of children. Mortimore & Sammons (1987) finds schools to be more important than background (sex, socioeconomic status, age, race) in terms of influence on behavior and performance of children. The policies and processes that are directly under the control of principals and teachers are crucial, and they can be changed. Bellon, Bellon, and Blank (1992) note also that, although student characteristics and background are important influences, school climate is one of the most important factors influencing the way children behave in school (see Exhibit 3-1). They note that teacher expectation is influential and that teachers can use effective strategies to mediate behavior. Teachers can also model the very behaviors they most want to promote in children in order to improve students' performance.

How do teachers and schools create a system of relationships that support the growth of acceptable and productive student behaviors? One way is to enhance a system of schoolwide management in which all constituents of the school play a part. Administrators can provide informed and committed leadership and implement effective policies, teachers and support staff can play an important role in developing and implementing effective school policies, and students can establish and maintain reasonable expectations that enable the school to function effectively (Bellon, Bellon, and Blank, 1992). Another solution is to try to establish and agree upon the factors that teachers do control and that do have significant influence over the behavior and achievement of students (Jones and Jones, 1990). One such factor is specific observable teacher behaviors that create a positive student-centered management climate. More specific classroom behaviors and strategies are explored in later chapters, but we can begin to think about general indicators of management that promote productive behavior in children. Exhibit 3-2 lists examples of such behaviors.

The teacher behaviors in Exhibit 3-1 are worth careful analysis. The teachers involved may sincerely believe that their actions are required by the behaviors of the children in the class. However, more

---

EXHIBIT 3-1   ***Negative Interactions in Poor School Climates***

Mr. Johnson teaches fourth grade in a school that serves low-income children. His belief that poor children lack discipline has led to rigid rules that he frequently enforces by shouting loudly at his students. The children must spend the first thirty minutes of each day sitting in silence at their desks with hands folded while Mr. Johnson checks homework assignments. They must then march single file to the bathroom and are not allowed to talk to one another. If anyone looks around the hall as they walk, Mr. Johnson yells, "Face forward!" Many children are silent and withdrawn, but a few look for opportunities to giggle, make silly noises, throw belongings on the floor, or misbehave in other ways.

Ms. Reira has taught first grade in a bilingual school near a housing project for fifteen years. She often confides in visitors that the children "are not civilized." Each September she obtains from the kindergarten teacher a list of children whose behavior posed difficulties last year. On the first day of school those children are placed in desks that face away from the teacher and toward the wall. Ms. Reira tells them, "In my room you must earn the right to turn around." The children facing the wall have difficulty seeing the blackboard and often stop trying to do their seatwork after the first few days. Several begin to act disruptively and attempt to distract their classmates at every opportunity.

reflection would lead to the somewhat uncomfortable realization that the teachers' negative attitudes and intentions are aggravating existing problems and may be creating new ones. Teachers must have a personal commitment to figuring out and implementing the strategies that encourage and enhance behaviors of all students. John Goodlad (1990) describes a strong level of commitment in teachers as the "moral imperative" to reach the highest level of success possible with every child. Goodlad notes that this sense of moral imperative can be missing from the language of teachers, including new teachers, when describing their sense of mission as educators. They may state a belief that all children should be treated in a kind and understanding manner yet also express the assumption that some children simply cannot learn (Zeichner 1992). The seriousness of such a negative assumption cannot be overstated. Teachers who believe that innate or circumstantial characteristics of children can render them unteachable will find it difficult or impossible to assume professional accountability for success. A lack of faith in your ability to teach children effectively is a potentially destructive force in a classroom.

How can teachers, new and experienced, develop and maintain a sense of moral imperative as they face the serious challenges ahead? It bears repeating that teaching is a human service occupation and that education is a powerful force in society. Educators must search for supportive approaches as they maintain enthusiastic efforts to teach all children successfully. One such approach has been described as invitational teaching (Purkey and Novak 1984). *Invitational teaching* is a perceptually based, self-concept approach to the educative process (see Exhibit 3-3). It centers on four basic principles:

- All people are able, valuable, and responsible and should be treated as such.

EXHIBIT 3-2   ***Specific Observable Behaviors Indicating Positive Climate***

Sincerity	Concern
Positive expectation	Cooperation
Respect	Credibility
Tolerance	Consistency

Source: J. E. Brophy, & J. Putnam. (1979). Classroom management in the elementary grades. In D. Duke, (Ed.), *Classroom management* (the 78th yearbook of the National Society for the Study of Education, pt. 2, pp. 182–216). Chicago: University of Chicago Press.

- Teaching should be cooperative.

- People have relatively untapped potential.

- Human development is enhanced by personally and professionally inviting people.

Wong and Wong (1991) states that invitational behavior can be verbal or personal and can be apparent in the physical environment of the classroom. In addition, invitational teaching must be present in *self-thoughts,* or the ways teachers actually process their efforts intellectually as they work. For example, a child may have a bad reputation and behave in difficult ways in the classroom at the beginning of the year. The teacher who thinks, "I knew this would happen, but I'll try to be calm and as nice to him as possible" is not processing invitational self-thoughts. In contrast, the teacher who thinks, "I know he's got lots of potential, so let's see how he responds to my suggestion that he be group leader this month" is processing invitational self-thoughts. The invitational thoughts of the second teacher will lead to invitational behaviors that can assist the student in changing his own behavior in the classroom.

Teachers should expect all their students to persist until they are reasonably successful at important tasks. Likewise teachers must expect themselves to persist with students until the students have achieved as much as they can. Because all people sometimes fail at tasks, it is only logical to anticipate that children will try and yet fail at regular intervals. Changing a person's behavior is a difficult undertaking. Therefore part of a sense of moral imperative and an invitational approach to teaching is the concept of forgiveness (Spaulding 1992). Forgiveness requires teachers to be stable and consistent in their efforts

---

EXHIBIT 3-3   ***The Four Basic Principles of Invitational Teaching***

People are able, valuable, and responsible and should be treated accordingly.

Teaching should be a cooperative activity.

People possess relatively untapped potential in all areas of human development.

This potential can best be realized by places, policies, and programs that are specifically designed to invite development and by people who are personally and professionally inviting to themselves and others.

Source: W. W. Purkey, & J. M. Novak. (1984). Inviting school success: A self-concept approach to teaching and learning (2nd ed.). Belmont, CA: Wadsworth.

and to willingly suspend judgment when children have been resistant or difficult.

| PROFESSIONAL DECISION | *Recognizing Bias* |

You are observing a kindergarten classroom at "circle time," a lesson of about twenty minutes' duration. The children are required to sit and listen to a story and then answer questions. Throughout the lesson various children frequently talk to others or lie down on the floor or fidget. The teacher either gives brief reprimands or ignores the behavior. By the time the questions are being asked, the whole group appears to be quite disrupted. At one point several children are talking or being inattentive, and the teacher is obviously growing impatient. The teacher suddenly corrects one girl in a loud tone and sends her back to her desk to sit for the rest of the lesson. After the lesson is over, you ask the teacher about that particular child. He expresses annoyance about her persistent talking during class. However, as an observer you saw many other children engaging in exactly the same behaviors as that child without repercussion. You extend the conversation to try to locate the source of the problem. The teacher then reveals that he knows this child's father is in prison for a robbery that took place a few years ago.

This situation should help you to think about three questions:

- How do you tend to respond to people who persistently annoy you or fail to respond to your requests?

- How can you work to develop self-thoughts that will help you to be a positive and encouraging professional with difficult children?

- Imagine for a moment that you were a kindergarten supervisor for the teacher described here. You might feel that the little girl who was punished was essentially acting like most of the other children at that time and that the information about the parent in prison has had a strong influence on the teacher's self-thoughts about the child. What might you suggest to the teacher in terms of management and invitational behavior?

This section has focused on the responsibility, or the accountability, of schools and teachers to create climates in which students can respond and interact in positive and productive ways. Up to this point the book has focused on understanding children and the many circumstances in their lives that require sensitivity and understanding on the part of teachers. The next section provides a brief overview of the problems and challenges facing professional educators. All who participate in the educational process need to be respected as individuals who at times encounter barriers to efficacy, or to the ability to be fully effective in the classroom. The more invitational schools can become to teachers, the more teachers will be able to maintain their commitments to their students.

PROBLEMS FACING EDUCATIONAL PROFESSIONALS

Many problems encountered by children in our society are experienced by teachers. The teachers may have grown up or be living in families experiencing economic stress. Teachers can be raising families as single parents and have children who experience difficulties in school or at home. Inadequate availability of high-quality child care, community crime and violence, unemployment, and chemical dependencies are just a few of the economic and social problems that teachers may face. In addition to personal challenges, teachers are confronted with many problems in the schools in which they teach. Consider the following scenario:

> Dr. Smith, a renowned college professor and researcher in the area of classroom management, has been invited by School District Z to provide a full day of in-service training. A popular and energetic lecturer, she begins the session filled with enthusiasm. But the more she continues to explain the needs of children, and the ways in which teachers must meet them, the more she feels that the teachers do not share her views. In fact, she senses that they may be angry and upset.
>
> At lunch Dr. Smith asks the principal if there is a problem of which she should be aware. The principal says, "Now that you ask, we are having serious problems in this district. The school budget has been cut, special education services have been withdrawn from this school, and the public is not supporting raises for teachers in the new contract." Dr. Smith says, "I feel foolish speaking to these teachers about how sensitive they should be to children at a time when they feel that their own needs as professionals are not being met."

Teachers, like any professionals who work hard to assist and support the growth of others, need to feel that their work is important and valuable. Teachers can become discouraged when they are steadily exposed to public disapproval or suspicion of the current system of education. Likewise, teachers become frustrated or demoralized when they encounter working conditions in schools that are neither financially adequate nor professionally supportive. As this anecdote suggests, teachers can have difficulty balancing directives to be kind and sensitive to children with their own sense of abandonment by administrators or alienation from the community. Realistically speaking, the problems, challenges, and frustrations in the educational process are by no means limited to the student population.

> Mr. Diaz is a teacher who attended Dr. Smith's in-service session. The single parent of two, he eats breakfast with his children while watching a news report on the ineffectiveness of American teachers. Once at school he cannot find parking in the small area reserved for teachers in the parking lot. His mailbox in the school office contains notes from his principal: two new children are joining his class of 34 fourth graders, and his new textbooks have not yet arrived. The school secretary contacts him at lunch to inform him that a parent came in to complain because her child, a student in Mr. Diaz's class, failed a math test; the parent could not stay to talk to Mr. Diaz because she had to get back to work. Mr. Diaz has a pleasant day with his students but hears several colleagues complain about the irrelevance of Dr. Smith's in-service session. Mr. Diaz says he enjoyed it but felt that she really did not understand what a teacher's day is like. He leaves school, picks up his children, goes shopping, makes dinner, helps his children with their homework, and then plans his classes for a few hours for the next day.

It is easy to understand why teachers like Mr. Diaz and his colleagues resent what they perceive as experts' insensitivity to the realities of their work environments. Actual professional circumstances of teachers vary widely around the United States, but dilemmas inherent in teaching as a profession are widely recognized (Nieto 1992; Banks 1994). Dr. Pearl Kane, a professor at Teachers College, Columbia University, published a letter she wrote to her daughter in college to discourage her from becoming a teacher (Kane 1990). Kane warns her daughter that more than 40 percent of all teachers leave the profession within the first five years. She also cites such problems as few opportunities for leadership, little control over what is actually taught, difficult working conditions inside schools, and lack of influence on the broader community. These are serious problems, and they deserve careful attention when so much is being asked of teachers today.

ACTIVITY AND DISCUSSION

As an educator you are going to be part of a larger professional environment with adult peers as well as young students. You can assume that those with whom you work in schools will have mixed feelings and attitudes about their careers as teachers. It is a good idea to find out more about how teachers really feel about their jobs. Plan to interview several elementary school teachers in your community. What questions might you ask them about the ways they handle the professional dilemmas described here and what they are doing to counteract barriers or feelings of discouragement?

Think about how your job as a teacher may, at least at times, challenge your morale or sense of being valued. How do you think you might react? Are there ways that you might prepare for this problem?

Why Teachers Feel Disillusioned

Many educators agree that more and more expectations are placed on schools and teachers without substantial change in the organization and structure of American education (Bellon, Bellon, and Blank 1992). Teachers are inundated with demands created by the many children in our society who are at risk for educational disadvantage. However, these same teachers may be as victimized as their students by certain societal forces. They may be underpaid or held in low esteem by those who hold elite positions in society. Teachers may also receive little respect in the large bureaucracies in which they most often function and be unfairly blamed by the public for problems beyond their control (Banks 1994).

When discussing problems faced by teachers, it is necessary to examine the term *teacher accountability* from a different perspective, because it takes on controversial overtones in today's political climate, which is prone to blaming schools and teachers for a host of larger social and political problems. This book defines teacher accountability as self-assumed professional responsibility for creating a positive and respectful learning climate and for designing educational interventions based on multiple fair student assessments and best available knowledge in the field. However, when politicians, bureaucrats, or the media raise the subject of teacher accountability, it is often within the context of pressure to raise the standardized test scores of students (Bredekamp 1987). Increased use of standardized testing in the guise of teacher accountability can depersonalize the entire teaching process and demoralize teachers who sometimes recognize a greater need to focus on the individual social, emotional, or academic needs of the children in their classrooms. When teachers believe that the only real importance attributed to their work is the production of adequately high scores on standardized tests, the result can be a rigidity in classroom structure and instruction that makes student-centered management extremely difficult to implement.

QUESTIONS TO CONSIDER

1. Have you ever stopped to think about how people generally respond to you when you say you are or hope to be a teacher? If you had to describe the general response, what would it be?

2. How much of your decision to pursue teaching as a career involved thinking about testing students? Do you think that a student's performance on a standardized test is an adequate measure of teacher accountability? Why or why not?

The next section discusses new ideas and reforms in education. However, many educators consider reforms to be problematic for classroom teachers. All too often teachers sense that they have been left out of initial reform-planning processes and that those who have designed the reforms have paid little attention to whether and how they can be implemented in classrooms. Teachers then feel they are in the position of being expected to implement and support ideas they did not develop, that they may actually strongly oppose, that have already been tried and failed in the past, or that reach them as demands that are either unfair or competing with other forces (Evans and Brueckner 1992). Another problem is that reforms may not be supplemented with time and resources for in-service teacher education. Teachers expected to implement sophisticated reforms without the opportunity to develop the necessary skills may begin to feel inept and defeated. This is particularly true when teachers are told that the reforms are being implemented, when in fact no real monetary resources or additional classroom materials have been provided. Unfortunately, justifiably negative feelings can lead to increased resentment of work conditions or hostility toward students.

Some reforms do attempt to improve the difficult circumstances faced by teachers. The 1986 Holmes Group Report, *Tomorrow's Teachers*, for example, proposes the following:

1. Make teacher education more intellectually sound.

2. Recognize differences in teachers' skill, knowledge, commitment, education, certification, work, and career opportunities.

3. Create professionally relevant and intellectually defensible standards of entry to the profession.

4. Connect institutions of higher learning to schools and school practice.

5. Make schools better places for teachers to work and students to learn (Soltis 1987).

Although many of these reforms hold exciting promise for the future, they will take a long time to implement. Meanwhile, teachers will need support as they continue to try to provide outstanding instruction and student-centered management in the classroom.

Bernard (1993) asserts that a nurturing school climate can overcome serious risk factors in the lives of students. But can teachers who do not feel nurtured meet the extra challenges involved in extending themselves to children with serious risks in their lives? In response, Bernard further suggests that teachers must accept responsibility for choosing to face their problems and for seeing the strengths they do have to be effective despite the barriers. In other words, teachers must call upon their resiliencies in order to foster the resiliencies of children. Bruner (1966), while recognizing the flux that so often exists in the field of education, also suggests that it is important for teachers to find the continuity that exists as change is taking place. A critical continuity in schools is the ongoing need of students for daily interaction with warm caring adults who can express personal concern and regard as they strive to teach effectively in the classroom (Wong and Wong 1991). Teachers who dedicate themselves to those continuous needs of students despite barriers and setbacks will serve as models both to their students and their professional colleagues. (See Chapter 8 for some additional suggestions of teacher survival skills.)

PROFESSIONAL DECISION

Make a Professional Decision

One day, Ms. Reese is approached in the local supermarket by a parent who recognizes her from church. This parent has been thinking of moving into Ms. Reese's school district and asks her, "Is it true that this school has gone downhill and that the teachers can no longer teach successfully in their classrooms?"

Write a paragraph in which you give what you think might be an appropriate response on the part of Ms. Reese. Express the dilemmas that exist while remembering her sense of moral imperative and her fundamental commitment to the needs of her students.

CURRENT TRENDS IN SCHOOL PRACTICE AND REFORM

Teachers preparing for the educational challenges of student-centered classroom management must be well versed in current trends in school practice and reform. Many readers of this book will undoubtedly attempt to implement student-centered management in an atmosphere of comprehensive change in the structure of the school in which they teach. There is widespread recognition of an urgent need to improve the American system of education. As discussed in the context of at-risk children, dissatisfied employers report significant difficulty in locating adequately skilled job candidates, and businesses are spending significant amounts of money to teach new employees basic skills they should have learned in school. Perhaps more important a prestigious series of national reports since the early 1980s has focused public attention on such educational problems as low achievement, high dropout rates, and substantial adult illiteracy. These reports, along with businesses' concerns, have resulted in serious discussion at all levels of government of the status of American education and the implementation of many local and state reforms. Today's teachers are living in a climate of change that may ultimately result in significant differences in how schools operate as well as how classroom instruction is conducted in the United

States (Levine and Havighurst 1992). This section discusses several ongoing reforms related to class-management issues: school restructuring, developmentally appropriate practice, changes in assessment and tracking of students, inclusion of disabled students, and parent and community involvement.

Restructuring

Demands for educational reform in the United States have led to the concept of school restructuring. Levine and Havighurst (1992) describe *restructuring* as a systemic attempt to create fundamental changes in the way schools are organized; Spring (1991) defines restructuring as the development of new methods for controlling schools and reorganizing school learning environments. Restructuring must deal with many complexities of the school system and must ultimately focus on the goal of increasing general student achievement (Levine and Havighurst 1992). Those who advocate restructuring often note that public schools control the distribution of knowledge and skills (and thus opportunities) in modern society (Spring 1991). Restructuring attempts to extend the power and control of schools to a wider circle of constituents through increased representation of those groups and individuals who have a stake in the outcome of public education.

QUESTIONS TO CONSIDER

1. Think back to your own elementary and high school experiences. How would you describe the way your schools were organized? Were you aware of any people—other than the faculty—who seemed to be active and powerful participants in the process of education?

2. As a current or future teacher how do you feel about people who are not professional educators having an important influence on what is taught in school and on the ways schools are organized and controlled? What are the potential values? What are the potential problems?

Deregulation and School-Based Management

Public schools are government sponsored and tax supported and are thus controlled by federal, state, and local legislation and policy. In the interest of restructuring and improving education states have attempted to deregulate, or to reduce rules and regulations that might prevent local school districts from making changes necessary for true reform. Some areas of deregulation include reduction of counterproductive testing requirements (which often emphasize low-level skills), waiving of policies that protect incompetent teachers, rigid attendance policies, or unnecessary external regulations.

There are two main kinds of school deregulation. One form of deregulation, designed to support and encourage school improvement, is called *conditional deregulation with waivers*, or temporary lifting of rules for schools that meet predefined standards (Levine and Havighurst 1992). Another form of deregulation, one which will have a greater effect on the personal experience of teachers in schools, is called *school-based management* (see Exhibit 3-4). This is an attempt to enhance parent and community involvement in schools and to build teacher empowerment and faculty collaboration. *Shared decision making*, a central component of school-based management, would break old patterns of school authority and give teachers and elected members of school governing councils the opportunity to share power in running the school (Levine and Havighurst 1992). A third aspect of restructuring that affects classrooms is *choice*, or an attempt to improve public schools through competition, by permitting families to select the public schools their children attend. Many public school districts have some form of choice, such as magnet programs or special schools, and teachers may be specially selected for these programs based on interests and abilities (Spring 1991).

All these proposed innovations will have at least some effect on the lives of teachers and students throughout America. Banks (1994) suggests that restructuring should actually be a fundamental examination of the goals, values, and purposes of schools, because most serious educational problems are inherent in the current system. Restructuring would thus question not just *how* schools are managed and controlled but *why* they exist and *what* they are trying to accomplish for all children. It is hoped that teachers will have a transformational effect on restructuring (Giroux 1993) and will be able to support efforts to convert classrooms into places where all children are having successful experiences in nurturing and caring environments (Banks 1994). In fact, McClure (1991) says

---

EXHIBIT 3-4   ***Example of Restructuring and School-Based Management***

The Fieldstone Elementary School is located in a moderate-income suburban community. Although the students tend to achieve average or above-average scores on standardized tests, many community residents believe that the school is mediocre and send their children to private schools. The superintendent has selected Fieldstone as the site for a restructuring effort in the district. An ad hoc committee of community residents, business representatives, teachers, and school parents has met for a year to design changes that will improve the school and make it more attractive to the community. They have decided to focus on smaller classes, more personal contact with families, introduction of a foreign language into the curriculum, and providing more opportunities for teachers to share in school leadership. Next year the school will elect a council that will collaborate on decisions concerning school curriculum, extracurricular activities, testing practices, and hiring of teachers and staff.

---

all restructuring will miss the point if it does not lead the way to pedagogy that liberates and empowers students. Such systemic changes in how students are taught and treated in schools would provide intrinsic support for the implementation of student-centered classroom management.

Developmentally Appropriate Practice

One important aspect of restructuring schools is a reexamination of the relationship of what is being taught, how it is being taught, and the response of the learner to what is required in the classroom. Disruption, apathy, and failure in school, although often blamed on students, can in many cases be directly related to curriculum and methods of teaching that can cause initially enthusiastic students to become increasingly negative toward learning (Bellon, Bellon, and Blank 1992). According to the National Association for the Education of Young Children, which published landmark documentation that children learn best when they are active participants in the process (Gartrell 1994), a major deterrent to student learning can be the failure to apply knowledge of child development to program practice (Bredekamp 1987). *Child development* refers to an accumulated body of knowledge about predictable ways in which physical, social, cognitive, and emotional growth takes place in children from birth to adolescence. Theories of child development are frameworks for understanding and predicting normal stages of growth and are based on intensive and scientific study of infants and children (Gardner 1982). Developmentally appropriate practice requires educators to use available knowledge of child development to plan a relevant and meaningful school curriculum. (See Chapters 4 and 5 for more detailed examination of child development theories and developmentally appropriate practice).

A basic premise of developmentally appropriate practice (DAP) is that the recent trend toward formally instructing young children in academic skills is based on misconceptions about how early learning takes place. Child development research consistently shows that children younger than eight learn best through concrete play and direct interactive experience with people and objects. *Constructivist theory* holds that children internalize knowledge of the world through these interactive experiences. Those who support constructivist theory argue that play is the primary active vehicle for and indicator of mental growth in children as they progress through developmental stages.

Unfortunately, many programs for young children that have changed in response to social, political, and economic needs have not been responsive to *developmental* needs (Bredekamp 1987). Children can miss critical developmental experiences when they are pressed academically and can actually lose their dispositions to use the knowledge they acquire in meaningful ways (Willis 1993). Although DAP began as an early childhood initiative, its focus has been extended through middle-level schools and beyond (Manning 1994).

What exactly is *developmentally appropriate practice?* It is defined as an approach to education that takes into account those aspects of teaching and learning that change with the age and experience of the learner (Willis 1993). There are two dimensions to developmental appropriateness: the age of the child and the individual characteristics of the child. The term *age* refers to universal and predictable stages of physical, emotional, social, and cognitive growth established through child development research, whereas the term *individual characteristics* refers to the unique personality, family background, learning style, and pattern or timing of growth found in each child (Bredekamp 1987).

As mentioned in the introduction, a major premise of this book is that student-centered management is inextricably linked to the concept of developmentally appropriate practice (see Exhibit 3-5). Later sections in the book elaborate on DAP in depth and draw connections between the appropriateness of the curriculum and the tendency of students to cooperate with the educational process through self-initiated engagement in meaningful learning activities.

EXHIBIT 3-5   ***Example of Developmentally Appropriate Practice***

Public School 37 is in a large eastern city. For the past ten years a series of superintendents has been hired with the promise of "raising district test scores." In this process the kindergarten changed from a half-day program with a focus on play and socialization to a full-day program that concentrates on preparation for standardized first-grade tests. Pressure on teachers resulted in "teaching to the test," and scores have risen to some degree, whereas teacher satisfaction has dropped, and student behavior problems have escalated. The teachers have expressed dissatisfaction with the pressure to drill the children in basic skills and report increased apathy and inattention in their young students.

This year a team of teachers and early childhood specialists has redesigned the district kindergarten program. The classrooms will have "centers" in language arts, mathematics, reading, and science. Teachers have asked for a commitment from the district to provide the resources necessary to buy more books and manipulative mathematics and science materials for the centers. They have also requested supplies of paper, crayons, and paints, which had been removed from their order lists some years earlier. The day will be organized into periods for centers, reading, and choice in play. Outdoor exercise will be included in the daily schedule. Although some teachers and parents oppose the idea, the district has decided to suspend all achievement testing in kindergarten and is considering suspending it in first grade as well.

ACTIVITY AND DISCUSSION

1. Take a moment to remember the three best teachers you ever had, and jot their names down on a piece of paper. Beneath each name, list the reasons that you liked these teachers so much and why you still remember them so clearly. After you have made your lists, analyze them for behaviors of the teachers that you found engaging and invitational and activities the teachers planned that you found exciting and meaningful.

2. Discuss your behaviors and activities with other students to find similarities in your lists. How many of you have remembered the teachers who created hands-on activities and included a great deal of interaction with people and objects as part of the standard curriculum? What implication does your list have for your future development as a teacher in a developmentally appropriate classroom?

Inclusion of Children with Special Needs

Many teachers are going to be asked to include students who are disabled in the daily lives of their regular classrooms (see Exhibit 3–6). Along with other reforms and changes in education has come the Regular Education Initiative, which has focused on increasing the extent to which children who are disabled are educated in the regular classroom (Jones and Jones 1990). *Inclusion* refers to a movement toward placing more students with disabilities in their neighborhood schools along with their nondisabled peers. Many educators who support inclusion expect that some students will continue to need special placements for part or all of the school day. Other educators support the concept of full inclusion and assert that the only option available should be placement in the regular classroom. Both the Education of the Handicapped Act (EHA), passed in 1975, and the more recently reauthorized Individuals with Disabilities Education Act (IDEA) contain strong emphases on inclusion whenever possible, but some educators believe that special education has remained unnecessarily segregative (Willis 1993).

Like many proposed changes and reforms in education, inclusion is controversial. Its advocates in the field of education charge that labeling children is harmful and that automatic placement of children with disabilities in special education classes violates the law. They cite the common practice of school districts to designate one school for children with certain disabilities and then to transport all those students to that school. Opposed to automatic assignment to

---

EXHIBIT 3-6   *Inclusion*

Barbara is ten years old and for the last three years has attended a special school for children designated as "educable mentally retarded." Her standardized tests in reading show that she is at the first-grade level, and her teachers report that she has difficulty getting along with other students in her special class.

This year Barbara has been selected to be "included" in the fifth-grade class of her community school as part of a special project. She will have an educational specialist assisting her in the classroom for two hours a day, and her teacher will be released during the year for ten days of intensive training in working with students with special needs. The children in her class attended an assembly designed to prepare them for a disabled classmate, and several have been selected by the teacher to include Barbara in their cooperative learning group. The district hopes that Barbara will be able to achieve at a higher level and gain more social satisfaction by interacting with her same-age peers from the community in which she lives.

special schools or classes, many argue that special education requires "responsible downsizing," and that all children who can function in regular classrooms despite their disabilities should have the opportunity to do so.

However, other concerned educators argue that it is not appropriate to generalize about all children with disabilities. Some children may have a better chance of reaching full potential in special classrooms, and in fact many advocates fought in the past to gain special education programs and facilities. Concern exists that districts may be eliminating special education programs simply to reduce operating budgets and that teachers in regular classrooms do not receive the information and support needed to help "included" students to function on an acceptable level (Willis 1993).

The challenge of inclusion provides educators with the opportunity to use many principles stressed thus far in this book—if they are willing to do so. Will regular classroom teachers who have disabled children in their classrooms be overly responsive to labels and deficit terminology? Or will they look with open minds at their promise and abilities? Will teachers assume active responsibility for the success of inclusion and use that success as an opportunity to foster multicultural skills, attitudes, and behaviors in all the students in their classrooms? It is clear that attitudes will play an important role and that teachers who hold themselves accountable for success will strive with diligence to learn more and work with support staff to fully incorporate the child into the classroom. Inclusion will require growth and improvement in management skills for many teachers (Jones and Jones 1990), but with that growth may come stronger development of student-centered management for all children in the classroom.

Testing, Tracking, and Authentic Assessment

Almost all educational reforms relate in some important ways to the current testing and tracking policies in schools. The uses and abuses of standardized testing and subsequent grouping or tracking of students are under scrutiny nationwide and are being considered in the context of new forms of authentic assessment of student progress that would allow greater latitude in school practice. (Chapter 6 offers a comprehensive discussion of authentic assessment as it relates to developmentally appropriate practice.) Testing, tracking, grouping, and assessment are centrally related to both the content and the methods of classroom instruction. Because there is also a strong connection between the content and method of classroom instruction and the quality of student-centered classroom management, teachers must give careful attention to testing and tracking issues.

Never in the history of American education have students been subjected to so much standardized testing. According to Perrone (1990), few of those who completed high school before 1950 took more than three standardized tests, and the results of those tests were rarely discussed in or outside schools. By comparison, the young people who completed high school in 1989 took eighteen to twenty-one standardized tests. The results of those tests were examined not only in educational circles but in the general public and even on the pages of local or national newspapers. The class of 1989 also spent an enormous amount of classroom time preparing for the standardized tests, and the focus on testing was by no means limited to the students' high school years. Preschool, kindergarten, and elementary school teachers around the country have reported increased use of standardized tests. Along with this growth in the testing of children from an early age has come increasing use of worksheets, workbooks, early ability grouping, tracking, grade retention, and other test-related policies that might be considered inappropriate for young children. Much of the testing has been related to or regulated by political concerns of state and local legislators, school boards, and superintendents whose continued employment depends on improving student scores on standardized tests (Kamii 1990.)

This widespread educational emphasis on early and extensive standardized testing is controversial. Many experts are concerned that it has had a negative effect on the learning and the attitudes of students in schools. One serious worry is that the quality of classroom instruction has been reduced because the curriculum is routinely narrowed to the topics that will be tested. The worksheets and practice materials used in classrooms resemble test materials, and children who spend a great deal of time working with these materials are pressured daily to obtain the one correct answer (according to teacher or test maker) rather than *think* of the many alternatives (American Educational Research Association 1991). Many professional groups have made formal statements that question the effects of standardized testing on children's thinking processes in the classroom. The Association for Childhood Education International (ACEI), the Association for Supervision and Curriculum Development (ASCD), the National Association for the Education of Young Children (NAEYC), the National Association for Elementary School Principals

(NAESP), the National Council of Teachers of English (NCTE), and the National Council of Teachers of Mathematics (NCTM), among other professional groups, have all raised concerns that the focus on testing has caused inappropriate drilling in isolated test-related skills (Kamii 1990). If testing practices are detrimental to learning, the subsequent harm to children raises critical ethical concerns. Advocacy for reasonable curtailment of standardized testing in schools may begin to counteract the potential negative effects of psychometry in the classroom (McGill-Franzen and Allington 1993).

Standardized testing is most often used as the basis for tracking or grouping students according to their ability. Although educators universally acknowledge that children do differ in terms of current levels of achievement, there is an ongoing debate about the positive or negative effects of tracking or grouping in schools. Some argue that tracking is particularly helpful for higher-achieving students, whereas others assert that heterogeneous grouping is more beneficial to all students than separating them according to assumed ability levels. Traditional educational research on the effects of tracking can yield contradictory results, sometimes indicating positive, negative, insignificant, or mixed results. Interpretive studies, on the other hand, provide detailed information about how tracking affects what teachers think, say, and do in real classrooms. Evidence exists that test scores and tracking have significant effects on student opportunities and outcomes in school (Page 1991). According to Oakes (1985), tracking may be a well-intentioned policy but, with no consistent research to support it, the actual consequences may be hellish for children. Slavin (1993) expresses concern that segregated groups of children cannot stimulate and challenge one another, that low groups have a discouraging stigma, and that teachers actually do not differentiate the curriculum according to tracks. Good and Brophy (1987) add concerns that social labeling connected to tracking affects teacher attitudes and expectations, that tracks tend to be permanent (of particular concern when young children are tracked), and that equity dilemmas arise when different groups of children are treated and instructed differently.

Many educators now look to the concept of authentic assessment for resolving the testing and tracking debates. The standardized tests, which have been a key feature of educational reform, are actually estimations of students' potential performance. Authentic assessment would replace the standardized multiple-choice test with real performance criteria requiring students to demonstrate what they have learned (American Educational Research Association 1991). Because authentic assessment must be built into the process of teaching and curriculum building, it is hoped that students would move from a focus on practicing for tests to more active and meaningful learning with built-in assessments. These assessments might be portfolios of work completed or in process, recorded observations of teachers, information from parents and other sources, self-reports of students, and other evidence of active learning (Leavitt and Eheart 1991). Part of the change in classroom structure that would accompany a change in the assessment process would be more opportunity for *cooperative learning,* or the opportunity for children to work with peers to achieve learning goals (Jones and Jones 1990). Clearly, teachers would need to develop different management and discipline techniques for heterogeneous classrooms in which students are engaged in active work than are required in tracked classes in which homogeneous groups of children focus on preparing for standardized tests (see Exhibit 3-7).

Parent and Community Involvement

Teachers and other professionals in schools know that they cannot help students to reach their full potential without the support and assistance of the parents (families) and other concerned citizens in the communities where they teach. Many experts in school reform are encouraging school systems to enlarge the democratic process by which the schools are run to include an increased role for parents,

---

EXHIBIT 3-7   **Example of Changes in Testing and Tracking**

Rural Valley Consolidated School District has one large elementary school for children who live on farms in a fairly large area around the school. For many years the children have been tracked according to their achievement scores at the end of second grade. A group of parents organized a few years ago to protest the tracking system, which parents claimed resulted in differential opportunities for children before they had a true opportunity to develop their skills in school. Many teachers supported the parents and added their concern that the tracks tended to reflect socioeconomic status and that children placed in the lower track in third grade tended to remain in that track through high school. A new superintendent, although insisting on continued standardized testing, has agreed to have heterogeneous class groupings in the elementary school. All the children will be assessed in a variety of ways each year, including teacher observations and portfolios. The children will be grouped for math and reading, but the ability groups will be flexible until the students reach high school.

constituents, and critical participants in education (Greenberg 1989). The earlier discussion of school restructuring in this chapter explored ways in which site-based management and shared decision making can involve parents and community members.

Educators generally agree on the importance of parent endorsement of schooling at home and of traditional parent support of school activities and requirements (Greenberg 1989). However, some teachers are actually reluctant to increase the participation of parents in schools. This reluctance can be based on several factors:

1. Engaging parents in the process of schooling usually takes extra time and energy on the part of teachers.

2. Parents can be angry or difficult to manage.

3. Teachers know that parents are often already burdened with family and employment responsibilities.

4. Teachers want to protect their classrooms from unfair scrutiny or blame.

Parents are often reluctant to become more involved with schools. Their feelings may be based on oppressive memories of their own school experiences, fear of professionals, guilt over problems they know their children are experiencing in the classrooms, or a belief that school should be left to the experts. These barriers can be alleviated by school efforts to help families fulfill basic obligations, communicate expectations of the school, involve families in positive ways in the school, and help families to be involved in learning at home (Weinstein and Mignano 1993).

Many educators will have to repudiate the traditional acceptance of family-deficit models. Greenberg (1989) notes that families that are culturally, economically, or structurally diverse have often been viewed as inferior and thus made to feel inferior. Vulnerable families can receive negative or harmful messages from schools that view them as deficient (Comer 1984). Edmonds (1979) refers to the effect of social science on school reform as pernicious because he believes that the persistent assertion that the family of the child is the principal factor in the acquisition of basic school skills has resulted in a loss of school accountability and subsequent lack of teacher effort. Although teachers must be realistic about the problems and limitations of parents and families, their expectations should be that most parents care about their children and will assist them if they receive useful and clear information about what they can to help (Weinstein and Mignano 1993) (see Exhibit 3-8).

EXHIBIT 3-8   ***Example of Parent Involvement***

Harriet Tubman Elementary School is located in a midwestern city. The small Parent Teacher Association for years has consisted of a few affluent mothers who are not working outside the home and who meet during the day. More than half the parents in the school are on public assistance, and more than 40 percent of the children live in single-parent homes. It has been customary among the few active parents and many staff members to assume that most parents don't care enough to be involved in their children's education.

This year a new principal (a single parent herself) has created changes in the school. She asked every teacher to write a letter home to families in September to share important school information and to tell parents the best way to get in touch with the school. In addition, she asked each teacher to plan one class event to which all parents are invited. The principal has surveyed all parents to see when they prefer school activities to be held, and the Parent Teacher Association has been asked to meet this year in the library meeting rooms of all three neighborhoods served by the school. In addition, the principal has monthly evening meetings to which all parents and teachers are invited to discuss school issues and to provide helpful information to parents who wish to support their children's schoolwork at home.

PROFESSIONAL DECISION   *Classroom Reform*

You are in the middle of a job interview in a rural school district. The principal says, "I guess you know we have a lot of reform going on all over the country. Here in this district teachers have a lot more freedom to make decisions than they might in larger and more complicated school systems. I'd like to know which current reforms you think are most important and how you think you might make them work in your own classroom."

Think about what your answer would be. Write a brief answer, listing reforms you find most engaging and identifying ways in which you as a classroom teacher might realistically fit them into your curriculum and instruction. If parent involvement was not on your list, be sure to also think of how you will enlist the support of family and community members.

ETHICAL CONSIDERATIONS FOR TEACHERS

The first two chapters of this book discuss many important issues and reforms that will have a major influence on the future of American education. Teachers, who will be playing a critical role in that future, will need to be guided by a professional code of ethics. This code, central to the development of student-centered classroom management, must establish personal integrity and professional conduct that reflects the highest principles of the teaching profession as well as an unwavering concern for the well-being of all students. A central component of a code of ethics for educators is a sense of responsibility for protecting students from any conditions that are harmful to learning (Evans and Brueckner 1992).

Ethics guide the day-to-day behavior of teachers and facilitate the many daily decisions that are of a moral or value-laden nature. When teachers encounter conflicting values in the school setting, the rights of children should be central to professional decisions and choices. Teachers' ethics must reflect recognition of the uniqueness of childhood as a vulnerable yet highly promising stage of life and the unique mission of the school in fostering respect, dignity, and a sense of personal value in students (Essa 1992).

How do busy teachers apply a code of ethics on a daily basis? They do so by reflecting each day on what they are doing and why they are doing it. It is personal reflection that supports rational and ethical choices of teachers about how and what to teach and when to discipline children, as well as a sense of responsibility for the choices they make. Responsible choices are based on such ethical questions as; What do children in a democracy need to know? What strategy will result in real learning? Which decision is based most on caring, fairness, equity, and justice for children? What evidence will there be that the choice has accomplished the goal you set for yourself?

Teachers also make daily choices in the areas of reform and restructuring outlined in this chapter. The National Coalition of Advocates for Children (1985) asserts that excellence in teaching and basic fairness for all children suffer when decisions result in a lack of flexibility in school structure, misuses of testing, narrowness of curriculum and teacher practice, and the lack of democratic governance in classroom and school. Classroom teachers do control many decisions in these areas and can be guided by their code of ethics in promoting the best learning environments possible.

Teachers often experience pressure to cover the required curriculum and to prepare children for formal standardized testing. However, Grumet (1988) reminds teachers that curriculum should not get in the way of the self-image and efficacy of children. When teachers see themselves as having a personal bond with students, rather than seeing students as "the other," they tend to be concerned with psychological and social development as well as educational gains (Zeichner 1991). How can teachers develop closer bonds with students? The simple ethical guideline offered by Grumet (1988) is that teachers should treat all children as they do their own. Because we do not "excuse our own children from their futures" (164), Grumet writes, we must not assume or allow failure in any children when it can be alleviated or avoided with a teacher's care, concern, dedication and hard work. Unfortunately, a complication in practicing this ideal is that many educational programs that work well for all children are not actually available to all children, and many services that counteract disadvantage are least available to disadvantaged children (Bastian, Fruchter, Gittell, Greer, and Haskins 1985).

Teachers who are determined to be ethical in promoting success for all children will have to acknowledge the dynamic of privilege that does exist in American education and that tends to assist more advantaged students and work against less advantaged students. Thus a well-functioning code of ethics for modern teachers must foster the development of social consciousness and moral commitment to equality (Zeichner 1991).

PROFESSIONAL DECISION | *Separate and Unequal*

Mr. Ramirez and Ms. Linder graduated from the same college and obtained teaching positions in the same small suburban school district that houses three elementary schools. Mr. Ramirez teaches in the school that serves the most advantaged families in the district. His class of 26 third graders has new reading texts and a new playground in the back of the school. Ms. Linder teaches in the least advantaged part of the community, and her class of 36 first graders does not have enough seats or texts. The children do not have a playground and often stay in the overcrowded lunchroom for the entire lunch period.

Ms. Linder and Mr. Ramirez have been talking about their situations during a teacher in-service day. Mr. Ramirez defends the discrepancies between the schools because the parents in his school pay much higher real estate taxes and "care more about education." Mr. Ramirez also points out that the students are better behaved, with far fewer suspensions than in Ms. Linder's school. Ms. Linder feels that her children do not get an equal chance to learn, and that their disruptiveness is the result of the larger class sizes and lack of time on the playground. She also thinks that the teachers in her school are operating at a disadvantage in terms of test scores, because the high quality of instruction can be offset by remedial but serious developmental delays caused by problems encountered by the children. Because the district utilizes standardized tests to some degree as a teacher-accountability measure, teachers often vie to be placed in schools where more advantaged children consistently attain higher scores. Indeed, the turnover in Ms. Linder's school is high while Mr. Ramirez's school has not had an opening in several years.

What do you think are the ethical standards that should guide the interaction of students and teachers in Mr. Ramirez's school? In Ms. Linder's school? What standards apply to both schools? Write a code of ethics for this school district, and discuss it with a partner.

CHAPTER SUMMARY

This chapter provided an overview of the issues affecting schools, teachers, and curriculum that are central to the creation of student-centered management. Teacher accountability and the responsibility of schools to children were discussed in the context of the interactive nature of behavior and the sense of moral imperative that should motivate teachers to act on the belief that all children can be successful learners. Invitational teaching was explained as an approach to classroom implementation of positive and productive interactive strategies; the ongoing professional concerns and challenges of teachers were also discussed. Current educational reforms and changing practices reflected in restructuring, developmentally appropriate practice, inclusion, authentic assessment, and parent and community involvement were explained; each will affect the development of student-centered classroom management. Finally, the ethics of teaching were discussed as a foundation for daily decisions of teachers in the current context of change and reform in education.

CHAPTER REFERENCES

American Educational Research Association. (1991, March). Interview on assessment issues with Lorrie Shephard. *Educational Researcher 20*(2), 21–23, 27.

Banks, J. A. (1994). *An introduction to multicultural education*. Boston: Allyn & Bacon.

Bastian, A., Fruchter, N., Gittell, M., Greer, C., & Haskins, K. (1985). *Choosing equality*. Philadelphia: Temple University Press.

Bellon, J. J., Bellon, E. C., & Blank, M. A. (1992). *Teaching from a research knowledge base: A development and renewal process*. New York: Merrill.

Bernard, B. (1993, November). Fostering resiliency in kids. *Educational Leadership, 51*(3), 44–48.

Bredekamp, S. (Ed.). (1987). *Developmentally appropriate practice in early childhood programs serving children from birth through age eight*. Washington, DC: National Association for the Education of Young Children.

Brophy, J. E., & Putnam, J. (1979). Classroom management in the elementary grades. In D. Duke (Ed.), *Classroom management* (the 78th yearbook of the National Society for the Study of Education, Pt. 2, pp. 182–216.) Chicago: University of Chicago Press.

Bruner, J. S. (1966). *Toward a theory of instruction*. New York: W. W. Norton.

Comer, J. (1984). Parent participation in the schools. *Phi Delta Kappan, 67*(8), 442–446.

Edmonds, R. (1979). Effective schools for the urban poor. *Education Leadership 31*(1), 15–23.

Essa, E. (1992). *Introduction to early childhood education*. Albany: Delmar.

Evans, J. M., & Brueckner, M. M. (1992). *Teaching and you: Committing, preparing and succeeding*. Boston: Allyn & Bacon.

Gardner, H. (1982). *Developmental psychology* (2nd ed.). Boston: Little, Brown.

Gartrell, D. (1994). *A guidance approach to discipline*. Albany, NY: Delmar.

Giroux, H. A. (1993). *Living dangerously: Multiculturalism and the politics of difference*. New York: Peter Lang.

Good, T. L., & Brophy, J. E. (1987). *Looking in classrooms*. New York: Harper & Row.

Goodlad, J. (1990). *Teachers for our nation's schools*. San Francisco: Jossey-Bass.

Greenberg, P. (1989). Parents as partners in young children's development and education: A new fad? Why does it matter? *Young Children 44*(4), 61–74.

Grumet, M. (1988). *Bitter milk: Women and teaching*. Amherst: University of Massachusetts Press.

Jones, V. F., & Jones, L. S. (1990). *Comprehensive classroom management: Motivating and managing students*. Boston: Allyn & Bacon.

Kamii, C. (1990). *Achievement testing in the early grades: The games grown-ups play*. Washington, DC: National Association for the Education of Young Children.

Kane, P. (1990, April). Love of learning is not enough. *Teacher Magazine, 1*(7), 84–85.

Leavitt, R. L., & Eheart, B. K. (1991, July). Assessment in early childhood programs. *Young Children, 46*(5), 4–9.

Levine, D. U., & Havighurst, R. J. (1992). *Society and education* (8th ed.). Boston: Allyn & Bacon.

Manning, M. L. (1993). *Developmentally appropriate middle level schools*. Wheaton, MD: Association for Childhood Education International.

McClure, R. M. (1991). Foreword. In S. B. Heath & L. Mangiola, *Children of promise: Literate activity in linguistically and culturally diverse classrooms*. Washington, DC: National Education Association.

McGill-Franzen, A., & Allington, R. L. (1993). Flunk 'em or get them classified: The contamination of primary grade accountability data. *Educational Researcher 22*(1), 19–22.

Mongon, D., & Hart, S. With Chris Ace and Anne Rawlings. (1989). *Improving classroom behavior: New directions for teachers and pupils*. New York: Teachers College Press.

Mortimore, P., & Sammons, P. (1987). New evidence on effective elementary schools. *Educational Leadership 45*, 4–8.

————. (1991). *The good common school: Making the vision work for all children*. Boston: Author.

Natriello, G., McDill, E. L., & Pallas, A. M. (1990). *Schooling disadvantaged children: Racing against catastrophe*. New York: Teachers College Press.

Nieto, S. (1992). *Affirming diversity: The sociopolitical context of multicultural education*. New York: Longman.

Oakes, J. (1985). *Keeping track: How schools structure inequality*. New Haven, CT: Yale University Press.

O'Neil, J. (1993, November). Inclusive education gains adherents. *ASCD Update 35*(9), 3–4.

Page, R. N. (1991). *Lower track classrooms: A curricular and cultural perspective.* New York: Teachers College Press.

Perrone, V. (1990). How did we get here? In C. Kamii (Ed.), *Achievement testing in the early grades: The games grown-ups play* (pp. 1–13). Washington, DC: National Association for the Education of Young Children.

Postman, M., & Weingartner, C. (1969). *Teaching as a subversive activity.* New York: Delacorte.

Purkey, W. W., & Novak, J. M. (1984). *Inviting school success: A self-concept approach to teaching and learning.* Belmont, CA: Wadsworth.

Slavin, R. F. (1993, November). Students differ: So what? *Educational Researcher, 22*(9), 13–14.

Soltis, J. F. (Ed.). (1987). *Reforming teacher education: The impact of the Holmes Group Report.* New York: Teachers College Press.

Spaulding, C. L. (1992). *Motivation in the classroom.* New York: McGraw-Hill.

Spring, J. (1991). *American education: An introduction to social and political aspects.* (5th ed.). New York: Longman.

Wayson, W., & Pinnell, G. S. (1982). Creating a living curriculum for teaching self-discipline. In D. Duke (Ed.), *Helping teachers manage classrooms.* Alexandria, VA: Association for Supervision and Curriculum Development.

Weinstein, C. S., & Mignano, A. J., Jr. (1993). *Elementary classroom management: Lessons from research and practice.* New York: McGraw-Hill.

Willis, S. (1993, November). Teaching young children: Educators see "developmental appropriateness." *ASCD Curriculum Update* (Association for Supervision and Curriculum Development), 1–8.

Wong, H. K., & Wong, R. T. (1991). *The first days of school.* Sunnyvale, CA: Harry K. Wong Publications.

Zeichner, K. (1992). *Educating teachers for diversity.* Madison: University of Wisconsin.

4 PERSPECTIVES ON CHILD DEVELOPMENT, MOTIVATION, AND BEHAVIOR

Teachers in the process of constructing a philosophy of student-centered classroom management need to include theoretical knowledge of child development, motivation, and behavior in their approach to children. They must also apply understanding of historical and current ideas about the ways in which children grow and learn. The management of groups of children in classrooms requires a lifelong habit of learning and reflecting on the complex ways that humans think and act in response to their environments. It also requires understanding of the different contexts of behavioral requirements in school and the ways in which these contexts serve the needs of institutions and professional adults as well as children. This chapter discusses the following topics:

- Applying child development theories in the classroom
- Motivation and behavior in school
- Historical ideas about children and education
- Child development and behavior
- Moral development in children
- Child behaviors that promote school success

APPLYING CHILD DEVELOPMENT THEORIES IN THE CLASSROOM

Almost every aspiring teacher is required to take courses in history and philosophy of education, as well as in child development. These courses can greatly enhance the practice of future teachers when they bridge relevant theoretical information with ideas for informed classroom practice. The goal of this chapter is to connect the theories and a philosophy of child-centered management in real schools. Why should theories of child development be included in a book on classroom management? There is a direct relationship between student-centered management and developmental interpretations of the way children act. The first three chapters of this book discuss current realities of children in America, responsibilities of schools to children, and perspectives on schools, teachers, and curriculum. To understand how that information relates to classroom management and discipline, it is necessary to focus on critical professional beliefs about the ways in which children learn and grow as thinkers.

Although some teachers have had intensive training in specific theories and their application to practice, most have surveyed a variety of theories in their courses. This chapter explores eclectic ways of thinking about theory to solve classroom problems and create a productive atmosphere for meaningful learning. In this chapter, and throughout the remainder of this book, student-centered and developmentally appropriate contexts of learning are presented as the single most important focus for helping children learn appropriate behavior and self-discipline in school and in life.

> You are visiting a first-grade classroom in an ordinary public elementary school. You notice that the children seem restless and distracted and that the room is warm and crowded. The teacher is exerting obvious effort in his attempt to help all the children understand and complete a reading readiness worksheet. The atmosphere seems to be a mix of tension and boredom. At a particularly frustrating point in the lesson the teacher turns to you and says, "The problem is that these children really don't want to learn!"
>
> A second teacher unexpectedly walks into the same classroom with a small cage. She says, "I wonder if anyone can guess what kind of baby animal I have with me?" Suddenly, the children become silent, and then they gather excitedly around the cage. They all crane their necks to see the animal and guess what

it is. They are talking and laughing, and when they find out it is a baby rabbit, they have many questions. Where did it come from? How old is it? Where is the mother? Can we pet it? Can we hold it? The second teacher says, "Everyone will get a turn at holding the rabbit, but first you must quickly sit in a quiet circle so it does not become too frightened." The children immediately sit in a circle, waiting for the baby rabbit to come out of the cage.

What is it that inspires a high level of curiosity in children, and why are they so much easier to manage and so much more cooperative when they are truly interested in what they are doing? This question has been asked and answered in different ways by many theorists throughout history. Examining their insights into the nature of human interest and motivation is helpful to teachers who are puzzled by some aspects of the behavior of children. Why is it that the same students who are bored and restless one minute can be totally absorbed in a task the next? Studying developmental theory can help teachers to balance and strengthen their personal beliefs about how children should behave and why they behave the way they do.

If teaching is to be considered a true profession, it must be based on well-established and -accepted theory. Applying the concept of developmentally appropriate practice, which is discussed fully in Chapter 5, requires substantial knowledge of child development. Every professional decision in the classroom should be based on the best available knowledge about the ways in which children learn and develop. Without comprehensive and consistent application of child development theory, teachers are in danger of making haphazard decisions that create resistance, boredom, and habitual inattention in children. Teachers also may be unable to adequately assess curriculum and related activities that school districts routinely use. Why focus on child development in school when so many American children do not experience optimal conditions in home and community? Responsible educators must recognize the even greater importance of respecting developmental needs and basing educational practice on best available theory when schools offer children their only real chance to thrive. The ultimate goal of all education is not to control but to motivate to learn and thus to enhance opportunities for life.

This chapter does not attempt to provide a thorough background of historical trends in educational thought or a comprehensive discussion of human motivation and child development theory. It is assumed that you have had, or will have, opportunities to study these topics in depth as part of your professional preparation for teaching.

The purpose of this chapter is to discuss several historical ideas and theories of child development in relationship to current issues in the child-centered management of behavior in classrooms. It stresses the need for teachers to turn to questions about how children learn best rather than to questions of what is "wrong" or missing in their home and community environment. It also stresses a positive approach based on the assumption that lifelong study of child development theory must be applied to ongoing observation, interpretation, and shaping of child behavior. An important part of this process is understanding the ways in which children can be motivated to learn. Successful motivation often eliminates the need to deal with distractions and discipline problems. This chapter emphasizes ways of thinking about behavior and its connection to requirements of the school rather than thinking about behavior as separate from institutional demands of schools on children. This discussion of developmental theory and its relationship to student-centered management introduces more detailed discussions of discipline and management.

QUESTIONS TO CONSIDER

1. Can you recall encountering a learning or behavioral difficulty when you were an elementary student? To what classroom conditions might you now attribute that problem?

2. Think about a class you found boring. What were your specific complaints about the teacher or professor? Why did you find the class boring?

MOTIVATION AND BEHAVIOR IN SCHOOL

The first and most important developmental concept involves motivation. Teachers need to consider motivation in the context of their professional requirements in the classroom. What does a teacher do all day? The answer is complex, but in truth teachers spend a great deal of daily classroom time attempting to shape general and specific behaviors of children. "Sit down," "Take out your books," "Be quiet," "Keep your hands to yourself," "Complete page fifty-five," "Line up single file,"—these are all familiar commands from teacher to students during a typical day. Teachers also spend a great deal of time explaining, demonstrating, and guiding each day, but they must continually monitor the behavior of the group and of individuals.

Obedience or Motivation?

If teachers spend much of the school day guiding behavior, it follows naturally that students spend much of the school day following adults' directives. Does this mean that the academic success of children is based mainly on the ability and willingness to follow the directions of teachers? If this were the case, learning would depend most on the child's willingness and ability to be obedient. However, we know that learning is an active endeavor that requires the cooperative participation of students in meaningful tasks. Although the more passive response of obedience may be viewed as an integral requirement of acceptable school behavior, academic success in school is far more dependent on a positive student response to intrinsic motivation to complete meaningful work. As Jerome Bruner (1977) writes in *The Process of Education*, "Somewhere between apathy and wild excitement, there is an optimum level of aroused attention that is ideal for classroom activity" (72).

It is that level of aroused attention, rather than a level of obedience, that should be the most important goal of educators. It is students' motivation to be attentive rather than obedient that will most help the teacher to engage the minds of the students. Children who are motivated to engage in an activity are likely to learn and repeat the skills involved. This view is supported by Piaget, who noted that children from birth seek stimulation and competence and tend to perform tasks consistently once they have mastered them (Ginsburg and Opper 1969).

The process of learning requires conditions related more to attracting and maintaining students' interest and less to superficially controlling isolated behaviors such as staying silent, sitting still, or "paying attention" (which can at times be a mask that children use while their minds wander to more interesting subjects). Engaging students in the process of learning requires such factors as a reasonable choice of learning activities, the opportunity to assume responsibility, and the development of a personal sense of accountability for completing the work required (Johnson and Johnson 1994). Teachers should note that environments conducive to learning do not derive from a focus on ways to foster obedience in children but from the creation of meaningful contexts for learning. These conditions require teachers to master ways to create a classroom environment that motivates students to become engaged in meaningful work. Students who are absorbed in work will be learning and demonstrating acceptable social behavior.

What Is Motivation?

Motivation can be generally defined as any internal condition that appears to produce goal-directed behavior (Gardener 1982). Theorists in human development and behavior have studied the forces that lead people to act in some ways and not in others. For classroom teachers motivation is never a theory so much as it is a discernable reality that dictates the success or failure of many classroom lessons. As partners in the learning process, students must be inspired to play an active role in the classroom. The motivation of children to play that active role is directly related to the tasks they are asked to accomplish in school. Students must have spontaneous and sustaining interest in the tasks and must be convinced that it is important and beneficial to complete them. Thus learning and motivation are often an individual rather than a group matter, because they are related to each child's current level of development, as well as interest and competence in required tasks.

Spaulding (1992) defines motivation as the key to all learning and suggests that human motivation is tied to personal competence (self-efficacy) and personal control (self-determination). In many instances a focus on competence and control can mean that students are more motivated when they perceive school tasks as something they do for themselves rather than something they do (with or without coercion) for adults. The child who is "well behaved" is usually the child who believes that important rewards exist within the setting of the school and that "good behavior" will result in satisfying and meeting valuable personal goals. The challenge for all teachers is to create goals and related rewards that act as incentives for all children in school.

QUESTIONS TO CONSIDER

1. How would you describe your behavior in elementary school? Do you recall it as generally consistent, or did it change from time to time? Did it change from teacher to teacher? Why?

2. However you described it, if you were asked to give a general explanation for your behavior in elementary school, what would that explanation be?

Motivation and Acceptable School Behavior

Many behaviors required of children in school are in truth related to operational needs of adults rather than learning needs of students. Although motivation is central to learning activities, children often are expected to "behave themselves" in a certain way simply because they are instructed to do so. Why should children, even those who are truly motivated to successfully meet all the learning tasks of the school, "behave" as adults wish them to? Because we assume that motivation is the driving force behind goal-directed human behavior, what exactly should we see as motivation for children to obey adults' directives in the school setting? This is not an easy question to answer, and it deserves serious thought on the part of anyone considering classroom teaching.

The reasons cited by adults for cooperation in school ("learn to be responsible" or "get better grades," for example) may be neither apparent nor convincing to students. Schools may be requiring behaviors very different from those expected in the home and community, and in some cases parents may not support the rules and expectations of the school. Although teachers traditionally remind children that they need to do well in school to get a good job when they grow up, there is not always a direct link between school achievement and adult economic or career success in modern America. Children may have unemployed parents who lost jobs for which they prepared in school for many years or may have siblings who worked hard to graduate from high school and then could neither afford to go to college nor find a job with a living wage. Role models for some children may be adults who dropped out of school and became successful through unusual circumstances (or even, unfortunately, illegal activities). Other children may live with one or two parents with one or two jobs who still do not have enough money to buy a home or a car or sometimes even food. Children living in poverty may have little personal experience with adults who have the good fortune of long-term successful employment. Although these realities do not mean that teachers should not continue to help children visualize potential connections between school and future employment, they do indicate that some of the difficulty in motivating children may stem from depressing or discouraging factors in their lives.

Children tend to "behave well" in school when school is a rewarding and pleasant place to be. If they can meet consistent levels of success in their undertakings, and maintain responsive and encouraging relationships with their teachers, children also are more likely to meet operational and institutional demands. Teachers must therefore also focus on ways to make daily learning meaningful and relevant to the lives of their students. Those goals are central to creating developmentally appropriate tasks that inspire spontaneous interest and meaningful task completion. They are also central to promoting an atmosphere of cooperation and indeed obedience when necessary.

Do All Children Want To Learn?

Many teachers experience moments or days of frustration during which they wonder, "Do all children really want to learn?" The answer is almost invariably yes, but educators should not confuse the desire of children to learn through their life experiences with the more specific motivation to learn in school. Bruner (1966) writes that the single most human characteristic is the ability to learn and indeed that learning is so deeply ingrained in the human experience that it is almost involuntary. Virtually all humans are motivated in some way (Spaulding 1992), and almost all children have intrinsic motives to learn simply because they are curious. Children are most strongly attracted to what is unclear or uncertain and stay attracted to it until it is clear and certain. The intrinsic reward in such circumstances appears to be solving a problem or acquiring knowledge (Bruner 1966). Thus, with the rare exception of intellectually disabling conditions, all children *do* want to learn. However, all children do not demonstrate the desire to learn inside the school.

Why isn't the desire to learn always in evidence in school? One reason may be that school is very different from home or other environments. Children in school are required to be orderly, they must function as members of a group, they are often restrained from doing what they most want to do at any given time, and the requirements of school are often inflexible (Bruner 1966). Also, the tasks required in school may not be those that capture the spontaneous interest of children in other settings. Although some children do seem to "take naturally" to school, and to perform at a consistently high level, many equally capable children have more difficulty adjusting to school requirements. Classroom teachers should thus assume that all children are motivated to learn but that connecting that motivation to requirements placed on children in an institutional group setting may require much coaxing or adjusting.

It may be helpful at this juncture to review the discussion in Chapter 3 of the school's responsibility in meeting the needs of the child. Even if some children resist the tasks required by schools (and this can happen even in a classroom in which the teacher is working diligently to motivate every child), educators are responsible for sensitive and concerned analyses of why students resist. The behavior of children is always linked to their motivation to complete required tasks. Teachers need to ask *how* the children are being motivated, *why* they are being motivated, and *why* it should appear important to children that they attend to the tasks at hand. It can be tempting at times to blame parents, community, television, and a host of other outside factors for the failure of children to want to learn in school. However, teachers must recognize that because all children are potential learners who want to demonstrate their competence, focusing on what students can do successfully is intrinsic to their continuing desire to complete their work. Motivation is an acquired competence, and teachers can help children become better motivated by telling them why tasks are important and by relating those tasks to their lives (Jones and Jones 1990).

Any assumptions about children's motivation and desire to learn must be linked to the honest recognition that some children attend schools that have less money than other schools do. In his 1991 book *Savage Inequalities*, for example, Jonathan Kozol documents enormous differences in American schools. Certainly it is difficult for students and teachers alike to maintain a positive attitude toward learning in a depressing and poorly funded school environment. Before the days of compulsory education, the most likely course for a discouraged and disenfranchised student was to drop out of school. Students today might be too young to drop out but old enough to express hostile and apathetic attitudes (Bellon, Bellon, and Blank 1992) that have been interpreted as making "little effort to learn" (Charles 1992: 114). Many of these students could be motivated to succeed on a higher level in school. Certainly no students should be labeled in negative and unproductive ways when their apathetic behavior is a direct and logical response to the underfunded and programmatically inadequate schools they attend. Glasser (1990) suggests that the commitment and personal warmth of teachers can overcome apathy. Teachers who are angry or upset by the inadequate resources with which they and their students must contend need courage and hope in order to continue to encourage their students and act as advocates for them in the greater society.

ACTIVITY AND DISCUSSION

1. In a small group recall your years in elementary school as well as any experiences you have already had with schoolage children. List the activities that always seem exciting and interesting to children. Then list activities that seem to create restlessness and boredom in children. Discuss the role that intrinsic motivation might play in the different responses of the children.

2. With a partner pretend that you are teaching in a classroom that contains two different groups of children. One group has affluent parents and enjoys comfortable housing, stylish clothing, and nice vacations. The other group has parents on public assistance, lives in housing projects, and frequently lacks appropriate clothing. List ways in which each group might be more or less motivated to try to be successful in school. Identify some ways that you think you could motivate all the children (as a group) to work as hard as they can in school.

Prevention Through Motivation

Motivation is the first developmental concept considered in this chapter because it is such a complicated and important factor in the school behavior of children. Children are motivated learners in many aspects of their lives (they may know how to care for siblings or use complicated public transportation systems, for example), and it is up to teachers to try to capture their motivation and direct it toward learning. Motivation is the first step in preventing behavior and management problems in the classroom, because it energizes the attention, emotions, and actions of children (Borich 1992). Motivation increases the likelihood of success with any individual task, and success in turn increases the likelihood that students will continue to make an effort. Bruner (1966) found that students either cope or defend in learning situations. If they cope, they can respect the requirements of the problem at hand and retain a sense of integrity. If students defend, they avoid or escape problems for which they believe there is no solution or that violate their sense of integrity. Teachers will encounter students who have built up defenses in school, and an intrinsic part of teachers' efforts to motivate these students will be to break down their defenses through repeated experiences of success (see Exhibit 4-1). Success in this effort requires a positive relationship, hard work, and mutual determination to make progress in the classroom (Weinstein and Migano 1993).

EXHIBIT 4-1   ***Coping and Defending in Schoolchildren***

Maryanna and Juliette are in the same fourth-grade class at Greenwood Elementary School. Their teacher starts this day by saying, "We have a surprise math test this morning. Books away please." Maryanna quickly puts her books away and silently recalls the homework examples she did last night. Juliette feels her mind go blank as she slowly places her belongings under her desk; she asks the teacher if she may go to the bathroom before taking the test. When her teacher says, "No, please wait," Juliette feels anxious and unhappy. She reaches over to the desk of the boy next to her and takes his pencil out of his hand. He tries to grab it back and falls out of his seat. A fight ensues. Chastised by her teacher, Juliette cries and refuses to complete the test. Maryanna, on the other hand, works enthusiastically and finishes quickly.

Maryanna is *coping*—she has a positive response to the requirements of the test and feels confident that she has the knowledge and experience to take it successfully. She is eager to demonstrate her competence.

Juliette is *defending*—the test poses a problem she feels that she cannot solve successfully. Unwilling to face the failure that seems inevitable (she failed the last two tests), Juliette avoids and escapes from the test through inappropriate behaviors. Her sense of integrity is less threatened by disapproval of her behavior than it is by attempting to take the test and failing it.

HISTORICAL IDEAS ABOUT CHILDREN AND EDUCATION

This chapter has discussed the link between motivation and appropriate behavior in school. Children are motivated to be attentive and to learn for some reasons that are directly related to well-identified stages of human development. Students are more interested in some topics and activities at some times rather than others because of the developmental patterns they experience. This chapter turns now from the discussion of motivation to an examination of theories about the way children learn and grow.

Dr. Hunter, a noted expert in the history of child development theory, has been invited to talk to teachers about the relationship of theory to classroom practice in the area of management and discipline. He carefully describes the approach of major theorists in his address and draws connections between theory and how teachers may interpret children's behavior in schools. After the lecture Dr. Hunter takes a few minutes to read over the audience evaluations of his address. To his surprise and disappointment, more then half the teachers feel that his talk is not useful to them. They write such comments as, "We are tired of hearing the same old theories again and again" or "We need some new ideas for controlling behavior." After carefully analyzing the evaluations, Dr. Hunter realizes that he must think of more meaningful ways to help teachers incorporate increasingly sophisticated understanding of the theories into the ways they plan to motivate and interpret the classroom behavior of children.

"Personal Theories"

All teachers come to the profession with a personal history of experiences with family, peers, community, and school. Along with this personal history are personal and informal theories—shaped by the teachers' experiences and interactions with others—of how children should be treated and how they should be expected to behave in school. Personal views and ideas are important, but they are often limited to the ways in which each individual experienced the culture of family and school.

Personal theories must be continuously informed and strengthened with knowledge of the history of educational thought and understanding of the various formal theories of human development and behavior. The challenge for teachers is to form a flexible balance of personal beliefs and theoretical knowledge to support their lifelong habit of reflective thought in the classroom. This balance protects teachers from bias in their analysis of and response to discipline problems in the classroom. Teachers need a repertoire of developmental concepts that they can use to support decisions and actions in the classroom that are fair and that give children a true chance to grow and improve. They can combine their basic understanding of the concept of motivation with expectations of how children naturally act at certain ages and stages. Many valuable and relevant concepts have evolved over history, particularly during the last century.

History of Education Theory

Many great intellectuals throughout history have given serious thought to the education of children. Teachers, the intellectuals who shape the minds of children today, can benefit from reflecting on the major themes that have emerged throughout history and the ways in which those themes continue to be important to educators (see Exhibit 4-2).

EXHIBIT 4-2   *Modern Reflection on Historical Theories*

Modern educators should reflect on the importance of historical beliefs about children and thus apply them to their own classroom practices.

Philosopher/ Educator	Contribution to Education Theory	Questions for Today's Teachers
Johann Amos Comenius	Play and choice are necessary to help children develop in harmony with their cultural settings.	Are play and choice possible to any extent when class size is large and curriculum is standardized? How might this theory apply to multicultural settings?
John Locke	Children's minds are blank slates shaped by environment and experience.	What are the roles of experience and innate developmental stages in the educational process? How can schools best deal with the diversity of childrens' personal experiences?
Jean Jacques Rousseau	Reason must be grounded in harmonious emotion and natural expression. Self-direction leads to self-acceptance.	How can teachers apply Rousseau's notions when children have had little or no opportunity to develop skills in self-expression? How can schools focus more on emotional health?
Johann Pestalozzi	Educators must rely on the natural instincts of the child to provide motivation for learning.	How would Pestalozzi see to the effects of television and movies on the play and learning behavior of children? How can standardized curriculum be altered to appeal to diverse natural interests?
Friedreich Froebel	Early education should be a process of natural development; play releases the inner power of children, and true discipline is embedded in feelings of human worth.	How can schools instill discipline in and protect the self-worth of children who bring problems from home and community into the classroom? How would Froebel view same-age grouping in terms of natural development?
John Dewey	Play carries children to a higher level of consciousness, and children need to experience real-world problem solving in the democratic process.	Should children explore real-world problems like violence or drug addiction? Can their play in school reflect realities in their lives?

When teachers wonder why a child is acting in a certain way or why their students are so disinterested in a subject, they can be certain that the question has been considered by other educators. Although many thinkers focused on young children, their ideas translate well to the education of older children.

One seventeenth-century intellectual who focused on education was Johann Amos Comenius, who suggested in his writing that children should be encouraged to play and make choices. He believed that this mode of education would bring them into harmony with their cultural setting. The ideas of Comenius are reflected today in developmentally appropriate practice, as well as in multicultural approaches to education.

In the late seventeenth century John Locke described the mind of the child as a blank slate (*tabula rasa*) that is shaped by environment and experience. Locke stressed that adults must avoid any behaviors that they would not want children to learn because of the strong tendency of the child to imitate. (Braun and Edwards 1972). His perceptions are reflected in the focus of modern behaviorists on environmental reinforcement as the major influence of child development and behavior.

Jean Jacques Rousseau was an eighteenth-century philosopher who wrote that the existence of reason, which is intrinsic to education, has to be well grounded in harmonious emotion and natural expression. He believed that education builds the character of children through inner development and self-direction and that self-acceptance is critical to surviving the challenges of adolescence. Rousseau's ideas are reflected in modern conceptualizations of child-centered curriculum that promote independence and self-esteem.

Johann Heinrich Pestalozzi was an educational philosopher whose life bridged the eighteenth and nineteenth centuries; he espoused the theory that educators must rely on the natural instincts of the child to provide motivation for learning and that positive early experiences promote positive moral reactions in later life. Modern developmental theorists still focus on appropriate educational experiences as the basis of values and moral development in children. Also, many educators continue to question whether discipline should be loving and permissive or restrictive (Weber 1985).

Friedreich Froebel was the founder of the first kindergarten in Germany in 1937. Froebel believed that early education should take place through a process of natural development that unites the individual with God and nature. He used the metaphor of the garden to demonstrate that children do grow according to nature if they are cared for properly (Spodek, Saracho, and Davis 1991). Froebel also believed that play releases the inner power of children and that true discipline is embedded in feelings of human worth and harmonious human relationships (Weber 1984). Froebel's beliefs continue to be relevant to modern educational thought about the importance of sensitivity to natural developmental patterns and the continuing need for kindness and human concern as a support for the development of ego and competence in children. Froebel's focus on the importance of play and the critical role of emotions in fostering learning in children are reflected in psychoanalytic theory and continue to be central to the question of discipline. Harmony in relationships remains important in development of self-control and skills in human interactions.

John Dewey, the progressive educator who lived from 1859 to 1952, also believed that play is the natural impulse that carries the child to a higher level of consciousness. He believed that children need the opportunity to experience real-world problem solving, including engagement in the experience of democratic group living. Dewey felt that the school can develop a code of values that determines the code of relationships between students and teachers. This code of relationships, as well as the values implicit in the study of realistic life activities in the classroom, is what Dewey believed would lead to the development of moral values in the child (Weber 1985). Today there is increased concern that students have the opportunity to engage in cooperative learning, which prepares them for the democratic nature of the group work that is increasingly required in business and other employment situations. Ethics, values, and morality have emerged as political as well as educational issues in public school districts around the United States.

Educators who reflect on the intellectual history of education have the opportunity to draw connections between past, present, and future concerns about the education of children. They can benefit from asking the questions that have emerged again and again throughout history. How can we foster the natural development of children? How can children be nurtured and protected as they develop their innate ability to learn and grow? How do children learn to become disciplined adults? That these and many other important questions continue to challenge those committed to children suggests that each generation must reanalyze and redefine the nature of its educational commitments. In the past hundred years an important component of educational history has been the emergence of theories from the systematic study of children and adults. These theories provide an organized framework for observing and interpreting the behavior of children, and they inform the decisions and interventions of the classroom teacher.

Reflecting on the Theories

Sometimes educators become cynical about developmental theories. They wonder whether the theories have real relevance or real application to the classroom. Teachers are decision makers, and their professional preparation qualifies them to think in critical ways about theory. Although it is not productive to dismiss theories, it is helpful to choose those that seem to support your personal philosophy of classroom practice. Perhaps one teacher will decide that Locke, like Skinner many years later, oversimplified human development by placing too much emphasis on environment. That same educator may recognize that modern schools do not often lend themselves to the more naturalistic ideas of Rousseau. Still, by shaping the classroom environment as much as possible to support skill development through ordered choice of multiple learning centers, the teacher is actually using the theories of Locke and Rousseau in practice. In agreeing or disagreeing with theories teachers use their intelligence and experience to strengthen their integrated approaches to successful classroom education.

ACTIVITY AND DISCUSSION

Think back once again to your favorite teacher(s) in elementary school. Identify specific ways in which these teachers reflected some of the views of the intellectuals discussed in this section. Then discuss with a partner or in small groups the specific ways in which these teachers were able to maintain discipline and promote self-esteem in students.

CHILD DEVELOPMENT AND BEHAVIOR

The field of education has been heavily influenced by more recent theorists who have provided extensive insights into the ways in which human beings grow and develop from birth and throughout life. These theorists have provided much important information to those who wish to create the most relevant and productive school experiences for children. Although all human beings are unique, most also fit into a predictable and sequential developmental process. From infancy until death every human being exhibits signs of individuality as well as predictable patterns of development. Child development theory and research have provided normative data to help parents, teachers, and all who are responsible for children to predict and nurture a fairly orderly process of growth. Children sleep, eat, cry, grow, speak, read, ride a bike, and master a host of other life skills within well-established time frames.

Teachers throughout the elementary grades and adolescent years make many assumptions about readiness and interest in students based on normative data and the expectation of sequential growth patterns. In fact, the field of education is permeated with developmental expectations, many of which shape such practices as age of school admission, selection of grade-level curriculum, and movement from one level of schooling to the next. These assumptions and practices are based on a variety of theories about ways in which children develop as thinkers and actors in the school setting.

Child development theory is central to any discussion of behavior and motivation in the classroom. The child who is at times restless and troublesome may be observed at other times to be completely fascinated by a learning task. Could the intermittent learning difficulty be the emotional ramifications of a problem at home? Is the child being inadvertently reinforced for inappropriate behavior? Is the required task beyond the current physical or intellectual abilities of the child? The answers to these questions should not rest merely on the hunches of educators; the answers should be informed and guided by current knowledge of child development. Children act as they do for a reason, and the educator who can successfully apply a relevant behavioral intervention from developmental theory is far more likely to make an appropriate and productive response.

Theorists in child development have formulated explicit (well-defined) and orderly explanations of predictable and sequential growth patterns or responses to the environment (Weber 1985). These assumptions about the human species are usually based on extensive studies of children or adults or both. Many theories cannot really be proved but are considered valid so long as they can be consistently applied and so long as scholarly disproof is not possible. By applying theory, educators and others concerned with human growth and development can interpret and support the systematic changes that take place as the person moves through the life cycle (Baldwin 1980).

Almost all educational practices are based on either implicit or explicit theory that has emerged over the past one hundred years (Weber 1987). It is important for teachers to study developmental theories and to develop a pattern for systematically applying theory in the classroom. It may be helpful to think of a wheel of ideas or guesses based on several major developmental theories that you can spin and apply. A variety of situations will arise every day that require reflection on the ways in which human beings can be expected to behave.

Theories of human development that have emerged in the last century have greatly enhanced our understanding of childhood as a foundational stage of growth (see Exhibit 4-3). The child study movement is considered to have begun with work of G. Stanley Hall (1844–1924), who studied children in natural settings in order to develop "scientific" data on child development. Hall believed that data on child development should provide the context for adapting school curricula to the specific learning needs of children. He postulated that every child retraces the evolution of human beings (Weber 1984) and further suggested that play helps children to lose their primitive behaviors (Spodek, Saracho, and Davis 1991). (Note that themes of play and natural development emerge repeatedly throughout history, along with suggestions that teachers supply flexible and creative opportunities for children in schools.)

Arnold Gesell, whose work spanned the turn of the century and continued into the early 1960s, persevered in the child study tradition by forming a systematic data base by observing children. Gesell's detailed descriptions of children were transformed into the norms and stages that undergird maturational theory. He believed that the behavior of children evolves with other forms of mental and physical growth in unified structure and consistent sequence guided by genetic predetermination. Gesell assumed the "ground plan" of child development to be beyond the control of parents or teachers and wrote that failure to interpret maturity and readiness in children results in wasted effort, harmful interference, and unjust discipline (Weber 1985). Educators who apply Gesell's theory continue to respect the natural developmental patterns of children and to observe students carefully to be sure that they are not frustrated by inappropriate school demands. In addition, schools around the United States routinely test for readiness, and maturity remains an important issue in decisions regarding age of school entry and appropriate curriculum for children throughout their educational careers. Some educators now question the use of readiness tests for children,

EXHIBIT 4-3   ***Developmental Theorists***

The developmental theorists listed here have strongly influenced educational practice. Teachers will benefit from reflecting on these theories to strengthen their approach to student-centered classroom management.

Philosopher/ Educator	*Contribution to Education Theory*	*Questions for Today's Teachers*
G. Stanley Hall	Scientific data on child development should provide the context for relevant school curriculum, and play helps children retrace evolutionary development.	To what extent has research on child development been applied to school curricula? How much opportunity for meaningful play has been built into school programs?
Arnold Gesell	Systematic data base on children provides information on genetically predetermined norms and stages; and failure to determine readiness results in wasted educational effort and unjust discipline.	Did Gesell base his developmental assumptions on a child population as diverse as the one that American teachers encounter today? How can readiness be applied to strategic adaptation of school curriculum?
Sigmund Freud	Psychoanalytic theory focuses on human emotional development and childhood conflicts created by unconscious urges toward aggression and sexuality.	How has the widespread exposure of modern American children to violence on television and in movies influenced their inner developmental conflicts? How can teachers best be prepared to allow for the psychodynamic conflicts that take place in childhood?
Erik Erikson	Psychosocial theory supports psychoanalytic theory of conflict and the focus on the role of ego in the integration of developmental timetables and social demands.	Are school demands realistic in terms of the developmental timetables of children? How do the social demands of school add to or subtract from positive ego development?
B. F. Skinner	Behaviorist theory views human developmental response as dependent on variable reinforcement in the environment.	How can this theory best be balanced against other widely accepted stage theories of child development? Is it possible for teachers to identify the appropriate reinforcements for all children in real classroom settings?
Jean Piaget	Intellectual development takes place as the child constructs knowledge of the world through interaction with people and objects.	How can appropriate intellectual tasks be designed for large groups of children whose developmental needs are highly diverse? What objects could most easily be incorporated in daily learning and teaching?

insisting instead that schools take the responsibility for being ready to meet the needs of all entering children.

Sigmund Freud (1856–1939) developed the psychoanalytic theory that focuses on human emotional development. A generally accepted idea of Freud's time was that childhood is innocent. Freud countered with the then-radical theory that children are conflicted with primitive and unconscious urges toward aggression and sexuality. Freud at first was surprised that his neurotic patients focused consistently on the experience of childhood, but as his theory developed, he drew greater attention to childhood as a significant stage in emotional development (Weber 1985). Freud built his theory on his conceptualization of a series of internalized conflicts that are based in biological patterns, basic instincts, and unconscious motives of the early years of life. The conflicts are based on innate desires that the child must transform into responsible social behaviors. Educators influenced by Freud understand that the normal process of human development includes natural emotional conflict for children. It is thus important for teachers to pay attention to the emotional needs of children by providing an educational environment that helps direct their instinctual energies toward socially acceptable outlets (Spodek, Saracho, and Davis 1991). Other educators question the use of psychoanalytic theory in the classroom and suggest that schools look instead at their procedures and curricula for potential causes of conflict or emotional distress in children.

Erik Erikson (1902–1994) supported Freud's belief that children experience internal conflicts centered on the need to create a balance between personal needs and desires and the requirements of society. He focused on the role of the ego of the child in integrating the organic timetable with social demands (Weber 1985). Erikson differed from Freud in his main focus on psychosocial (rather than psychosexual) forces and encouraged awareness of the increasing hazards of sociocultural stress as it affects the human experience. Erikson identified eight conflicts that humans confront throughout the life span, the first four of which relate to children from birth through early schooling (Erikson 1963). He believed that children first need to develop social trust in the world as a stable and encouraging place and then to explore that world with independence while retaining access to social guidance that fosters self-esteem. As children continue to develop, according to Erikson, they feel more comfortable with the task of contemplating goals and taking initiative. Eventually, they acquire the knowledge and skills necessary for successful completion for adult-created and -defined rules and tasks. Erikson, like so many others, believed play to be essential to the development of healthy social and emotional abilities in children (Weber 1987). Educators who incorporate Erikson's theory are sensitive to sociocultural stress and help children to meet the demands of school through experiences that strengthen their feelings of competence and self-esteem. However, other educators feel that competence in appropriate school activities provides meaningful self-esteem and that the focus should be on school curriculum and skill building.

Whereas these theorists focused on internal stages, conflicts, and timetables, B. F. Skinner (1904–1990) focused on environmental factors external to individual organisms. His rigorous experimentation and observation built the behaviorist theory, which views human response as highly dependent on variable external conditions. Reinforcement in the environment, according to Skinner, determines the probability that certain behaviors will be continued and others discontinued. In his view the environmental consequences of any behavior control the replication or extinction of that behavior. Thus educators who accept behavioral theory assume that they can use consequences to strengthen or weaken identified behavioral responses of students (Weber 1985). They accept as their task the need to observe behavior and analyze ways in which they might restructure environment to assist the child in developing self-control and positive learning strategies. Other educators question the use of behavioral strategies, which they believe may be neither adaptable to individual needs nor conducive to a primary focus on curriculum and warm interpersonal relationships between children and teachers.

In contrast to maturational, psychodynamic, and behavioral developmental theories, the cognitive theories of Jean Piaget (1896–1980) focus on the development of intelligence (which he defined as knowledge of the world). Piaget was a scientist who conducted and recorded intensive observations of his own three children and designed "semiclinical interviews" to explore how children actually think about specific conceptual problems. He theorized that every child constructs knowledge of the world through actions and interactions involving people and objects rather than through impassive mental registration of material to be learned. Piaget postulated that active children develop changing structures of thought and concept through equilibration of two separate processes: assimilation into existing mental structures and accommodation through alteration of mental structures (Weber 1987). Educators influenced by Piaget try to assist children in the development of a thought process that leads to intellectual growth through appropriate learning activities. They believe that telling children information is less valuable than helping them to conceptually explore material through meaningful activity (Spodek, Saracho, and Davis 1991).

Why do these theories of child development remain relevant to modern considerations of behavior and motivation in children? Formal education in our society is an intersection of two powerful forces: the natural development of children and the institutional demands of the school as it represents society. The intended outcome of this intersection is learning, but learning cannot take place without the participation and cooperation of the children. Teachers who know *how* children learn, and who focus on the preparation and implementation of appropriate activities, are far more able to successfully engage their students (see Exhibit 4-4 on page 92). Behavior and management are inextricably tied to the creation of a school environment that respects the learning needs and developmental realities of children.

ACTIVITY AND DISCUSSION

1. Think about a child you have seen misbehave in the classroom. Try to apply psychoanalytic, behavioral, psychosocial, and cognitive theory to the problems this child exhibits. How might each theorist suggest that the teacher intervene?

2. Discuss your ideas in a small or large group.

MORAL DEVELOPMENT IN CHILDREN

This chapter has covered motivation, historical thinking about ways in which children should be educated, and theories of human development. We now turn to the topic of moral development for two reasons. The first is that many human development theorists have studied moral development and its relationship to critical developmental experiences. The second is that many teachers apply overt or subtle moral meaning to their behavioral expectations and interpretations in the classroom. Consider this hypothetical situation:

Ms. Sharpe has had to correct Juanita more than ten times today for misbehavior. Juanita has been whispering to the children seated around her during lessons, failed to follow directions for three separate activities, and went to the bathroom without asking permission. Toward the end of the day Ms. Sharpe has come to the end of her patience. She says, "Juanita, I am very disappointed in you. Tomorrow when you come into this room I expect you to be a good girl!"

What did Ms. Sharpe mean by being "good"? Being obedient? Being quiet? Making appropriate choices? Following orders? Does being good mean completing well-established task expectations? Does it mean being demure and compliant? Does it mean facilitating the task of the teacher, who must control a large group of children all day? Does it mean being true to your inner self by choosing the work that best reflects your personal interests and abilities? Morality (which is often what is presumed in the concept of goodness), like motivation, goes well beyond the concept of obedience in complexity and relates closely to the absence or presence of developmentally relevant school tasks. Teachers in student-centered classrooms often are in the position of making value judgments about behavior. They will be assisted by insights into the dynamic forces and social experiences that help children to develop values. Several theorists who focused on moral development and the educational process offer important perspectives.

Maria Montessori (1870–1952) drew powerful connections between morality and the freedom to develop a sense of personal power (competence or self-efficacy.) According to Montessori, this sense of power is developed in children through self-initiated engagement in meaningful tasks that require full mental concentration. She stressed her belief that children who misbehave need to work at interesting educational "occupations," and that "if the child is placed upon a path in which he can organize his conduct and construct his mental life, all will be well" (Montessori 1967: 200). Montessori claimed that her schools solved the problem of discipline by allowing children to freely seek their own work and to become absorbed in different kinds of tasks. Children could thus construct their personalities not through domination and repression but through "motives for activity" that were so well adapted to the child's interests that they "provoked deep attention" (206). Montessori was concerned that the concept of freedom not be misconstrued as chaotic permissiveness. Rather, educators need to design a progressively interesting world of study in which the character is strengthened through the search for intellectual knowledge (Montessori 1967).

EXHIBIT 4-4

Thinking About Theory in Practice

A Classroom Scenario

Mr. Washington is a new teacher for a fifth-grade class that has a bad reputation. He wants to focus on using developmental theory to foster improved behavior in the students. After several weeks careful observation and anecdotal records have given him some important information about his class. The students fight constantly over the placement of seats (but only during large group instruction) and are particularly unruly after lunch every day. Some students have been retained in grade and are physically advanced, whereas several others appear to have entered school early or close to the district's age cutoff. When Mr. Washington presents learning activities based on movement, music, or student choice, he generally can obtain the cooperation of the class. Most disruptive behavior begins when he attempts to teach new concepts while students listen for more than fifteen or twenty minutes. There is constant interruption over the loudspeaker from the principal and assistant principal during the last hour of the day, which makes retaining his students' attention nearly impossible.

Mr. Washington thought through the theories of maturation, behaviorism, psychodynamics and psychosocial dimensions, and cognitive growth and has decided to attempt the following five interventions:

1. Maturationist	Several students are immature and appear not to be ready for some of the material to be covered. Mr. Washington is going to try to adapt the curriculum for individuals, and look for parent volunteers to assist as tutors. In addition, students who are more mature will be used as peer tutors and given some additional responsibilities in the classroom.
2. Psychosocial	Fighting over seats seems to be related to emotional stress in gender relationships. Both boys and girls seem more comfortable when they are separated for large group direct instruction, so Mr. Washington redesigns the seating chart but retains mixed-gender small groups, which are working well.
3. Psychodynamic	Mr. Washington observes a lunch period and finds that his students are not getting an opportunity for active play in an overcontrolled playground situation. He asks the lunch monitors whether the students may have more time for free play, which allows them to relieve emotional stress.
4. Behaviorist	Mr. Washington knows that he must help his students to develop listening skills that will allow them to absorb at least twenty minutes of direct instruction a few times a day. He gives clear behavioral guidelines and rewards the class with five minutes of in-class free time after each successful direct instruction period.
5. Cognitive	Mr. Washington continues to develop independent and group activities that foster independent learning each week. In addition, he asks students to start writing weekly journals about their mathematics and language arts interests to help him shape appropriate ideas for class projects.

Jean Piaget included moral behavior of children in his constructivist theory of development. He believed that moral behavior is related to the practice of rules and that much can be learned about children's conceptualization of rules by observing their play. Piaget believed that children aged 4 to 7 do not really know or follow rules, although they insist they do. Their characteristic egocentrism affects their moral behavior and is reflected in the fact that they focus on themselves and cannot really understand the perspective of another. Children gradually grow into what Piaget referred to as *incipient cooperation* in games by ages 7 to 11, when they are willing to apply greater understanding of rules to social expectations for mutual cooperation during games. In Piaget's theory conflicts and difficulties over rules continue until age 11 or 12, when children know and understand rules well and enjoy elaborating on them (Ginsburg and Opper 1969).

Piaget's theory thus suggests that children construct morality along with knowledge and intelligence through their social experiences with rules and cooperation. He believed this construction has to take place through active education characterized by interest, play, and experimentation. Devries and Kohlberg (1987) remind us that cognitive organization is present in every area of a child's development at any point "where a self thinks about the physical and social world and its own relation to that world" (xii). The social experiences required for the development of morality lead to reciprocal friendships, the meeting of mutual interests, common understandings, and forgiveness when needed. Well-developed morality in children supports the behaviors that most teachers expect: truth telling, taking turns, respecting the rights of others, following class rules, and keeping promises (Devries and Kohlberg 1987).

Piaget and Montessori both focused on the *will* of the child as central to the development of morality. Montessori believed that the child's freedom to select the most absorbing intellectual activity strengthens later tendencies to choose productive and appropriate behaviors. Piaget stressed the role of will in the child's pursuit of intellectual activity, because as children work at interesting tasks, they also elaborate on their sense of moral rules intrinsic to completion of the tasks. He believed that constraint or coercion do not lead to the development of the mutual respect that ultimately overcomes egocentrism in the developing child. Piaget stated that the act of following the rul of others through a morality of obedience never leads to the kind o' reflection necessary for commitment to a set of internal principles of moral judgment (Devries and Kohlberg 1987).

The theories of Montessori and Piaget should not be misconstrued as support for chaotic and undisciplined classrooms. Rather, these theories underscore the need for well-structured learning activities that provide choice and independence and that motivate children through natural and consuming interest in developmentally appropriate activities. More simply put, the child who chooses an activity because it is interesting is not likely to misbehave while engaging in that particular task.

Misbehavior can be an indicator that a particular task is boring or frustrating and therefore developmentally inappropriate for the child at that time. When the hypothetical Ms. Sharpe tells her student Juanita to "be good," she is saying that Juanita should reflect on her misbehavior, decide to change, and then identify more acceptable behaviors in which to engage in the classroom. However, it is entirely possible that Juanita has little or no experience with making choices and reflecting on the effects of different kinds of behavior in the classroom. Montessori and Piaget, within their separate theories, suggest that a child like Juanita has to practice making choices in the classroom every day in order to construct an internal code of behavior through social interactions defined by reasonable rules. Her "goodness," like her development of knowledge, must be a time-consuming and personalized construction of the intellect.

Lawrence Kohlberg (1927–1987) was a developmental psychologist who also constructed a theory of morality in children and adults. Kohlberg, like Piaget, focused on the reasoning that takes place when a child is confronted with a moral or ethical dilemma. Rather than characterize an individual as bad or good, Kohlberg suggested trying to ascertain the student's current level of thinking about problems or situations involving moral decisions. Kohlberg's six stages of moral reasoning move from (1) an initial punishment and obedience orientation through (2) satisfaction of desires and needs, (3) an interpersonal concordance or "good boy–nice girl" orientation, (4) a "law and order" orientation, (5) a social contract (legalistic) orientation to (6) an orientation of universal ethical principles. Kohlberg's constructivist approach to morality mirrors the approaches of Montessori and Piaget and illustrates the role of intellectual experience in formulating morals and ethics in children (Gardener 1982).

Note that none of these theories states that the character or intrinsic personality of a child should be judged on the basis of observed levels of moral development. Rather, those concerned with the development of the child should identify the developmentally appropriate activities that may provide growth in self-knowledge and ability to improve in social behavior. Morality as we commonly define it in modern society implies the ability to think in a reasonable way about alternatives and to choose the most socially responsible alternative. Because it is often necessary to require specific behaviors in school situations, it might at first appear unrealistic to suggest that children can choose their behavioral responses in school. However, each school day provides some opportunity for children to experience choice, and teachers can assist them in doing so whenever possible. Choices can frequently be provided through a variety of interesting activities that require interactions with people and objects in potentially cooperative social situations. The child who is allowed to make responsible intellectual choices in the classroom is not only growing in mind but in spirit—and in morality. This discussion of morality draws a true connection between the actual tasks required by the school, the cognitive experience provided by those tasks, and the ability of students to make appropriate behavioral choices. Teachers in student-centered classrooms should have confidence in the connection between meaningful work and positive moral development in children.

ACTIVITY AND DISCUSSION

Take some time to reflect on recent conversations you may have heard about morality and values in American society. What do you think people usually mean by these terms? List some social indicators of morality and values in adults. Then apply concepts from Montessori, Piaget, and Kohlberg to ideas about how children can develop those social skills in school. Discuss your ideas in a small group.

CHILD BEHAVIORS THAT PROMOTE SCHOOL SUCCESS

This chapter has examined motivation, historical and current theories about child development, and morality as an integral aspect of child growth and learning. All these aspects of child development can and should be enhanced by the educational experience. All children are developing organisms who respond to internal physical and emotional structures as well as to external social expectations and reinforcements. Regardless of the level of advantage or disadvantage a child may be experiencing in family and community, educators can focus on the power of each individual to maintain progress on a developmental continuum. The intellect of the child is constantly energized by events, people, and objects, and every task and intervention helps to guide that intellect to new areas of developmental achievement.

It is important to relate the information about motivation, behavior, and development discussed in this chapter to the actual child behaviors expected in school that inhibit or reinforce the process of education. It is at this point that reflective educators can begin to apply historical and developmental thought to the real problems of children in schools. Rather than exhibit school behaviors that are generally good or bad, children act in ways that closely relate to the social and educational task-related expectations of the school. When so many teachers cite difficult student behavior as their most pressing problem in the classroom, everyone concerned with education must wonder whether school expectations are poorly correlated with developmental needs. Can the curricula and teaching strategy most commonly used in classrooms across America capture the natural interest of children and thus motivate them to engage in productive work? This question does not and should not discount the fact that children can be disruptive and difficult in the classroom for a variety of reasons, including outside influences that affect their attitudes, dispositions, and social skills. However, the role of the school is to meet educational needs, and the job of the teacher is to motivate and instruct. When evidence exists—as it does—that both teachers and students are experiencing stress in the process of education, institutional practice must be questioned. Children need the opportunity to become interested in relevant work, and teachers need the opportunity to identify and implement those interventions that can interest and motivate their students.

One such important intervention is an effort to identify child behaviors that promote school success and to work as hard as possible to assist children in the development of those behaviors. Always keep in mind that school behaviors of children never exist in isolation from the tasks that the school requires. Teachers must assess the realities of school and classroom requirements and take steps to help all students meet those requirements as successfully as possible.

Child Development and School Realities

Part of the gap that sometimes exists between educational theory and classroom practice is created by ideas that appear to be sensible in the college classroom but are actually quite difficult to apply in the elementary school classroom. Why is this? One important reason is that schools are complex institutions that require a great deal of specific cooperative behavior from children simply so schools can function in some orderly pattern. The behaviors required of children in order to facilitate large group function differ from behaviors that should be required in an ideal sense from developmentally appropriate tasks (see Exhibit 4-5). For example, the school may have a large assembly every Friday. The first-grade children may be expected to sit without moving or talking for fifteen minutes waiting for an activity to begin and then to attend to a twenty-five-minute presentation geared more to the intermediate grades. They might then be required to line up, wait five more minutes to exit, and to walk silently back to their classrooms. Children who lack the maturity or skills to meet all these expectations may be corrected or even punished by adults. Their teachers have a valid point when they say, "I know this was much too long a time period and not really interesting to my students, but I have to enforce these rules to do my job."

Because schools as institutions so often require students and teachers to act in ways that are not the best practice, developmental

---

EXHIBIT 4-5

The Four Contexts of School Behavior

Institutional Requirements	Children support the maintenance of order in the school by following rules in such areas as dress, bus conduct, promptness, and courtesy.
Teacher Requirements	Children support the maintenance of order in the classroom by following rules in such areas as silence during lessons, lining up and moving through the building in a specific pattern, and following directions during lessons and tests.
Group and Peer Requirements	Children support the maintenance of a positive and productive social environment by cooperating with small groups and partners and helping others to complete required tasks.
Developmental Learning Requirements	Children support the learning environment by selecting and completing tasks that reflect their interests and abilities.

theory may seem irrelevant to practitioners. Why focus on development and theory when it cannot always be applied? First of all, it is important to be aware of and be committed to best practice even when it cannot be fully implemented. There are always long-range goals in education; always ways to improve and reach for new attainments. Also, teachers can always take the most humane and understanding approach to children in any situation, thus alleviating some of the stress of institutional requirements on schoolage children. Most important, many school learning activities are directly influenced by individual teachers, and it is therefore within the power of committed teachers to build developmentally appropriate interventions into their daily practice. Some contexts of schooling can be much more sensitive than others to the developmental needs of children, and it is helpful to teachers to differentiate between them as they plan their daily work.

The Four Contexts of School Behavior

When educators reflect in an analytical way on the behavioral requirements of school, they realize that many different behaviors actually are expected from students in a variety of school contexts. This section considers four major contexts of child behavior in school that require the attention and planning of teachers: institutional requirements, teacher management and control requirements, group and peer requirements, and learning and related task requirements (see Exhibit 4-5). Within each of these four contexts teachers can identify the most productive behavioral responses of children and help their students to understand and develop these behaviors. Part of this process is analyzing the difference between child-centered requirements and those that actually serve the needs of adults or of institutions. It is important to recognize that children are often being asked to cooperate in supporting institutional and adult needs. Institutional and teacher-centered requirements that focus on group management may be based more on the need of adults to manage groups effectively, whereas group cooperation and developmental learning requirements can be based more closely in the needs of individual children.

Institutional Requirements

Every school has rules and policies that children must follow. These may include a dress code, times of arrival and departure, breakfast and/or lunch procedures, playground rules, parent permission for trips and certain activities, codes of behavior in the halls during class transitions, and rules for behavior on school buses or with crossing guards. Schools may use serious disciplinary techniques for such infractions as fighting, cheating, lateness, or truancy and may have in-house or out-of-school suspension policies (even for kindergarten and primary grades in some schools) for children who fail to follow school rules.

Children and their families need more than simple information about these institutional rules, requirements, and consequences. They also need to know how to follow these requirements, some of which may be unclear (appropriate dress, for example, may have a variety of cultural interpretations) or difficult to follow (children who walk to school may encounter traffic or weather delays of which parents are unaware, or different bus drivers may have different rules regarding noise or seat partners). Although individual classroom teachers often do not create school rules, they play an important role in helping children to understand and follow them. They can incorporate discussion of school rules in classroom activities and play an active role in reminding children of expectations before transitions, lunch, departure, and other times when they will be out of the classroom.

Some potential problems, like fighting, may be alleviated by efforts of classroom teachers to mediate disagreements, promote group cooperation, and eliminate unnecessary frustrations such as long waits for transitions. Other problems, such as lateness and failure to follow dress codes, may be related to family situations beyond the control of the child. Teachers can try to communicate with families and administrators about these problems. They can also speak personally with children who are having institutional difficulties to be sure they understand school expectations and to help them deal intellectually and emotionally with those requirements in a positive way. It is important for classroom educators to realize that institutional requirements exist for the smooth operation of the school and may not always be sensitive to the individual needs of some children and their families. Children as classroom learners should always have the right to be valued as potentially successful individuals, even if they or their parents encounter institutional difficulties.

Teacher Management Requirements

Classroom teachers must successfully meet their contractual obligations and the expectations of administrators, other supervisors, parents, and community. Central to meeting these requirements is effective management of an assigned group of students. Teachers are expected to adhere to the school schedule and to move children in an orderly way within the building at specific daily intervals. Examples of such intervals are trips to the lavatory, movement to lunch or gym, and entrance or exit at the beginning or end of the day. Teachers also may be required to teach certain subjects at specific times every day and to conduct countless in-class transitions from small group to large group, from one learning center to another, and from one activity to another. Within these requirements are numerous smaller tasks that must be completed in a safe and orderly fashion. These may include opening and closing desks, lining up, taking out books and putting them away, walking from one part of the room to the other, passing out and collecting papers, conducting tests, and helping a group of children to sit, stand, walk, or work without disorderly behavior.

Although children must exhibit specific behaviors in this category, the behaviors are often required to meet the institutional needs of adults who are attempting to maintain group control. Teachers know that school administrators consider class management and control a critical classroom skill. Therefore as teachers establish rules and routines in their classrooms, the professional stakes are often high. Those teachers who have large classes and who do not have support from paraprofessionals or resource personnel can experience considerable stress as they work to maintain control of their students. One way to help alleviate this stress is to help children understand why their cooperation is needed and to develop a sense of pride in the behavior of their class.

Teachers need to establish reasonable rules and to help the children see the connections between these rules and the maintenance of a pleasant and functional classroom environment. Rules are discussed in greater detail in Chapter 7. For now, suffice it to say that teachers can explain and demonstrate that rules and routines make the classroom a safer, friendlier, and more productive place. Teachers can also make a systematic effort to inform the families of their students about their class management procedures, perhaps in a letter in the beginning of the school year. Although rules and routines are not always completely sensitive to the needs and feelings of individual students, they can provide all children with a sense of predictability and order as each school day progresses. The classroom thus can appear to be a reasonable although structured environment, which can in turn alleviate stress as teachers and students work together to meet the requirements of their work at school.

Group and Peer Management Requirements

The classroom is a social environment, and children learn from each other as well as from their teachers. Added to the teacher management requirements are those necessitated by general interstudent social relationships, cooperative small group work, tasks to be completed by partners, and any other areas in which children are responsible to each other for completion of learning tasks. Unlike institutional and teacher management requirements, group and peer relationships can be designed and regulated with a more personal and developmental view of the individual students in the classroom. Also, unlike institutional and teacher management requirements, each grade has different social needs and interests as the students' interpersonal sensitivities, interests, and skills change.

One other way in which group and peer relationships differ from the first two areas is in the opportunity for moral and value development. Schools and classrooms must have rules to function as safe and orderly environments for learning, but obedience in and of itself does not offer the reflection required by the developmental process of moral development. Group or partner work governed by reasonable rules, often those that the children help to create, provide an environment of thoughtful cooperation that allows children to apply their intellects to why rules have important social value.

At this level of management teachers thus move from a product ("Everyone must stand and move to the doorway quickly when the bell rings") to a process approach ("Let's plan together how we want to design our group social studies project this month"). They are role models for key social skills, and they facilitate the development of social skills that lead to more complex levels of intellectual and value development. Of particular importance in our society is encouraging peaceful and respectful student relationships and the development of conflict mediation skills. Unlike institutional and teacher management skills, which essentially facilitate adults' requirements, group and peer management skills allow for choice, independence, and student control over developing competencies. Cooperative learning is discussed at greater length in a later section of this text.

Developmental Learning Requirements

It is in the area of developmental learning requirements that the child-centered approach to management emerges as a central concern. Developmentally appropriate learning requires that children have the opportunity to select the learning activities that reflect their current interests and abilities. For children in kindergarten and primary grades these activities are focused more in play-based active exploration of subject matter. As children move into the intermediate grades, they become more competent in organized academic tasks. In all cases students should have opportunities for choice and active problem solving. In developmental learning requirements a large measure of responsibility for behavior shifts sharply to teacher observation, planning, and facilitation of appropriate activities. There is also a shift toward student independence and personal responsibility for task completion. Student behavior requirements become largely self-directed, except in the cases of individuals who are impeded by more serious behavioral problems. The next chapter focuses on the concept of developmentally appropriate learning in the child-centered classroom.

PROFESSIONAL DECISION | *Helping Students Follow the Rules*

Melba Rankin has just taken a teaching position in the fourth grade of a large urban public school. She has found many of her students to be poorly disciplined and difficult to manage. Many children come to school late every day, and several are suspended each week for fighting or shouting at teachers. Ms. Rankin has trouble maintaining attention during her lesson, and some children laugh and make fun of each other in class. Social studies, which Ms. Rankin teaches after lunch, presents the worst problems. The textbook is old, and the children are restless and bored during the lessons. Some pass notes and others look out the window.

Analyze Ms. Rankin's problems using the four contexts of behavioral requirements in school discussed in this chapter. Make recommendations for Ms. Rankin in each area. How can she explain the requirements and work with her students to develop appropriate skills in each area?

CHAPTER SUMMARY

This chapter bridged discussion of realities of American children and schools in Chapters 1 through 3 with important perspectives on historical and developmental views of child behavior. It stressed that teachers who seek to create student-centered classrooms must be aware of ways to reflect on theory and apply it to practice. Theory is important because it informs the ways in which teachers interpret and understand behavior and helps schools to balance institutional requirements with real needs and abilities of children. This chapter contrasted concepts of motivation and obedience. All children are motivated to learn, although not all are motivated to learn in the ways and means stressed in some schools and curriculum standards. Student-centered management is dependent on learning activities that truly motivate and interest students rather than on obedience of children.

This chapter acknowledged the importance of personal theories, which usually are based on a teacher's specific cultural and educational experiences. It further suggested that teachers continue to learn about past and current educational and developmental theories and use them to reflect on the ways in which children respond to teaching and learning strategies in the classroom. Ideas of historical figures and theories of experts in child development were discussed, and examples of reflective questions were provided. Because values and morals are often discussed in terms of schools and society today, this chapter also discussed developmental views of the growth of morality in children. This discussion reinforced the critical importance of choice and relevance in curriculum to growth of positive behaviors in students.

Finally, this chapter described the four different contexts of school behavior: institutional requirements, teacher management requirements, group and peer management requirements, and developmental learning requirements. By reflecting on the relationship of school rules and expectations in each context, teachers are better able to clarify the nature of behavior problems and identify the best solutions. These four contexts of school behavior also illustrate that children are often asked or required to support the needs of institutions and adults through such behaviors as silence, lining up, and other forms of group cooperation. Group and peer management requirements, as well as developmental learning requirements, were stressed as the two areas in which teachers can most strongly encourage the intellectual, personal, and moral development of children. Constant encouragement of student growth through curriculum and activities informed and supported by theory can make student-centered management a reality in the classroom.

CHAPTER REFERENCES

Baldwin, A. L. (1980). *Theories of child development*. New York: John Wiley & Son.

Bellon, J. J., Bellon, E. C., & Blank, M. A. (1992). *Teaching from a research knowledge base*. New York: Merrill.

Borich, G. D. (1992). *Effective teaching methods*. New York: Macmillan.

Braun, S. J., & Edwards, E. P. (1972). *History and theory of early childhood education*. Belmont, CA: Wadsworth.

Bruner, J. (1966). *Toward a theory of instruction*. New York: W. W. Norton.

————. (1977). *The process of education*. Boston: Harvard University Press.

Charles, C. M. (1992). *Building classroom discipline*. New York: Longman.

DeVries, R., & Kohlberg, L. (1987). *Constructivist early education: Overview and comparison with other programs*. Washington, DC: National Association for the Education of Young Children.

Erikson, E. H. (1963). *Childhood and society* (2nd ed.). New York: W. W. Norton.

Gardner, H. (1982). *Developmental psychology* (2nd ed.). Boston: Little, Brown.

Ginsburg, H., & Opper, S. (1969). *Piaget's theory of intellectual development*. Englewood Cliffs, NJ: Prentice-Hall.

Glasser, W. (1990). *The quality school. Managing students without coercion*. New York: Harper & Row, Publishers.

Johnson, D. W., & Johnson, R. T. (1994). *Learning together and alone: Cooperative, competitive, and individualistic learning*. Boston: Allyn & Bacon.

Jones, V. F., & Jones, L. S. (1990) (3rd ed.). *Comprehensive classroom management*. Boston: Allyn & Bacon.

Kozol, J. (1991). *Savage inequalities*. New York: Harper Perennial.

Montessori, M. (1967). *The absorbent mind*. New York: Henry Holt.

Spaulding, C. L. (1992). *Motivation in the classroom*. New York: McGraw-Hill.

Spodek, B., Saracho, O. N., & Davis, M. D. (1991). *Foundations of early childhood education* (2nd ed.). Englewood Cliffs, NJ: Prentice-Hall.

Weber, E. (1984). *Ideas influencing early childhood education: Theoretical analysis*. New York: Teachers College Press.

Weinstein, C. S., & Mignano, A. J., Jr. (1993). *Elementary classroom management*. New York: McGraw-Hill.

5 DEVELOPMENTALLY APPROPRIATE PRACTICE AND CHILDREN'S BEHAVIOR

The goal of education is the optimal growth and development of children as members of society. This goal is best achieved when children are active learners who are motivated to cooperate with the learning process in school. The behavior of children in schools cannot be separated from the tasks that schools require. If educational tasks are poorly matched to the developing abilities and interests of students, a negative student response is the predictable outcome. Teachers who understand the principles and rationale of developmentally appropriate practice (DAP) can plan and implement meaningful lessons and activities that support positive behavioral responses from children. This chapter discusses the following topics:

- Looking at the power of curriculum
- Developmentally appropriate practice and positive school behavior
- Contrasting developmentally appropriate and psychometric practice
- The four areas of developmentally appropriate practice
- The relationship of constructivism to behavior
- Developmentally appropriate practice and the real world of classrooms
- The important role of teachers in implementing developmentally appropriate practice
- Linking personal competence to discipline

LOOKING AT THE POWER OF CURRICULUM

Chapter 4 turned from discussing the lives of American children and the challenges faced by their schools to examining theories about ways in which children learn and develop. The ideas and theories discussed in Chapter 4 can and should have a direct bearing on the creation of student-centered curriculum and learning activities. This chapter discusses the concept of developmentally appropriate practice. This philosophy and approach to education, more briefly discussed in Chapter 3, attempts to base classroom practice on developmental interests and needs of children.

Developmentally appropriate practice provides an opportunity to conceptualize behavior, discipline, and management as concepts that are interwoven in the structure of learning experiences in the classroom. Chapters 6 and 7 focus on more specific aspects of behavior, management, and discipline as separate aspects of classroom life. However, you must remember that the behavior of children is always responsive to the design of lively and relevant learning activities. Consider this situation:

> A businessman looks out the window of his office in a major American city and sees a group of fifth graders in the adjacent empty lot. Some children are taking photographs of the lot, which contains a community vegetable garden. Other children are interviewing community residents who maintain the garden. Another group of children is sitting in a corner of the lot observing a large medical complex that owns the lot and now plans to convert it into a parking lot for its employees. The owners of the medical complex had originally lent the lot to the community for its garden but are resisting community attempts to retain it.
>
> The fifth-grade students are trying to think of ways to simultaneously meet business and community needs. The children's teacher moves from group to group and asks many questions about what the children are thinking and how they are planning to investigate the problem. The businessman shakes his head as he watches, wondering what happened to the kind of classroom education he experienced as a child. But he cannot help but be fascinated with the lively interest of the children and the relaxed interaction they enjoy with their teacher. He decides to go down at lunch to learn more about what the class is doing.

At lunchtime he approaches the group and learns that it is working on a class project that integrates math, science, social studies, and language arts. Part of the class investigation will include a study of traffic patterns in the area, ways to design a parking lot so that the garden can remain, alternative sites for employee parking, and interviews of employees and residents to learn more about the stress of city living. The students plan to publish an illustrated report of their investigation. The businessman realizes on his walk back to his office that his conversation with the students has interested him in the issue of the community garden.

This fifth-grade class is enjoying an exciting activity that reflects many aspects of developmentally appropriate practice as it was introduced in Chapter 3. Educators now widely recognize the value of curriculum methods that allow children to construct an internalized knowledge of the world through interactive activities and projects. Many teachers around the United States are being encouraged to move beyond the four walls of the classroom and the four corners of the textbook to structure more dynamic and complex classroom activities. Often this more active curriculum allows children to explore real problems. The purpose of this chapter is to elaborate on the design of developmentally appropriate practice and to connect it to the support of child-centered classroom management in elementary schools.

QUESTIONS TO CONSIDER

1. Reflect for a few minutes on the example of the students who are investigating the community's concerns about the garden and parking lot. Did you ever have the experience of such a project as an elementary school student? If you did, what kind of projects did you do with your class?

2. If your elementary school experience was exclusively based on traditional academic work in the classroom, how do you think you can prepare to feel comfortable with creating developmentally appropriate projects for your students?

DEVELOPMENTALLY APPROPRIATE PRACTICE AND POSITIVE SCHOOL BEHAVIOR

School districts across the United States are facing the challenge of restructuring. The widespread interest in restructuring is a response to recommendations such as that of the Holmes Group, that educators need to make school better places for teachers to work and students to learn (Soltis 1987). An important aspect of restructuring is understanding that the behavior of both students and teachers is highly related to what is actually happening every day in real classrooms. Children's personal and interpersonal behaviors are shaped not only by the work required by school but by the emotional and physical climate in which that work must be done. Schools that create a climate of encouragement and support for intellectual growth of students are also empowering their growing abilities to act in positive and productive ways.

Developmentally appropriate practice is intrinsic to the process of school restructuring, because it seeks to make school more relevant to and interesting for children. Such a change holds promise for minimizing the stress created by school expectations that are unrealistic and unfair because they are not matched to students' real interests and abilities. Positive changes in curriculum that generate more interest and enthusiasm in students also support and encourage the many teachers who are frustrated by or even exhausted from attempting to engage resistant students in required but seemingly inappropriate curriculum.

Changing Definitions of Student Success

Restructuring is about change, including change in the way the school success of children is envisioned and assessed. Meaningful change in the definition and assessment of positive student outcomes cannot occur until teachers alter increasingly outdated conceptualizations of school success in children. According to Brooks and Brooks (1993), traditional schools tend to teach within a narrow band of issues, to focus on preestablished facts, and to require short and simple answers to questions. Student success within such a climate is rarely based on demonstrated understanding of complexities, possibilities, or discrepancies that emerge in the process of study. Rather, the assessment of student success is often based on the ability to function in elementary classrooms that reflect:

1. Classrooms dominated by teacher talk

2. Instruction based mainly on textbooks

3. Students isolated from one another through individual and often competitive completion of low-level tasks

4. The devaluation of *thinking* in favor of "right" answers

5. A curriculum based on a fixed conceptualization of the world that students are expected to know

These realities of school often require teachers and students to unquestioningly accept an inflexible, preestablished curriculum, to focus on covering rather than understanding that curriculum and to be satisfied with continuous completion of short-term rather than long-term goals (Brooks and Brooks 1993).

What student behaviors are required in this traditional conceptualization of success? Clearly, a central task confronted by the student is that of figuring out the "right" parts of problems and the "right" answers demanded by a fixed curriculum. What the student thinks often is secondary to such skills as discerning which answers the teachers will accept as correct, obeying teachers' directives, attending to textbooks, completing worksheets whether they are interesting or boring (or indeed whether they make real sense or not), depending on teachers to do all the planning, and waiting for adult approval before taking initiative in the classroom. All students, from those who appear highly gifted to those who seem to struggle with basic skills, can find their creativity and intellectual curiosity stunted in such a narrow school environment. Misbehavior of children within this traditional context of success can result from stress created by tasks and expectations that are too confining. Students who cannot correctly anticipate what the teacher wants them to think, or who cannot obtain adult approval for a variety of reasons (which may include bias, labeling, and low expectations as well as inadequate behavior or performance) will find themselves increasingly ill at ease in the social and intellectual climate of the classroom. Teachers who repeatedly confront serious discipline problems in their classroom may often ascertain from observation and analysis that these problems are related to students' low interest levels in subject matter, long duration of tasks requiring inactivity, and a lack of connection between tasks and the lives of students.

Selma Wasserman (1990) points out that no responsible adult sets out to create mental handicaps in the lives of children. However, school situations that focus on adult control more than children's intellectual power can unwittingly create educational hazards. The "can do" child who approaches school tasks with interest and enthusiasm requires the support of "can do" adults who understand the importance of flexibility and respect for individual interests and learning styles. Wasserman believes that schools can release positive power in children by allowing them to try, guess, fail, and persist in a climate that values learning more than right answers. She restates Glasser's point of view, that all behavior is our best attempt to satisfy such basic psychological needs as a sense of belonging, power, freedom, and fun. Teachers cannot initiate positive relationships with students when they are engaged in a battle of wits over constraining and developmentally inappropriate curriculum. Elkind reminds his readers in *The Hurried Child* (1981) that Sigmund Freud's view of human happiness as the ability to "*lieben und arbeiten*" (love and work) still holds true today. Children in schools that are building developmentally appropriate practice have the opportunity to become effective workers who can care for and accept themselves and others. Such a climate cannot help but improve the quality of discipline in classrooms.

ACTIVITY AND DISCUSSION

Jawanda and Tamika are friends in a large public school kindergarten. They are both successful and capable students but have different behavior and learning styles. Jawanda seems to understand concepts almost immediately and frequently says, "Teacher, what else can I do?" Tamika seems more distracted and needs to hear directions several times. Her teacher sometimes has to coax her to complete her work. However, at the end of the year Jawanda and Tamika have achieved the same unusually high scores on math and reading readiness tests. Their teacher is asked to recommend one or both for an advanced first grade. How important a role do you think Tamika's behavior during lessons should play in whether the teacher recommends her for an advanced class?

   With a partner list reasons that Tamika might or might not be recommended. What would each of you recommend, and why?

CONTRASTING DEVELOPMENTALLY APPROPRIATE AND PSYCHOMETRIC PRACTICE

Developmentally appropriate practice is based on the relatively simple idea that curriculum in schools should match the child's level of mental ability. However, further examination of this concept reveals its depth and complexity. Assessing a student's current level of mental ability (not to be confused with fixed mental ability) requires observation, discussion, and an interactive method of teaching. Such assessment is different from the psychometric approach in traditional schooling, which is based on behaviorist rather than developmental viewpoints and highly dependent on standardized testing (Elkind 1981). Developmentally appropriate practice is also unlike the psychometric approach because it is a philosophy based on general principles rather than a prescriptive methodology for classroom practice. In DAP the teacher honors the child's sequential patterns of development as well as children's individual differences and exercises informed judgment based on training and reflection (Willis 1993). Teachers and students experience greater freedom of thought, expression, and respect for current levels of developmental competence in the DAP classroom. Also, there is no assumption that the current level of competence determines the child's ultimate potential for school achievement.

Much can be learned about DAP by comparing it to current psychometric practices in elementary classrooms throughout America (see Exhibit 5-1). Elkind (1981) suggests comparing the two philosophies in four major areas:

- Conception of the learner

- Conception of the learning process

- Conception of knowledge

- Conception of the goals and aims of education

As Exhibit 5-1 shows, DAP approaches learners as people with *developing* mental abilities. The presumption is that all students can achieve but that not all can achieve the same knowledge and skills at the same age. Furthermore, early achievement is not valued over achievement in and of itself and may actually be a detriment if it is pushed before basic skills are developed. Therefore DAP requires that curriculum be matched to the current interests and abilities of developing students. In contrast, the psychometric approach

EXHIBIT 5-1   *Comparing DAP and Psychometry*

Developmentally Appropriate Practice	*Psychometric Practice*
Conception of Learner	*Conception of Learner*
Children have developing mental abilities and achieve similar knowledge and skills at different times if curriculum is adapted to current needs.	Children have measurable mental abilities as indicated on IQ or other diagnostic tests and are matched with children of similar ability.
Learning Process	*Learning Process*
Learning is creative and constructive and requires problem solving, trial and error, active learning, and sudden insight.	Learning is passive and based on behavioral principles; students rely on textbooks and worksheets to acquire basic skills.
Conception Knowledge	*Conception Knowledge*
Knowledge is gained through an interactive process with the world of people and objects.	Knowledge is derived from instruction and textbook and worksheet tasks and can be measured on standardized tests.
Goals/Aims of Education	*Goals/Aims of Educations*
Facilitate development and construction of intellect to produce critical thinkers.	Produce students who demonstrate acquisition of basic knowledge and skills with high scores on standardized tests.

Source: Adapted from D. Elkind. (1989, October). Developmentally appropriate practice: Philosophical and practical implications. *Phi Delta Kappan 71*(2), 113–117.

assumes mental abilities are measurable, fixed in nature, and can be assessed through IQ or comparable tests. The curriculum in this approach remains fixed, and children are matched with other students of similar ability. The learning process in DAP is creative, and students need to stamp the content of the curriculum with their personalities, experiences, and interests. Students construct knowledge through active exploration that creates the opportunity to use trial-and-error approaches to solve problems and to gain sudden insights. In the contrasting psychometric approach students passively follow prescriptive behavioral principles to acquire basic skills in adult-directed and -structured classroom activities.

In DAP knowledge is always under construction and remains consistently subjective as well as objective. Children gain knowledge by interacting with the world of people and objects around them. In the psychometric approach knowledge is derived mainly from attention to textbooks, worksheets, and the verbal instruction of teachers. Furthermore, knowledge in the psychometric approach can be measured through standardized tests. It follows from these comparisons that the goals and aims of education are quite different in DAP and psychometric design of instruction. The goal of DAP is to facilitate the construction of knowledge in children so they can become intellectually competent adults capable of critical thought. The goal of the psychometric approach is to teach the information and skills that produce students who score high on achievement tests—the presumed indicator for intellectual competence in adulthood (Elkind 1981).

QUESTIONS TO CONSIDER

1. List the ways in which your education reflected psychometric practice and developmentally appropriate practice. What was your response to testing and test scores? Do they still influence your concept of yourself as a learner?

2. Try to recall a time in your education when you were able to make a choice and take independent responsibility for an activity. How did you respond to that opportunity in terms of your feelings and actions?

THE FOUR AREAS OF DEVELOPMENTALLY APPROPRIATE PRACTICE

The National Association for the Education of Young Children (NAEYC) first brought the concept of DAP to national attention with a focus on children from birth to age eight (approximately third grade). The NAEYC book *Developmentally Appropriate Practice in Early Childhood Programs Serving Children from Birth Through Age 8* (Bredekamp 1987) identifies guidelines for DAP within four separate areas of education: curriculum, adult-child interaction, relations between home and program, and developmental evaluation of children. Although Bredekamp's book focuses on early childhood education, national efforts to restructure schools reflect the same focus on curriculum, the quality of student-adult interaction, parent and community involvement, and testing and assessment of students. Therefore it is useful to explore these four areas and expand them as appropriate to all levels of elementary schooling and beyond. Each of the four areas reflects positive opportunities for child-centered management, which is always linked to developmentally appropriate practice.

A curriculum that is developmentally appropriate should cover all subject areas through an integrated approach that is based on observation and recording of students' behaviors and interest while learning. A wide range of children's interests should be met with an equally wide range of activities and relevant materials. Students should have the opportunity to make meaningful choices and enough time for satisfying involvement in the activities they select. Multicultural nonsexist books and materials should be available for all children to support the growth of self-acceptance and positive relationships with others.

Important connections exist between flexible and interesting curriculum and child-centered classroom management. Teachers who once might have concentrated on techniques for maintaining the attention of a whole group during a single lesson would instead be able to focus more on techniques for encouraging children to pursue meaningful tasks individually or in small groups (see Exhibit 5-2). Teachers also have time to observe their students as individuals. Data from these observations enable teachers to chart the personal interests of students and to continue to encourage their interests. Children who see themselves and their experiences in materials and books have more opportunity to build personal connections between academic skills and their lives.

EXHIBIT 5-2   *Language Arts Curriculum in Mr. Rudell's Third-Grade Classroom*

The thirty-two children in Mr. Rudell's classroom are seated at eight tables. The class is developing skills researching and organizing material for written essays, and Mr. Rudell has integrated science in the activity. The children have been grouped this day according to their interest in animals that live in water. They chose these animals after a class trip to a science center with a large aquarium. Mr. Rudell encouraged girls as well as boys to develop curiosity about amphibians, even though several girls were reluctant at first. Two children who recently moved from Puerto Rico have decided to investigate amphibians they saw on the island.

Some children have brought books from home, some have books from their local libraries, and others have selected books in the school library. Each student has at least one book to supplement the science textbook. Today Mr. Rudell's students have a choice of several activities. They may use dictionaries to develop vocabulary for their essays, begin to write rough drafts, continue to read their selected books, or work on the origami representation of their selected amphibian with paper and a book Mr. Rudell brought from home. Mr. Rudell has created a check list for observing and discussing with each student his or her progress with the project, any difficulties the student is encountering, and questions that have emerged in the process of research.

The second area of DAP, interaction of adults and children, encourages timely and caring responses to the needs and messages of students in the classroom. Students and teachers alike should be able to ask questions and express ideas in a comfortable climate of classroom communication. Teachers who observe excitement, interest, or distress can communicate to encourage, calm, or provide further direction for exploring the material. A sensitive level of teacher and student communication requires the teacher to move around the room to be close to individual students in order to provide focused attention and verbal encouragement. Teachers facilitate self-control and support self-esteem by observing, guiding, and suggesting behavioral alternatives. Although teachers remain responsible for planning and facilitating all the activities of the day, relaxed communication with students helps them to facilitate choice, independence, and flexibility in the design of lessons and activities.

The area of teacher and student interaction is important in the development of student-centered classroom management. Teachers are daily role models, and their responses to stress and challenges in the classroom support their students' growing abilities to develop appropriate behaviors. Children feel more confident when they can communicate with their teachers throughout the day and when they have relaxed opportunities to ask questions and discuss projects and interests. Children cannot always be certain when they choose certain aspects of projects or problems that their choices will continue to hold their interest. If they become bored or frustrated, their stress and subsequent tendency to misbehave can be redirected by a teacher who helps them solve the problem or choose a different aspect on which to work. When students do misbehave or fail to complete assignments, their teachers can help them reflect on their behavioral difficulties and support greater self-control and self-esteem through eventual task completion (see Exhibit 5-3).

The third area of developmentally appropriate practice, relations between home and school, reflects the current national focus on the importance of family and community support for school achievement in children. Home-school contact may be easier to maintain with younger children if a parent or care giver is available at home or comes to school each day to drop off or pick up the child. However, the parents of many students are under considerable stress as they try to manage family life and earn enough money to support their children. Teachers may experience uneven success in engaging parents and families in activities that support learning in school, but they must strive to make positive home-school communication an annual goal. Teachers who help children build and maintain connections between home and school, and who help parents to understand and appreciate the work their children are doing at school, make learning more relevant and important to their students. How can relations between home and school be created and maintained? Traditional report cards are useful to a degree, as are phone calls to parents when teachers have concerns about individual students. However, teachers should remember that many parents may still have some uncomfortable memories about school and teachers and may remain fearful that any contact with the school indicates failure or problems in their children. Such parents need consistent encouragement from the school if they are going to develop trust and confidence in teachers. They also need specific information about meaningful ways to support their children's interests and activities at home. Teachers must remember that some parents do not have extra money to enrich the home environment with learning materials, and some do not have the knowledge or skills to assist with schoolwork. It is often

---

EXHIBIT 5-3   ***Adult-Child Interaction in Mr. Rudell's Third-Grade Classroom***

As the third-grade students continue to work on their projects integrating language arts and science, Mr. Rudell circulates from table to table with his individual check lists. Although he takes care not to interrupt children who are concentrating on their tasks (he notes their interest in the specific activity), he does intermittently answer questions, solicit information, and check students' progress. Mr. Rudell reminds children who are behind schedule that the final essay is due at the end of the week and discusses work they may be able to complete at home to catch up. One student, Sheila, is already finished, so she and Mr. Rudell decide that she can draw some illustrations to hand in with her essay.

One student, Ronald, has been demonstrating emotional difficulties in the classroom. He becomes angry over his repeated failure to complete the origami frog he is working on and throws it across the room. Mr. Rudell quietly removes Ronald from his group and reminds him that throwing is neither permitted nor useful in solving problems. He suggests that Ronald might try the frog again, ask Sheila to help him with it, or wait until tomorrow to make a decision about that aspect of the project. Ronald decides to use the dictionary for the rest of the period.

Toward the end of the language arts period some students are giggling and others are looking out the window. Mr. Rudell suggests that all students who are no longer working on their project come to the front of the room and sit in a circle, so they can discuss any problems they are having and be sure that they have planned to complete their project on time. Before moving to the next subject Mr. Rudell encourages his students to continue to work hard and to complete projects of which they can be proud. He briefly shows the students two origami frogs he made at home that actually jump when he presses their backs. The children laugh and enjoy the frogs and are more relaxed as they begin their mathematics lesson.

helpful to design ways for students to bring something from school to show to or do with their parents at home.

Some useful ideas are class newsletters or family "newsgrams" that tell parents about current projects and ask them to write about their interests, experiences, or questions about the subject matter in a space at the bottom of the page. Students can be encouraged to develop small activities to complete at home with a parent or family member at regular intervals. Positive feedback to individual parents, even when students have been difficult in some areas of schooling, supports parents in their ongoing efforts to build self-esteem and confidence in their children (see Exhibit 5-4). Teachers who have more structured classroom time to observe, interact, and record student progress have more meaningful feedback to share with parents and families.

The fourth area of developmentally appropriate practice is developmental evaluation. Although screening and developmental testing yield useful information, particularly in early identification of special needs, the National Association for the Education of Young Children expresses caution about overall uses of tests in early childhood. It

---

EXHIBIT 5-4   ### *Home-School Interaction in Mr. Rudell's Third-Grade Classroom*

Each child in the third grade has a language arts portfolio with a section titled "I Communicate with My Family About My Work at School." Students write a letter to their parents or guardians at the end of each month, telling them what project they have completed in school. Family members are asked to respond with written comments at the bottom of the letter.

Mr. Rudell knows that one student is in foster care, one has a father in federal prison, one lost her mother to cancer last year, and three have parents who simply will not respond to school communications. The foster parents are responsive and enjoy being called parents, and both the father in prison and aunt with whom the child lives enjoy receiving the letters and writing back. Mr. Rudell maintains a high level of confidentiality regarding the parent in prison but knows that prison officials encourage communication with families as an important component of rehabilitation. The student whose mother died is still very sad and prefers to write to her father instead of her father and new stepmother. Both parents respect her feelings and trust that she will mature into acceptance of her situation. Mr. Rudell has "classroom grandparents" who have volunteered to respond to the letters of the three students whose parents fail to write back, and the students seem fairly comfortable with that arrangement. The other families are responsive to the letters and seem to enjoy receiving them and communicating with the school.

Mr. Rudell calls each family once a year with a positive report about a child's progress on a school project and has developed a class newsletter that is printed on a biannual basis. In addition, he has a fall and spring event, usually a play written by his students, to which all parents are invited. The classroom grandparents also attend, and each has a specific child to support during and after the play.

suggests that single assessments or screening devices should not be the basis of decisions that have a major influence on placement, enrollment, or retention of young children. Rather than use psychometric tests to group children, DAP uses test results to adapt curriculum to meet the specific needs of children. As children progress through elementary school, questions about appropriate uses of test scores remain important. As discussed in Chapter 3, the issue of testing and tracking children has permeated the movement toward restructuring schools in the United States. Many classroom teachers continue to be affected by the pressure of standardized tests, which can be used not only to track students but to assess the performance of teachers. Developmentally appropriate practice can be undermined by testing pressures, which can create an environment in which children spend much of the school day completing work and drill sheets that are actually a rehearsal for tests. Those children who do not test well may be stigmatized and segregated in lower-track classrooms that are not exposed to exciting and motivating curricula (Oakes 1985).

Clearly, teachers who emphasize practice for test taking also require large groups to be silent, long periods of inactivity and attention, and cooperation on the completion of worksheets. Students who sense the pressure created by high-stakes testing may become defensive and difficult to manage. Also, teachers who must prepare students for a test are unable to individualize the curriculum and encourage students to develop their interests and activities. Both students and teachers can be caught in this dilemma.

Although more comprehensive solutions continue to emerge, individual teachers must develop coping strategies. Observation, anecdotal record keeping, and work sampling can help teachers to retain a perspective on meaningful student progress. Teachers can help to reduce student stress by balancing required test-based activities with activities that allow greater freedom of choice and personal expression. Finally, it is important for teachers to avoid stereotyping and lowering their expectations based on standardized test scores. They must maintain the greatest focus possible on developmentally appropriate practice and respect for developmental potential, while the school or district continues to focus on testing as a central indicator of teacher and student success (see Exhibit 5-5).

In summary, the four areas of developmentally appropriate practice are directly related to the successful development of child-centered classroom management. Students who encounter an

EXHIBIT 5-5   *Testing and Evaluation in Mr. Rudell's Third-Grade Classroom*

Mr. Rudell has incorporated strategies of authentic assessment in his teaching method. His school district appointed a team of third-grade teachers to design approaches to assessment several years ago. Mr. Rudell supported the decision of the team to end language arts ability grouping, and he has been pleased with the results. Some students test in the upper and lower ranges of the yearly standardized reading tests; most are in midrange. Two disabled students are in Mr. Rudell's third grade. One is a student with a physical disability who is an exceptional reader; the other is a student who is learning disabled in language arts. Mr. Rudell is confident in his ability to challenge upper- and middle-range students with a developmentally appropriate curriculum but feels less confident about the amount of attention and assistance he is able to give lower-range students. His school district has a learning support team of three teachers with expertise in special needs from which he has requested assistance for several students who appear to be falling behind.

Mr. Rudell tries to build in to every lesson and project "challenge activities" for both higher and lower ranges and project, and encourages all children to attempt them when they are interested in doing so. Two of his midrange readers have initiated complex critical thinking activities. Mr. Rudell is concerned about tests, because they play an important role in the middle school and high school placement of his students. He and his colleagues do hold reviews of basic skills in reading and test taking in the month before standardized tests are given. However, he has consistently found that observation, anecdotal record keeping, and maintenance of check lists during individual projects help him to learn more about individual students and figure out their strengths and interests, which helps him to motivate them.

In this language arts activity Mr. Rudell has the following categories on his check list (which also has room for anecdotal notes):

1. Ability to maintain interest in task
2. Ability to plan and follow an independent timeline
3. Evidence of grade-level reading skills
4. Evidence of grade-level writing skills
5. Evidence of creativity and enthusiasm
6. Ability to handle difficulty and frustration
7. Cooperation with peers
8. Specific questions, problems, interests or abilities that become apparent

interesting and individualized curriculum, who are encouraged by observant and communicative adults, who perceive the connections between home and school, and who are neither pressured nor hampered by the existence or results of standardized testing are more likely to cooperate with the requirements of school. Their teachers can also respond in a more positive way to the flexible and interactive nature of the developmentally appropriate classroom.

ACTIVITY AND DISCUSSION

You are preparing for your first year as an elementary classroom teacher. You want to be sure that your classroom reflects all four areas of developmentally appropriate practice discussed in this section. Draw an organizational chart you might use to plan a full year that pays attention to each area.

1. What specific approaches or activities would you include in each area (for example, phone calls to parents, learning projects, grouping, design of classroom communication)?

2. Compare your organizational chart with others' in a small group discussion.

THE RELATIONSHIP OF CONSTRUCTIVISM TO BEHAVIOR

Developmentally appropriate practice is based on a *constructivist* theory that holds that learning must involve activity and exploration. According to the constructivist philosophy, knowledge is a temporary, developmental, social, cultural, and often not objective concept (Brooks and Brooks 1993). It is the process rather than the content of learning that makes it appropriate for the developmental needs of students. This process must be self-regulated and must allow the student to resolve cognitive conflicts by working with materials and thinking about problems.

The Relationship of Action to Discipline

Many developmental theorists link the acquisition of knowledge with the acquisition of a moral sense and social skills. Acquisition always implies activity. How many discipline problems occur in school when children are required to be inactive? Many a classroom observer notes the frequency of student misbehavior during long lessons as teachers alternately instruct and admonish to "sit still" or "be quiet" or "pay attention." Teachers must reflect carefully on the relationship of constructivist DAP to the developing behaviors of children. Greenberg (1990) identifies the following key phrases as central to developmentally appropriate practice:

Moves at will

Makes choices

Initiates work

Discovers

Assembles

Discusses (peers or adults)

Grapples with

Constructs

Plans

Solves

Creates

Works with

Evaluates work

Curriculum that provides for all these actions creates a shift in the concept of school discipline. The ability to take an active part in acquiring knowledge becomes more important than the ability to sit still, be quiet, and pay attention to lengthy verbal communication from adults. The "discipline" that children need to internalize in a constructivist setting (just as Montessori and Piaget theorized) is the completion of tasks that they choose and that hold their interest. Castle and Rogers (1993) identifies skills and/or emotional responses that result from the opportunities available in a constructivist curriculum:

Reflection

Connection of meaningful concepts

Respect for rules

Sense of community

Problem solving

Cooperation

Inductive thinking

Sense of ownership of work

These skills and emotions support social and moral behavior through the development of reason and increasing students' understanding of feelings, fairness, reciprocal relationships, and logical consequences (Castle and Rogers 1993). Some educators have become accustomed to school environments that assume that discipline is acquired by learning to attend to and obey adults in more passive teaching situations. However, students who are repeatedly coerced into behaving as though they are interested when they are not, or as though they understand concepts when they do not, may feel stupid and powerless (Willis 1993). Such "discipline" does not support moral or intellectual growth and in fact invites resistance. Today's teachers must equate the concepts of behavior and discipline with the creation of learning climates and activities that allow a great deal of activity and exploration.

Play and Constructivism

Play? In school? In the minds of many adults the concept of play belongs only in free time and is never applied to "work." However, within a constructivist philosophy *play* is any activity that enhances the creativity, imagination, and productivity of a student at any age. Throughout the life span people respond with positive emotions and dispositions to instruction that has room for spontaneous, voluntary, and enjoyable activity. Consider this description of a sixth-grade classroom:

> Dr. Baldwin, the new principal of Horace Mann School, was hired by the school board in large part because of her success in raising the test scores of students in her last position. She enters the sixth-grade classroom of Ms. Glick and finds what appears to be a commotion. Four groups of students are talking and laughing in different corners of the room. Some are drawing, some are making paper hats, and some appear to be playing the parts of characters in a play. She glances at student-made murals around the room, which appear to reflect Shakespeare's *Romeo and Juliet*. Dr. Baldwin approaches Ms. Glick to inquire about the lesson and learns that the students are preparing to act out scenes they have rewritten from Shakespeare. It is the end of a five-month unit on Shakespeare, and the culminating activity has integrated social studies, language arts, and literature. The students are rewriting scenes based on their insights into gender roles, cultural conflict, and parent-child relationships in modern America.

The hypothetical Dr. Baldwin would surely notice that the work of these students seems more like play. They are enjoying themselves and obviously enthusiastic as they anticipate their performances before the group. In fact, the activity of these sixth-grade students does take the form of play, even though it is related to serious and disciplined learning of established subject matter. Fromberg (1990) describes play as the ultimate integrator of human experience, because it involves imagination, social competence, language, culture, and cognition. She further explains that play can be defined as voluntary and purposeful activity that has spontaneous appeal for students over a period of time. Although play has been suggested and defended throughout history as a prime modality for learning in young children, altered forms of play are appropriate learning experiences for students throughout elementary school.

The hypothetical Ms. Glick has designed a developmentally appropriate strategy for motivating her students to read and write about Shakespeare and to express their interests by synthesizing their knowledge of the original play and modern multicultural concepts. As they write and rehearse, these sixth-grade students demonstrate meaningful play in their work. Pelligrini and Dressden (1992) write that play can be defined by the presence of nonlaterality (pretending), intrinsic motivation, attention to process, exploration of material, freedom from arbitrary rules, and active engagement of persons involved. Ms. Glick knows from experience that her students are far more likely to read Shakespeare and retain important information about plays if they have the active opportunity to be creative as they relate socially to one another in the classroom. (For example, they must actually read and understand a scene from Shakespeare before they can rewrite it.) Furthermore, the groups make their own rules about assigning parts and presenting plays, which supports the development of their social competence and morality. Ms. Glick has also noticed a sharp decrease in misbehavior in her classroom when students are independently involved in intrinsically motivating activities.

Play serves other important purposes in groups of all ages, particularly groups of young students. It reduces stress and builds confidence in students who fear failure in more traditional activities. Spaulding (1992) states that novel, uncertain, and discrepant lessons often hold the interest of the largest number of students. Opportunities for creativity and expression, important components of developmentally appropriate practice, are often playful in nature. Meaningful play, structured within educational disciplines, helps students develop concepts, generate ideas, and take an open-ended approach to learning (Wasserman 1990). Many educators may need some time to get used to the concept of play as meaningful throughout elementary school curricula and to feel comfortable with fun as a critical mode of developmentally appropriate learning. However, students who are busily engaged in work that allows them to be spontaneous, humorous, and communicative with their peers are more likely to be learning—and less likely to be creating discipline problems in classrooms.

QUESTIONS TO CONSIDER

1. Why do you think so many adults feel that play is less important than academic "work" in classrooms? How do you think most adults would define the concepts of play and work?

2. How might you explain the importance of play as it is described in this section to a friend or colleague who is concerned that a child who is allowed to play will fall behind in academic progress?

DEVELOPMENTALLY APPROPRIATE PRACTICE AND THE REAL WORLD OF CLASSROOMS

The progressive implementation of developmentally appropriate practice in public schools is a time-consuming and sometimes controversial process. Educators need patience and determination as they work to steadily replace psychometric practice with a child-centered curriculum and management. Developmentally appropriate practice can be controversial because it ultimately requires substantial changes in school practice and policy, particularly in ways students are grouped, instructed, tested, and tracked (see Exhibit 5-6). Educators accustomed to the step-by-step approach of test- and textbook-driven methods in the psychometric tradition may feel confused by the more philosophical and developmental approach of DAP. Many teachers feel uncertain about using DAP when their districts have not invested in training, materials, and the smaller class size that can enhance more individualized and hands-on approaches to education. In truth, DAP often requires intensive preparation, facilitation, and cleanup. Worksheets and texts can be more orderly and manageable, particularly in large classes.

To add to the DAP dilemma some parents and communities express caution concerning the educational pendulum that they perceive as swinging between "back to basics" and "progressive education." These parents may have children who are highly successful

EXHIBIT 5-6   ***Controversial Aspects of Developmentally Appropriate Practice***

Ms. Caroll has been a first-grade teacher in an advantaged suburban school district for fifteen years. Her district has always publicized its high test scores, and the good reputation of the schools in the district continues to attract many professional families to the area. Ms. Caroll has a routine for following the curriculum and helping her students prepare for standardized tests. She, like many teachers in her school, has a family of her own and many other responsibilities to meet as soon as school is over. Ms. Caroll is highly organized. She leaves her classroom ready for the next day thirty minutes after her students are dismissed and limits her work at home as much as possible to spend time with her family.

This school year a new superintendent and new principal in Ms. Caroll's school have collaborated to begin developmentally appropriate practice. Their plan is for teachers to begin to individualize instruction and to teach some subjects without textbooks or teacher manuals. The teachers, including Ms. Caroll, have become upset and confused. Their main concern is the standardized tests at the end of the year. Several teachers in the school are also parents of children in the district, and they have alerted other parents to their concerns. A group of parents has organized to block efforts to move away from the standard curriculum. They are concerned about college admissions and are comfortable with their children's progress in the current system.

Because of the questions that have been raised, the administrators have planned several evening meetings and asked the teachers to attend. They have also begun to require anecdotal record keeping in primary classrooms and asked the teachers to set up classroom learning centers in science, math, language arts, and social studies. The teachers are finding the new demands for an innovative curriculum time consuming, and several have investigated whether the union would carry a complaint. Some parents and teachers are completely opposed to a proposal to end ability grouping before third grade. They are not convinced the individualized projects, mixed age groupings, and trial-and-error activities will help all children reach their full potential.

Ms. Caroll, to her own surprise, has become interested in DAP. She has tried several projects with her students and has been impressed with their enthusiasm and interest. Ms. Caroll has rearranged her schedule to set up her classroom centers at the end of the day and spends time most evenings either planning or writing anecdotal records. She has explained to her family that she needs more preparation time each night because she now has more control over what she teaches and how she teaches—which she likes very much. Her organizational skills are helping her learn to balance new demands on her time. When parents ask for her opinion, she tells them about ways in which her first-grade students have become more excited about learning. Ms. Caroll is starting to feel a renewed excitement about being a teacher.

in the current structure of schools and who therefore are highly competitive for gifted programs and elite college admissions. Helping all children to function on equal levels of success is not always a goal accepted by communities accustomed to competitive school structures. Teachers (who are often parents as well) may share concerns about changes that create classrooms different than those in which they were educated as children and in which they were trained in their teacher education programs. In truth, developmentally appropriate practice requires the same intrinsic motivation, active work, and trial-and-error approach to problem solving from teachers as it does from children. Determined educators will not allow problems and setbacks to deter them from school practice that supports intellectual growth and the development of positive and productive behaviors in their students.

Teachers Must Support DAP

In the real world of developmentally appropriate practice in the classroom teachers need to take responsibility for articulating and defending new approaches to education. However, many teachers are just learning how to balance the more behaviorist and psychometric requirements of their school districts with the new interest in developmentally appropriate practice. Some teachers may feel that they are getting double messages from their school administrators: "We encourage you to be as creative and flexible as you wish in your classrooms, so long as your standardized test scores do not drop." Despite the problems, however, many teachers are finding that they and their students are functioning on a higher and more productive level in DAP classrooms. How might these teachers describe and defend their support for developmentally appropriate practice? Willis (1993) outlines the specific values inherent in developmentally appropriate practice that help others to become more aware of the ways in which it truly enhances educational experiences. Benefits of developmentally appropriate practice include:

1. Promotion of human interaction and construction of knowledge

2. Encouragement of active learning through meaningful choice

3. Fostering of exploration and inquiry rather than passive acceptance of teacher-based "right" and "wrong" answers

4. Development of concepts through intellectual construction

5. Embodiment of realistic and attainable goals for children

6. Encouragement of social interaction between children and children, and children and adults.

Teachers can also explain that developmentally appropriate practice is related to many other school reforms underway in the United States (see Exhibit 5-7). Children in developmentally

---

EXHIBIT 5-7   *Explaining Developmentally Appropriate Practice to Parents*

Ms. Caroll has been asked by her principal to describe changes in her classroom to parents at an open meeting. She is prepared to give a presentation but is somewhat surprised at the level of anger or anxiety expressed by some parents at the beginning of the meeting. This is the first time Ms. Caroll has taken a public position on a curriculum issue, and she feels somewhat nervous and uncertain. Still, the parents are responsive when she makes the following statement:

> *The adult success and happiness of your children is going to depend on their ability to make good choices and to work with others to attain realistic goals. Test scores alone cannot tell you about your child's ability to inquire into aspects of important problems or to interact cooperatively with others. Think for a moment about who you want your child to be when he or she is around twenty-three years old. Don't you envision a confident individual who has chosen meaningful work and is able to create and maintain productive relationships with others? Every day the children in our district who learn disciplined inquiry, engage in discourse with others about their work, and develop products or performances are preparing to be competent adults. I enjoy helping your children to construct knowledge in new ways, and I invite you to visit my classroom to see for yourself the excitement and interest of your children.*

---

appropriate classrooms are meeting the three criteria sought most commonly in restructuring schools (Newmann and Wehlage 1993):

- Students actively constructing meaning and producing knowledge

- Students using disciplined inquiry to construct meaning

- Students aiming for discourse, product, or performance

Even when administrators, parents, or teachers continue to support traditional classrooms strongly rooted in textbooks, worksheets, and testing, DAP activities can be systematically included to improve the overall quality of education in the classroom.

THE IMPORTANT ROLE OF TEACHERS IN IMPLEMENTING DEVELOPMENTALLY APPROPRIATE PRACTICE

Teachers are required to make adaptations and to solve problems throughout their careers (the very skills promoted in developmentally appropriate practice). Many teachers have important questions and concerns about DAP: What about grades? How will I cover the required curriculum? Won't my classroom be too noisy? Can I trust my students to really complete independent work? How will I handle the disruptive behavior of students who can't handle freedom? Will the parents accept DAP? How will I know my students are really learning anything? What about my own need to feel successful through the performance of my students on standardized tests? These questions must be respected (Wasserman 1990), and many are answered in different ways in each school and classroom. The philosophical approach of DAP respects teachers, as well as students, as learners in the process of building understanding about ways to create constructivist classrooms.

Developmentally appropriate practice changes the rules about the ways in which students and teachers interact in classrooms (Wiske 1994). Learners can become teachers, and teachers can be learners in the more generative constructivist curriculum. Teachers do not relinquish their authority (Dopyera and Dopyera 1990), but a climate of respect for intellectual growth does mean that teachers and students share roles as intellectual authorities in the uncovering of knowledge. Perrone (1994) stresses that teachers must be passionate about learning and respectful of students' point of view in the process of acquiring knowledge. Although teachers are still responsible for establishing operant structures and frameworks for learning subject matter in the classroom, they can decide when to maintain and relinquish control in order to foster choice and active learning in students.

Chapters 4 and 5 stressed the critical nature of interaction in the process of child development. Teachers are powerful mediators and models in the process of learning as they create and support interactive classrooms. They are "cognitive partners" (Brooks and Brooks 1993) who form relationships with students. These relationships are built on mutual respect for inquiry rather than continual concern about right or wrong answers to questions.

It is impossible for teachers to individualize their attention at all times, but they can always try to be sensitive through caring forms of communication. Even when school budgets have not been adjusted to provide more developmentally appropriate materials, more adaptive classroom furniture, or smaller class size, teachers can interact through books, pictures, creative and inventive activities, and opportunities for students to relate classroom learning to their experiences and interests. Students will still be distressed, bored, frustrated, and disobedient at times. But interactive teachers in developmentally appropriate classrooms can keep them from slipping further and can provide incentive and motivation through intrinsically interesting tasks (Wasserman 1990). Supportive and individualized interaction enhances opportunities for students to construct a positive approach to self-discipline in classrooms.

Teachers are the key to successful implementation of developmentally appropriate practice. Their insistence on meaningful classroom activities that help all children to develop critical skills at an appropriate developmental pace will play a major role in the growth of this philosophy. As teachers face the challenges ahead, they can also be confident that appropriate educational opportunities help all their students to be more competent and cooperative in the classroom.

LINKING PERSONAL COMPETENCE TO DISCIPLINE

The discussion of child development theory in Chapter 4 relates morality to the processes that exist in the active acquisition of knowledge. Developmentally appropriate practice also focuses on the acquisition of knowledge, which suggests that it is more closely related than more traditional approaches to the development of morality in children. This is an important connection to make in a book that focuses on student-centered classroom management. When the rules of school are related to interesting and active work, rather than sitting and listening or lining up and being quiet, students have more opportunities to reflect on choices and alternatives in the ways they can think and act. Their behavior becomes less of a response to adult rules and directives and more of a self-initiated and responsible reaction to meaningful work environments. Students who can seek work that holds their interest are able to see themselves as competent. It is competence, and the accompanying self-regard, that can lead the way to disciplined behavior in school.

Wasserman (1990) reminds educators that it is easy to disrespect students in school. They are physically smaller and have less ability to control their needs. Furthermore, children can be tiresome, stubborn, and otherwise difficult to manage. Most adults believe that they have the right to tell, show, direct, and manipulate children—and that such interventions are positive. It is important for all teachers to realize that they are role models for children in the use of power. Elkind (1981) relates the misbehavior of children to inappropriate school demands that build stress and tension.

Greenberg (1990) also suggests that tasks that appear to be arbitrary, uninteresting, or too difficult to students can be a cause of children's lack of self-discipline. Although young children may be inattentive, disobedient, or disruptive, problems can escalate as students grow older. Current statistics on crime and assaults in American schools certainly attest to a level of frustration and anger in some students. Educators must pay attention to the climate created by the adults as well as the students in schools. If children are expected to be reasonably polite, cooperative, and attentive, they must experience the same behavior on the part of their adult role models. Every teacher who strives to implement student-centered classroom management must take seriously the responsibility for being a model of exemplary behavior.

Schools that focus almost exclusively on academic achievement can fail to take into account different but equally important categories of learning. Katz (1989) identifies four categories of learning:

- Knowledge, or the specific subject matter to be learned

- Skills, or small repeatable units of action

- Dispositions, or habits of response to learning situations

- Feelings, or the subjective emotional state experienced by children in schools

Dispositions and feelings are closely related to issues of discipline and management. Children who feel a sense of incompetence and frustration are prone to develop the defensive school dispositions (Bruner 1966) discussed in Chapter 4. Katz (1989) further suggests that self-esteem, critical to the development of self-discipline, is related to the child's sense of intellectual competence. Children need success to build self-esteem, and academic excellence in education cannot be achieved by making children feel like failures (Greenberg 1990).

Competitive school environments often reward students who do it right the fastest. Children who require more time, better explanations, and second or third chances to achieve the same level of success as "quicker" students may be unfairly regarded as less capable. When the result in cooperative classrooms is competence and successful learning, goals are achieved equally by students, regardless of the time taken to reach them. A stronger focus on cooperative learning can eliminate the race to the right answer, because students have the opportunity to think, talk, and weigh alternatives. Developmentally appropriate practice focuses on active learning and construction of knowledge, rather than achievement of high test scores, as the most important indicator of competence. Eliminating unnecessary competition can also bring about the elimination of stress, which distracts children from their work and often is expressed in classroom discipline problems.

ACTIVITY AND DISCUSSION

Craig is a student in your second-grade classroom who appears to be highly anxious about reading activities. Whenever you hand out books for reading time, Craig begins to sing out loud or tap on his desk. While other students read silently, Craig generally is looking away from his book but sometimes turns pages.

As a group, analyze silent reading time in terms of the knowledge, skills, dispositions, and feelings required by the task. Which of these four areas of learning might you address, and how would you do so, to try to help Craig develop a stronger sense of competence in silent reading activities?

In the next two chapters this book focuses more exclusively on issues and problems in classroom management and discipline. Readers are urged to approach the next chapters with the philosophy of developmentally appropriate practice foremost in their minds. There is no real way to separate discipline and management from curriculum in actual classrooms. Children who "can't learn" or "won't behave" always need the support of teachers who have the courage to question the appropriateness of the curriculum before they judge the child. Many changes discussed in this chapter have the power to motivate children and alleviate the stress that can cause behavioral difficulties in less appropriate educational settings.

CHAPTER SUMMARY

This chapter turned from the discussion of developmental theories in Chapter 4 to developmentally appropriate practice, which is a philosophical model of applied theory in the classroom. Connections were made between the nature of learning activities in the classroom and the ways in which both children and adults behave in classrooms. Curriculum was described as a powerful conduit for interest and activity that can and should be informed by knowledge of how children learn best in various stages of their development. Developmentally appropriate practice was linked to overall positive school behavior, and ways in which schools could change to better meet the learning needs of children were described. A specific contrast was drawn between DAP and psychometric school practice, which is heavily based on standardized testing. Developmentally appropriate practice was described as appropriate to both age and the individual, and the four most important areas of DAP were explained in detail.

This chapter also addressed controversies that can emerge as teachers and communities are asked to change their thinking about the ways in which schools should function to best meet the educational needs of children. Developmentally appropriate practice is part of the process of change in American schools today. Just as schools are engaged in restructuring efforts that will be implemented over time, appropriate practice is in developing stages in most school districts. Indeed, DAP is closely linked to many other important aspects of educational restructuring and reform. This chapter stressed that teachers must rise to the responsibility of implementing and representing the positive aspects of change, not only in the classroom but with parents and other concerned adults. The role of teachers in implementing as well as explaining and defending DAP was outlined. Finally, connections were made between the focus on developmental theory in Chapter 4 and developmentally appropriate practice in Chapter 5 to the more specific focus on management and discipline in Chapters 6 and 7.

PROFESSIONAL DECISION

Balancing the Demands of Teaching

Ellen Stillman has just begun her first year as a third-grade teacher in a prestigious suburban school system. She was selected from more than one hundred candidates and is both honored and apprehensive as she begins her career. Ms. Stillman studied in college with several professors who had strong commitment to developmentally appropriate practice, and she completed her student teaching in a first-grade classroom that reflected many principles of the DAP philosophy.

Ms. Stillman has begun to realize that her district prizes high scores on standardized achievement tests. Although she was originally told by her principal that the district had a commitment to DAP, it is becoming obvious that many teachers are spending a great deal of time preparing their students for tests. Several parents have already made appointments with her to discuss their children and have made it clear that they are concerned with competitive high school and college admissions. One teacher in the school has warned Ms. Stillman that "people whose students don't score at the top don't last here very long." Ms. Stillman decides to call a former professor to discuss the situation. The professor says, "I'm sorry, Ellen, but now you are in the real world. You have got to make sure your students do well on those tests, and you have to try to be a developmentally appropriate teacher." Ms. Stillman decides to try to balance the two competing demands.

Outline the plan of action you think Ms. Stillman should take to create a constructivist classroom that incorporates the reality of testing in her district.

CHAPTER REFERENCES

Bredekamp, S. (1987). *Developmentally appropriate practice in early childhood programs serving children from birth through age 8.* Washington, DC: National Association for the Education of Young Children.

Brooks, J. G., & Brooks, M. G. (1993). *In search of understanding: The case for constructivist classrooms.* Washington, DC: Association for Supervision and Curriculum Development.

Bruner, J. S. (1966). *Toward a theory of instruction.* New York: W. W. Norton & Company, Inc.

Castle, K., & Rogers, K. (1993–1994, Winter). Rule creating in a constructivist classroom community. *Childhood Education. 70*(2), 77–80.

Dopyera, M. L., & Dopyera, J. E. (1990). The child-centered curriculum. In C. Seefeldt (Ed.), *Continuing issues in early childhood education* (pp. 209–220). Columbus, OH: Merrill.

———. (1989, October). Developmentally appropriate practice: Philosophical and practical implications. *Phi Delta Kappa, 71*(2), 113–117.

Elkind, D. (1981). *The hurried child: Growing up too fast too soon.* Reading, MA: Addison-Wesley.

Fromberg, D. P. (1990). Play issues in early childhood education. In C. Seefeldt (Ed.), *Continuing issues in early childhood education* (pp. 224–238). Columbus, OH: Merrill.

Greenberg, P. (1990, January). Why not academic preschool? (Part I). *Young Children, 45*(2), 70–80.

Katz, L. G. (1989). *Early childhood education: What research tells us.* Bloomington, IN: Phi Delta Kappa Education Foundation.

Newmann, F. M., & Wehlage, G. G. (1993, April). Five standards of authentic instruction. *Educational Leadership, 50*(7), 8–12.

Oakes, J. (1985). *Keeping track: How schools structure inequality.* New Haven, CT: Yale University Press.

Pelligrini, A. D., & Dressden, J. (1992). In V. J. Dimidjian (Ed.), *Play's place in public education for young children* (pp. 19–25). Washington, DC: National Education Association.

Perrone, V. (1994, February). How to engage students in learning. *Educational Leadership, 51*(5), 11–18.

Soltis, J. F. (1987). *Reforming teacher education: The impact of the Holmes Group Report.* New York: Teachers College Press.

Spaulding, C. L. (1992). *Motivation in the classroom.* New York: McGraw-Hill.

Wasserman, S. (1990). *Serious players in the primary classroom.* New York: Teachers College Press.

Willis, S. (1993, November). Teaching young children: Educators seek 'developmental appropriateness.' *ASCD Curriculum Update* (Association for Supervision and Curriculum Development), 1–8.

Wiske, M. S. (1994). How teaching for understanding changes the rules in the classroom. *Educational Leadership, 51*(5), 19–24.

6

A CLOSER LOOK AT MANAGEMENT AND DISCIPLINE

Teachers and students together must create a meaningful and positive behavioral climate. Mutual positive behavior depends on a spirit of respect and cooperation in all school participants. Teachers, however, bear the greatest responsibility for the climate and quality of classroom life. All students depend on their teachers to have the professional skills and personal dispositions that motivate students to behave appropriately. Teachers must view the behavior of children as dependent not only on classroom curriculum and activities but on their own well-established procedures and interventions. Through personal modeling, careful observation of students, analysis of problems, and application of appropriate interventions, teachers can manage orderly and productive classrooms. Neither children nor teachers should be dehumanized in the process of building a community of reasonable and responsive learners in schools. Thus the focus of behavioral intervention is always enhanced learning and participation rather than coercion or control. Such a focus requires in-depth understanding of management, discipline, and special discipline problems. This chapter discusses the following topics:

- Behavior as a separate classroom phenomenon
- Categorizing classroom problems
- Is the problem discipline or management?
- Thinking of discipline as guidance
- Developing student-centered discipline
- The reality of serious behavior problems

BEHAVIOR AS A SEPARATE CLASSROOM PHENOMENON

Chapter 5 invites the reader to begin to examine the specific issues of discipline and management more closely. Today's teachers are likely to feel challenged by the behavior of many children in the classroom. No matter how thorough their preparation or appropriate the curriculum they implement, teachers also need the opportunity to plan and implement positive management strategies in their classrooms. Teachers need to conceptualize management and discipline as distinct but integrated challenges that are greatly affected by their skills and attitudes. On the one hand, teachers must always connect the issues of management and discipline to their curricula and activities. On the other hand, they must learn skills that are effective in managing groups of children and helping them to learn appropriate behavior. The ways in which teachers view appropriate behavior and communicate their behavioral expectations have a direct effect on the organization and productivity of their classrooms. Consider this scenario:

> Ms. Dean is a student teacher in the third grade of a large elementary school with departmentalized classes in reading, mathematics, social studies, and science. Therefore her students move from classroom to classroom and teacher to teacher throughout the day. Ms. Dean's cooperating teacher suggests that she follow the children in her homeroom for the entire day. While doing so, she makes a surprising discovery. "I couldn't believe my eyes when I saw the children changing so much from room to room," she told her cooperating teacher later. "With some teachers they were so well behaved, and with others they did not act appropriately at all. I had no idea that this happened. What is going on?"

Ms. Dean was well trained in developmentally appropriate curriculum. However, like many prospective teachers, she had assumed without fully realizing it that "good" or "bad" behavior is related to the personal habits and characteristics of the children. She had heard many people refer to "single-parent families," "too much television," or "no discipline at home" as the sources of behavior problems in school. However, after one full day observing the same group of children with different teachers, her assumptions were definitely challenged. Now she has a greater sensitivity to the responsibility of teachers for setting a tone and creating a climate that shape and control the behavior of children. She observed that some "problem children" actually behave appropriately with some teachers. She feels a much greater responsibility for developing the skills and dispositions that will help her to support positive behavioral skills in her own students.

All teachers should recognize that children do indeed behave differently with different adults. Although some children have developed negative habits or dispositions, and others have serious behavior disorders, *all* children respond to the level of preparation, organization, and expectation of individual adults. School behavior is always contextual; it never takes place apart from the activities, interactions, and emotions in the classroom. Teachers communicate, either directly or indirectly, their level of tolerance, their enjoyment of and commitment to teaching, and their intention to teach successfully. Students can often articulate the differences in their teachers, as Mr. Williams learns:

> Mr. Williams, a student teacher in a sixth-grade class, has been asked to design a writing project for remedial readers. He decides that his students might enjoy writing a handbook for next year's sixth graders, so he asks them to write down any advice new students might find helpful. To his surprise almost all the students write about their different teachers. Some teachers are described as mean, whereas others are "nice but you have to work really hard." Certain teachers are described as "strict but you do fun things," and others "sound like you have to do a lot, but you can get away with skipping your homework." Mr. Williams spends quite a while thinking about what the students have written. He had never realized that students (even those identified as disabled or remedial) observe their teachers carefully and ascertain both negotiable and non-negotiable expectations in the classroom. He becomes determined to have his students describe him as "nice but strict, you have to work hard but you have fun and learn a lot."

Mr. Williams has developed some important insights about the ways in which students assess and evaluate their teachers. They know what is expected, what they can get away with, and how hard they will have to work to be successful. You are or were undoubtedly aware of the same phenomenon on your college campus. Professors might be described by students (on some campuses in official published evaluations) is such terms as "easy *A*s," "unprepared," "hard but interesting," "boring," or "excellent and well prepared." Students pass this information on to one another, and professors (like all teachers) get a reputation for certain professional behaviors and expectations. Teachers who want to improve the behavior of students in their classrooms must reflect first on their own level of preparation, lesson design, interaction with students, and communication of expectations. The behavior of teachers directly shapes the behavior of students in schools.

This chapter, on strategies that promote positive classroom behavior, is founded on the preceding chapters. You are encouraged to use all previous chapters as the context for this discussion, which focuses more closely on the behavior of children in schools. Dedicated teachers must care about and reflect upon difficulties in the lives of their students as well as on the professional issues and challenges in their schools. They must understand that innovations in education can help students improve their behavior by enhancing their interest and active learning. Equally important is applying knowledge in the areas of child development and intrinsic motivation to the ongoing construction of developmentally appropriate classrooms.

The ideas and suggestions in this chapter for shaping and intervening in classroom behavior assume that you have been developing an overall sensitivity to the lives of children and the responsibility of schools and teachers for meeting the needs of all children as much as possible. At this point you should also be developing the habit of relating behavior problems to questions about the appropriateness or interest level of related school tasks. This chapter provides the opportunity to reflect on and analyze discipline and management problems as separate and distinct from other classroom occurrences. However, all discipline problems are discussed within a continuing focus on the responsibility of school and teachers to foster competence and confidence in children.

Discipline and Management— Interesting Problems

All successful teachers must manage functional classrooms that incorporate enough discipline for the majority of school tasks to be completed at a reasonable level of success. This book has discussed many difficulties that can interfere with smooth classroom functioning. Unless teachers develop a proactive and optimistic method for approaching behavior problems, they are in danger of becoming antagonistic toward or fearful of their students. Without professional and attitudinal skills in behavior management teachers may focus on control and obedience more than on connecting appropriate behavior to interesting and rewarding school tasks. Thus it is important to avoid thinking of classroom behavior as a negative problem and instead to conceptualize it as an interesting problem. Discipline and management in school are colorful and intricate puzzles with many pieces. Teachers who are willing to learn, grow, and improve their skills become increasingly competent at putting that puzzle together every day.

One way to approach the interesting challenge of behavior is to apply some scientific thought and research to problems before confronting them. This means that teachers need to be observers who suspend judgment and form hypotheses about reasons for behaviors. Viewed as an interesting problem, misbehavior tends to be less threatening or stressful to the teacher's sense of expertise and professionalism. Teachers can take the time to observe, document, and analyze the problem and react with a purposeful plan. All teachers should anticipate some interesting behavioral challenges. The successful teacher does not seek to avoid difficulties; rather, the successful teacher intervenes with confidence based on professional skills. A trial-and-error process is always necessary, and interventions that work with one class of children might fail with another. The first line of intervention often is simple instruction that explains the behavior desired and redirects students' attention in the classroom (Kameenui and Darch 1994).

QUESTIONS TO CONSIDER

1. Think of a recent argument or misunderstanding with a friend or family member. What do you think caused the problem? What events led up to it? What points or issues needed to be clarified? What decisions did you make in terms of changing yourself or the relationship? What might you do differently if you could resolve this difference now?

2. Talk in a small group about the ways in which you tend to respond to misunderstandings and ways in which more methodical documentation and analysis of personal problems might help you to make thoughtful decisions about behaviors and relationships.

Classrooms—Busy and Demanding Places

The general suggestions here, like so many that are offered to class-room teachers in the area of behavior management, cannot be helpful without the recognition that teachers are doing many important things at the same time. The class may be misbehaving while the teacher is looking for the transportation money that someone requested over the loudspeaker in the middle of a hands-on mathematics lesson involving new materials. Or one child may be too disruptive to ignore while the teacher is trying to supervise six different language arts groups. It is wrong to assume a level of concentration that often cannot really exist in the classroom. Teachers who have smaller classes, aides or assistants, parent volunteers, and guidance resources are better able to implement behavioral strategies than those who don't, but all teachers are meeting many challenging and simultaneous demands.

The next step is to hold to a simple line of defense for approaching discipline and management: teachers must *know* what they want, *teach* students the behaviors they want them to master, and *reinforce* those behaviors every day. The importance of consistency cannot be overstressed. Even when classroom life becomes chaotic (and it does at times), students and teachers with established habits can function with a good level of organization.

Think back for a moment to the hypothetical scenario with which this chapter began. Ms. Dean, the student teacher, may not have realized it, but she was observing the behavioral habits that teachers and students had formed in each classroom. In a classroom that seemed more positive, the teacher had probably developed strong routines and organized activities that had helped her students to trust her to be consistent, have high expectations for appropriate behavior, and have interesting lessons. In a classroom that seemed less positive, the teacher may well have made the incorrect assumption that children would "obey" without offering a logical explanation of the behavior he expected and the way it supports classroom learning. The students may also have realized that this teacher was not well organized and that he did not prepare interesting lessons. The observer would guess that this second teacher really cannot improve his classroom discipline and management until he improves habits that depend on how well he prepares the lessons and communicates his expectations in the classroom. Once that is accomplished, he can fit effective skills into his busy but better-planned and -organized day.

Communication—Building Strong Classroom Habits

All prospective teachers should be aware that they sometimes overlook the simplest ideas. Teachers may design complex lessons but fail to give basic behavioral instructions before they begin. It is not good practice to assume that young students know or should know by now how they are expected to behave in school situations. Children come to school with diverse experiences, and they may have received different social messages and expectations at home, in day care and other preschool experiences, and in other classrooms.

Basic classroom communications should not be confused with some of the formal behavioral methods discussed in Chapter 7. First and foremost, teachers must take the time to *explain* the specific behaviors they require (hang coats on hooks, speak quietly in halls, raise hands to ask questions) and then must consistently *repeat* the explanations whenever necessary. Most adult learners (graduate students, for instance) need several explanations and reminders about assignments and directions for projects. Teachers must *organize* the routines and spatial arrangements in the room to reinforce the behaviors they expect and should model appropriate behavior as well. ("Children, I will not interrupt you when you are speaking to me. Please do not interrupt one another.") A fundamental rule of classroom management can be summed up in a few words—take the time to tell the children what you expect them to do and how you expect them to do it.

ACTIVITY AND DISCUSSION

Mr. Banks has decided to have a Focus on Library Books Month in his classroom. He has 37 fourth-grade students and 40 library books. Mr. Banks's plan is to divide his students into six groups and have each group select one library book and read it aloud. Then he wants each group to prepare a short skit on the book and perform it for the rest of the class. Mr. Banks has ninety minutes set aside for this activity.

In a small group, analyze this project:

What explanations will Mr. Banks have to give?

Which directions should he repeat more than once?

How might he organize the classroom for the activity?

What routines should he put into place?

How can Mr. Banks model appropriate behaviors?

CATEGORIZING CLASSROOM PROBLEMS

Many classroom teachers around the country say they have serious concerns about behavior problems and discipline problems in schools. However, further analysis often reveals that they use terms like *discipline problems* to describe many different problems. It is important to understand some specific aspects of discipline and behavior problems in order to more fully appreciate the sources of the problems (often more than one) and to identify remediation for which schools and teachers can and should be responsible. Some aspects of discipline problems may be beyond the reach of even the most dedicated and skilled educators, whereas other aspects of the same problems may be fairly easily resolved through intervention at school.

What's the Problem

General discussions about behavior and management risk being nothing more than fruitless rehashing of age-old conflicts in the desires and expectations of schools, teachers, students, families, and communities. Each specific school, class, group, or individual child experiencing behavioral challenges is different. No problem can be addressed until it is well defined. Consider this example:

> A school psychologist is conducting an in-service training session for all the second-grade teachers in the district. He has been asked to speak about discipline problems because most teachers say that classroom discipline is their most serious professional problem. However, when he asks four teachers to describe the actual discipline problems they are facing, he gets four different responses:

> *The parents of my students are not cooperating at all with our homework policy. The children are not doing their work and the parents seem to take no interest whatsoever. I can't even reach parents during the day to discuss the problem.*

> *I have two children whose behavior is so difficult I cannot control it. One was in a special class for children with emotional problems until this year and is upset about being moved. Another is on medication for psychiatric difficulties. They cry, yell, and demand attention.*

> *My whole class refuses to pay attention. No matter what I do, they will not listen to me or be quiet.*

I have several students who come in late every single day. There is always some excuse, but the problem has not been resolved. Even detention after school for lateness has no effect on them.

In truth, these teachers are describing very different problems. Many questions immediately emerge in each situation. Do the children have the opportunity to write their assignments down in a notebook? Do they have homework folders? Is there an organized effort to communicate with families about homework? Can family members review and sign assignments? Is there school support for emotionally disabled students, and has it been made available to the teacher? Are attention problems related to the curriculum or actual delivery of lessons? Are there home, school bus, or personal transportation problems causing lateness? The teachers in every case must make several important decisions:

1. What is the most pressing problem?
2. What part of the problem is under the teacher's control in terms of planning intervention?
3. What is the best plan of action?
4. What is the best way to implement that plan?

See Exhibit 6-1 for a discussion of how one teacher solved a classroom problem.

The danger for teachers is that they can come to feel frustrated, or even defeated, by their classroom discipline problems. To counteract this danger beginning teachers need to develop the habit of thinking about behavior management in an efficient and systematic way. Teachers who anticipate problems and consistently implement strategies to improve behavior do a great deal of work. However, teachers who have a proactive approach to discipline also avoid a great deal of frustration and negativity and build a positive rapport with students who come to trust their consistency. Whenever teachers encounter a difficult problem in the classroom, they should take some time to outline its basic dimensions. When did it occur? Why did it seem to occur? How might it be circumvented or solved? Teachers also benefit from placing all problems within one or more of the four contexts of behavior problems mentioned in Chapter 4 (see Exhibit 6-2 on page 145). These are:

Institutional requirements

Teacher management requirements

Group and peer management requirements

Developmental learning requirements

The mental habit of categorizing problems in the appropriate school context also helps teachers to analyze them, focus on important aspects, and select suitable solutions.

EXHIBIT 6-1   **Teacher Tackles Homework-itis**

Mary James is a third-grade teacher encountering a frustrating problem with homework. The children are not completing their work, and parents do not seem to be helping their children at home. Ms. James has tried to telephone a few parents, but they have not been at home during the school day. Here are the steps she took in analyzing her problem:

1. *What is the most pressing problem?*
   The problem is that more than 60 percent of the children in the class are not bringing completed homework to school on a daily basis.

2. *What part of the problem is under the teacher's control in terms of planning intervention?*
   I can actively work with my students to make sure they have the materials and organized opportunity to make note of daily assignments and to carry those assignments back and forth from home to school. I can consistently reinforce proper behaviors and also be sure that my assignments are relevant, interesting, and age appropriate. I could also make an organized attempt to solicit more parental assistance.

3. *What is the best plan of action?*
   I can ask the school PTA, which has started a fund to help teachers buy materials that help us to include families, to provide thirty-five small homework notebooks and also ask that the PTA note in the newsletter my request that parents check and sign these notebooks daily. I can work intensively with my students for a few weeks to be sure that they develop the habit of writing down all assignments and placing all work in designated home-school folders. I can form a Class Homework Club to assist children still having difficulty completing homework and maintain an observation chart on homework completion. At the end of four weeks I can prepare a Homework Information Sheet to help make all parents aware of the efforts my class is making. I hope the students will become more organized in carrying assignments and notices home and more parents will receive and read the sheet. I need to find out the best time and method of reaching parents whose children still have difficulty completing assignments.

4. *What is the best way to implement that plan?*
   I can have a "homework party" with popcorn and show that movie about the importance of homework. After the movie I'll introduce the homework notebooks, Homework Club, and new rules about homework. For one month I'll spend ten minutes at the beginning and end of each day helping students to organize their folders and notebooks. I'll design a weekly form for my observations and anecdotal notes about homework, so I can weed out specific problems. (Anecdotal notes will be the children's explanations of problems in remembering or completing homework.) I'll telephone all parents whose children continue to have difficulty at the end of the month.

EXHIBIT 6-2

School Behavior and Homework-itis

Ms. James is almost ready to implement her homework improvement plan, but she decides to analyze her problem further to identify the relevant contexts of school behavior:

Institutional requirements:	The school has an informal home work policy, but each teacher is responsible for designing and implementing a plan.
Teacher management requirement:	Much of this problem falls into the category of teacher management. I cannot teach effectively unless I can design and carry out organized homework directives.
Peer and group management requirements:	I think my students may be better motivated to complete their homework if I include a peer dimension to the assignments. I am going to give time for small groups to discuss questions about homework at the end of the day, and ask cooperative groups to check one another's homework each morning.
Developmental learning requirement:	I can better address the developmental needs of my students by giving more choice in homework assignments, and by relating assignments more closely to the long-term projects my students are working on in school.

Whenever they think about management and discipline problems, teachers need to focus on what they *can* do. If children in the class have chaotic home lives and continue to have difficulty doing homework, for example, the teacher needs to identify small steps that can help the students develop better skills. It is difficult to get into the habit of checking your own efforts to improve and your responsibilities for doing so when so many children and families pose challenges. However, teaching is a human service profession, and teachers never stop being responsible for planning and designing behavioral interventions. Personal and professional growth always requires trial and error, reflection, and willingness to change. Teachers who are always willing to consider their own role in the classroom problems grow increasingly skilled in student-centered classroom management.

When Is the Problem Misbehavior?

The word *misbehavior* is always judgmental and has many interpretations. It cannot be discussed without first defining *behavior*. Charles (1992) defines behavior as all the physical and mental acts that humans perform. Behavior is simply what a person does; no value judgments attached. Misbehavior, however, is defined as an action considered inappropriate to settings or situation. Adults usually assume that children know when a behavior is wrong and that they do it anyhow. In fact, many management and discipline problems are not actually misbehavior. Problems can be caused by misunderstandings, conflicting or inconsistent messages, lack of knowledge or skill in behaviors required, or the natural human tendency to become forgetful or inattentive at times. Most adults have mature friends or relatives who often confuse directions or who simply do not listen when others are talking to them. Schoolchildren, who are still in varying stages of maturity and development, will understandably be distracted or forgetful at times. Successful teaching requires patience, understanding, forgiveness, and a willingness to overlook smaller problems that are a natural part of dealing with groups of children.

Teachers do encounter intentional misbehavior in the classroom. Children are sometimes willful and disobedient. They recognize directives but fail to follow them or try to circumvent what is required or expected of them. Children might also be disruptive or aggressive in the classroom. Charles (1992) has identified five overall types of misbehavior:

Aggression: Verbal or physical attacks

Immorality: Cheating, lying, or stealing

Defiance of authority: Refusal to obey

Class disruptions: Talking, calling out, throwing materials, being a "clown"

Goofing off: Daydreaming, not doing work, wasting time

Although these five misbehaviors can take many different forms and pose problems ranging from mild to severe, most school misbehavior falls into one of these categories. Misbehavior might be caused by emotional problems, difficulties in the home or community, or deficits in the earlier experience or education of the child. However, misbehavior might also be caused by a failure to teach and consistently reinforce what is expected, by failure to create a sensitive and caring school environment, by unclear or confusing messages and instructions, or by boredom related to inappropriate activities. Recall the discussion of the development of morality in Chapter 4. Creative and relevant school activities that provide choices for students promote the morality that can diminish many of the disruptive behaviors teachers face in schools.

It is not easy for adults to deal with misbehavior, but difficult or confusing behavior is part of the maturation and learning process for many young people. Effective teachers know they are going to encounter some problems with misbehavior and seek to improve their skills in maintaining an instructional climate that helps children to become more disciplined. Remember that classroom management is best conceived as an interesting and challenging problem rather than an automatic indication that students or teachers are deficient. Teachers who are skilled and inventive in the area of classroom management are far more likely to enjoy successful and enjoyable careers in the field of education.

QUESTIONS TO CONSIDER

Sherry and Miko are doing their first classroom observation during their sophomore year of college. Their original assignment is changed because the teacher is absent, and they enter a kindergarten class that appears to be in absolute chaos. It is "free play period," but most children seem to be disorganized. Several children are running around the room, two children are throwing blocks at each other, and there is a great deal of shouting and loud laughter. The teacher explains that she is a substitute and that she is having a terrible time dealing with the class. By the time they go back to their university, Miko and Sherry are visibly upset. Miko says, "I really wonder if I want to teach," and Sherry says, "I certainly would never want to teach in a school like that."

Their professor later apologizes for the less-than-ideal observation experience, but also points out that it gave Sherry and Miko a realistic opportunity to reflect on poor classroom practice. Identify the most serious problems which they observed. How could you plan as a teacher to avoid or address those problems?

Competence or Compliance?

Is compliance or competence the desired outcome of management interventions in the classroom? Chapter 4 stresses the concept of motivation rather than obedience as the goal of student-centered classroom management. This chapter is designed to further develop that concept by suggesting that teachers seek competence in students more than compliance with adult directives as the goal in creating and maintaining control in the classroom. What does this mean? *Compliance* can be defined as getting children to do what adults tell them to do (Dangel and Polster 1988). It is, without doubt, often important to gain the attention and full cooperation of children in school. However, the request for students' compliance should be accompanied by respect and logic. Children should be able to understand why compliance is required and to see the connection between compliance and successful group functioning or individual learning. Children who have a sense of reasonable connection and logical choice in school obey adults more consistently and with less anger or resistance. A consistent habit of responding positively helps students become more competent in and assured of self-control and their ability to make meaningful choices in other areas of their lives.

Because teachers must be able to gain compliance from students when necessary, how might they think of the relationship of compliance and competence? One helpful method is to develop professional skills in fostering compliance that are matched with skills in maintaining the interest and motivation of students in appropriate learning activities. Compliance, in other words, should be connected to instructional or learning goals (Kameenui and Darch 1994). (Specific skills in gaining compliance from students are stressed in Chapter 7.) The concept of compliance is always connected to the need to protect a sense of competence (see Exhibit 6-3). Children cannot be reflective about their behaviors in a negative climate that is destructive to their self-esteem. Thus it is important for teachers to link the steps they take to gain compliance or correct misbehavior to supporting students' knowledge and skill. It is also important for teachers to think about compliance in the context of whether it could cause students stress. Are the students bored? Have they been sitting in one place for too long? Is the room too warm or too cold? Are student antagonisms exacerbated by crowded classrooms? Are student problems escalating in response to antagonism or hostility of adults? Misbehavior created by environmental problems can be solved only by eliminating negative and counterproductive circumstances.

EXHIBIT 6-3   ***Compliance Versus Competence***

Jennifer is a fifth-grade student who recently transferred into Hilltop School. She and her mother moved after her parents divorced earlier in the year. Jennifer has been apathetic in school and often refuses to do assignments. Today in math class she has been avoiding her independent work and making fun of the boy next to her. When her teacher asks her to stop, she shouts, "You can't make me! You can't make me do anything! You are stupid and I hate you."

Clearly, Jennifer is exhibiting several misbehaviors in the classroom. Her teacher, upset and angry about her insulting comments, decides not to provoke more of a confrontation in front of the class. He says, "Jennifer, I know you can calm down and try to complete your work. We will talk after class today." Jennifer does not do her work but does sit quietly for the rest of the period. Her teacher meanwhile thinks through the best way to approach the problem. He must make clear to Jennifer that her school behavior must improve. Continued failure to complete assignments and comply with behavioral guidelines will compromise her considerable potential for social and academic success. However, he does not want to simply provoke a punitive confrontation. He focuses instead on goals for Jennifer that he believes he can clarify and enhance.

If his focus is compliance, the teacher might use punishment to deter future incidents. If so, he will probably write an official complaint about Jennifer's defiance and recommend a day of "in-house suspension." He will tell Jennifer that she does have to listen to him, that he will not tolerate her rudeness, and that she will suffer serious repercussions for defiance. Also, he will call her mother to complain about her behavior.

If his focus is competence, the teacher might think with professional sensitivity about the effects on Jennifer of her parents' recent divorce, her loss of contact with one parent, and her move from her former community, school, teachers, and friends. Clearly, she needs help in adjusting. He thinks he should call her mother and discuss the possibility of counseling or a support group for children who have experienced divorce or death and subsequent relocation. Although her mother must be informed of Jennifer's problems, the teacher will also talk about his plans to help Jennifer enjoy school more. Next, he will talk to two student leaders in the class and ask them to include Jennifer in lunchtime activities. He plans to initiate a serious discussion with Jennifer and will consider the adaptation of independent work if necessary to accommodate her adjustment. His intention is to agree with Jennifer on several goals they can try to reach together in the weeks ahead.

ACTIVITY AND DISCUSSION

1. Talk in a small group about Exhibit 6-3. How do you think you might prepare to manage your emotions in a busy classroom when behavioral events like this take place? How would your former teachers have handled this situation?

2. When students reach Jennifer's level of defiance, how do you think the goals of compliance and competence might be integrated to motivate students to improve their behavior and to have more interest in independent classwork?

IS THE PROBLEM DISCIPLINE OR MANAGEMENT?

The process of analyzing and categorizing problems as a way of approaching educational intervention is enhanced by a clear understanding of the difference between *management* and *discipline*. Both concepts must be studied and analyzed so they can be practiced in effective ways (Bellon, Bellon and Blank 1992). Although management and discipline problems frequently are interconnected, they are also dissimilar in many regards. Management as an educational concept is usually based in the responsibility and ability of the teacher to create and support an organized and productive learning environment. Discipline (a component of management) is an educational concept based in the responsibility of the teacher to encourage and maintain appropriate and cooperative behaviors on the part of students in the classroom.

What Is Classroom Management?

The best way to begin to conceptualize and define classroom management is to imagine the following situation:

> Sarah, who has just begun her student-teaching experience in the sixth grade, is faced with a sudden emergency. A child has fainted, and her cooperating teacher has left her with the whole class. The students are preparing for a class trip, and as she rushes from the room, the cooperating teacher says, "Make sure they have everything and get them on the bus." Sarah realizes that she has to regain control of the class and maintain a level of silence and attention as she gives instructions. The trip money needs to be counted, the permission slips have to be checked, the lunches are not yet distributed, and two students recovering from strep throat have to take medication at lunchtime. Sarah realizes that the bus is at the back door, which means a walk through the entire school. All the students need coats, and identification tags have to be distributed as well. Being in charge suddenly seems to be a great challenge as Sarah begins to organize her efforts.

Clearly, Sarah's most important focus must be on managing all the details and activities that are required for the transition from the classroom to the bus. She must identify all the tasks and then rank them in order of importance. Sarah must also decide how to explain the entire process to the class. She has to think problems through and be explicit in her directions and expectations. Undoubtedly, Sarah is going to make some mistakes this time. Perhaps someone will forget his medication, or the children will run in the hall and another teacher will complain about the noise. The class may get all the way to the bus before Sarah realizes that some children do not have their coats. The more she experiences life in school, the better Sarah will get at planning and structuring classroom events.

ACTIVITY AND DISCUSSION

You are in Sarah's situation. Complete the following activities in a small group:

1. List all the tasks Sarah must complete.

2. Rank the tasks in order of importance.

3. Identify all the directions Sarah must give to her students.

4. Troubleshoot by predicting problems that might occur and plan to avoid them.

Sarah's situation is an illustration of the complexity of the school environment. School requires daily movement through a maze of rules, routines, activities, and lessons. Children need to maintain their belongings, hand in "business" items such as permission slips and lunch money, use the bathroom, eat lunch, get a drink when they are thirsty, sharpen pencils, and solve individual problems (such as illness) when they arise. Teachers need to manage their supplies and belongings, meet their administrative responsibilities (such as taking roll and placing book orders), take care of their personal needs, handle emergencies and special problems (such as irate parents who suddenly demand a meeting before or after school), and create an organizational structure strong enough to support the demanding daily requirements of teaching. It is up to the teacher, not the students, to develop strong competencies in classroom management.

How is *classroom management* defined? Classroom management is the overall planning and implementation of procedures that create an orderly and productive environment for teaching and learning (Bellon, Bellon and Blank 1992). The role of planning cannot be overemphasized. Teachers who think through lessons and other learning events carefully can design procedures and methods that circumvent many potential problems. For example, if children are going to walk outdoors to gather colorful leaves in the fall, the plan must account for appropriate clothing, safety procedures, expectations for behavior in public places, appropriate bags to put the leaves in, behavioral guidelines for crossing streets, assignment of walking partners, and time for exiting and reentering the school (children who ride the bus may have to be back earlier than children with private transportation). Keep in mind that this level of management planning is separate from the actual planning of lessons and learning activities. Many other professional classroom responsibilities fall into the category of management, including scheduling, pacing lessons, planning social events and interactions, designing and maintaining materials, organizing classroom space, and recruiting class volunteers for tutoring or special events.

Relationship of Discipline and Management

According to Jones and Jones (1990), about half the time spent by teachers and students in classrooms involves aspects of management—generally organizing and arranging learning events and handling misbehavior and other discipline problems. Thus it is probably most helpful to think of discipline as part, or one important aspect, of overall classroom management. Many management skills that teachers need fall into the category of discipline: building positive peer relationships, establishing behavioral rules and routines, maintaining student achievement, sustaining intrinsic and extrinsic motivation of students, and responding to class or individual disruptive behavior (Jones and Jones 1990).

What Makes Management "Student Centered"?

The purpose of education is the growth and development of students. Because classroom management is an important and time-consuming component of every school day, its focus must be on positive outcomes for students. Unless teachers place their primary focus on students, classroom management can become insensitive or grounded more in the interests and convenience of adults. Vigilant professionals must guard against the danger of giving higher priority to institutional requirements than to the developmental needs of the children for whom the institution was created. This challenge is particularly great for teachers who work in schools that are overcrowded, understaffed, and underfunded. Unfortunately, such schools do exist throughout America. However, teachers who work hard to maintain a professional level of concern and commitment to children are also able to maintain successful levels of student centeredness in most classrooms.

Management becomes student centered when it is focused on several important aspects of every classroom-teaching situation:

1. The emotional life of students

2. The developmental needs of students

3. The interests and abilities of students, and

4. The increasing competence and accompanying self-esteem of students

Previous chapters explored all these aspects of student-centered management. Obviously, an environment in which children are shouted at, ordered about, unnecessarily confined, and coerced into compliance is unacceptable. However, in the difficult climate of modern education, teachers must work hard to build and maintain positive student-centered management. To be successful they must accept their role as the final authority and decision maker while respecting the feelings and needs of students through sound instructional practice. Successful teachers must anticipate and circumvent as many problems as possible. Finally, they must develop effective classroom discipline by preventing and correcting behavior problems (Bellon, Bellon, and Blank 1992).

ACTIVITY AND DISCUSSION

You will be facing your first classroom of students in a few weeks. Identify the most important management planning you think you should do. What problems or challenges should you plan for now? Write down ideas you have for planning for

1. The emotional needs of your students

2. The developmental levels of your students

3. The interests and abilities of individual students

4. The need for increasing competence in your students

What Is Classroom Discipline?

Classrooms are places in which students are required to demonstrate self-control, willingness to cooperate with others, and the ability to obey the requests of numerous adults. This is true because schools by their very nature deal with groups of individuals who must be coordinated to function in an orderly manner. Charles (1992) refers to discipline as steps taken by adults to cause students to behave acceptably in school. These steps should encompass prevention of as well as response to discipline problems. Teachers should keep in mind that the concept of discipline is not necessarily a negative concept. They should question any assumption that children will behave inappropriately unless warned and controlled by adults with strong disciplinary procedures. Chapter 4 establishes the idea that appropriate tasks in an interesting learning environment foster self-discipline in children. The most important act of the teacher in fostering discipline is establishing a positive and productive learning environment. Once that is accomplished, teachers must also anticipate positive and negative student behaviors and plan to deal with them in an effective way. Thus another way to define discipline might be the ongoing response to appropriate as well as inappropriate classroom behaviors that promotes growth in skill as well as a successful learning environment. The thoughtful and encouraging response to appropriate behaviors should be as important to a system of discipline as any plans to remediate misbehavior.

THINKING OF DISCIPLINE AS GUIDANCE

Few if any readers would claim that their behavior in elementary school was always appropriate. Their maturation into people who are willing to obey rules and contribute to the well-being of a community in all likelihood is the result of process of growth that depended on consistent guidance over many years. Behavior, like many other school subjects and skills, is learned through steady interactions with people and events in and out of school. Because most behaviors required in school are emphasized because they make it possible for a group to function successfully, part of learning to behave appropriately is understanding the value of personal contribution to group function. Gartrell (1994) stresses that a guidance-based approach to discipline empowers productive human activity and assumes the potential for good. Caring adults can help children to develop personal strength and the insight necessary for ethical decisions. Guidance, in Gartrell's view, also transcends traditional school discipline to promote goals for a democratic society.

Once again, in the guidance point of view, teachers must decide between discipline as enforcement of compliance to adult standards or discipline as guidance toward socially responsible personal skills. After all, for adults the underpinning of democratic participation is not simple obedience of laws. Rather it is the adherence to mutually agreed-upon laws that enhance the well-being of the entire (and participatory) group. Guidance-based discipline helps children to participate in the process of building positive group dynamics in schools and later in society.

Guidance and the Basic Needs of Children

Why should children behave? Motivation, as discussed earlier in this book, plays an important role in all human behavior. Sometimes adults who recall that they always obeyed their parents and teachers when they were young become aware later of the many motivating factors in their early environments. There may have been many "hidden rewards," such as resources made available by parents or interesting curricula and learning activities provided by teachers. They may also have been rewarded with a feeling of belonging to a unit that was capable of meeting their needs as individuals and a sense of personal competence as a member of that unit. Children who have developed the disposition to "obey" have often enjoyed many rewards in their home and school environment for their cooperative behavior. Put another way, they had tangible and intangible rewards for good behavior. In addition, the presence of parental love and affection, as well as material resources, in all likelihood served to reinforce their cooperation.

On the other hand, some children in schools today are not enjoying intrinsic or extrinsic rewards in their stressed and impoverished families or their crowded and underfunded schools. The sad fact is that some children may sense that they have nothing to gain or lose through their behavior, whether positive or negative. Children, like all human beings, have an instinctive drive to meet their most pressing needs. What can teachers do when children are frustrated by their home or community circumstances? Most certainly, they can organize their own classrooms to meet some of the basic needs of children that schools can provide (see Exhibit 6-4).

EXHIBIT 6-4   ***Meeting the Needs of Children in School***

Mr. Roger is a teaching volunteer in a school that serves children whose parents are almost all unemployed and impoverished. Although he received intensive training, Mr. Roger was still unprepared for the sadness and frustration exhibited by many children in the school. He was initially confident that he would be able to reach the children but has had several encounters with children who have said, "What do you care, anyhow?" or "You can't make me do anything I don't want to do." Mr. Roger is determined to live up to his commitments to the children but is unsure of what to do. His supervisor tells him, "These kids are fighting for their survival. Remember what that means! They need to have a sense of belonging and power in your classroom. Give them some freedom, and be sure that some of what you do is really fun for them."

With that in mind, Mr. Roger plans a monthlong activity to try to foster satisfying personal feelings for the children. He develops a project called Building Our Classroom in which he seeks to express his caring about his students as they develop a mutual sense of belonging in the classroom. Some children decide they would like to decorate the windows, and others decide to focus on the door or walls. The themes chosen by the class are winter sports, science facts, and books we are reading. One group of children decides to build a small hut in the back of the room to replicate one built by an explorer in a book they are reading. Another designs a bird feeder and figures out how to hang it outside the classroom window. Three boys and a girl decide to build a pair of snowshoes they will try during the winter. Mr. Roger encourages all the children to develop an artist's signature or symbol and to place it in the part of the room to which they think they contributed the most.

Glasser, as noted in Charles (1992), describes children's basic needs as survival, belonging, power, fun, and freedom. If classrooms are indeed structured to meet the common good, these needs of children must be a priority (Banks 1994). Activities that respect children by reflecting these needs provide ample opportunity for discipline through guidance while motivating children to cooperate and behave appropriately.

ACTIVITY AND DISCUSSION

Reflect on the problems faced by Mr. Roger in Exhibit 6-4. In a small group identify the components of Mr. Roger's idea that may promote feelings of survival, belonging, power, freedom, and fun. Think of some ideas or activities that would enhance this project and meet more basic emotional needs of the students.

DEVELOPING STUDENT-CENTERED DISCIPLINE

Children want to be competent and comfortable in school. Almost all are capable of developing the abilities that will enable them to have successful relationships with their peers and teachers. (Exceptions might be children whose disabling emotional difficulties require more intensive intervention than classroom teachers can reasonably be expected to provide. These children are discussed in a later section of this chapter.) Student-centered discipline meets the desire of children to belong and be competent by creating and maintaining a school community that works for the common good (Banks 1994). It assists children in building the knowledge, skills, and attitudes they need to become competent and productive adults.

Thinking about student-centered discipline as a social rather than individual endeavor emphasizes the mutual interpersonal responsibilities of teachers and students. Discipline as a concept of social cooperation is found in the flow of daily activities and interactions within the entire group and is not focused on behavioral confrontations between teachers and only individual students. Children want to know that the adults who are with them all day really care about them. Warm and personal interactions with adults are prerequisites for learning responsible and prosocial behaviors in the classroom. Teachers who are considerate and supportive are excellent role models and create an environment that motivates their students to imitate them. Over time children not only acquire knowledge of how to act in social situations but also develop trust in their sense of belonging in a supportive classroom environment (Gartrell 1994).

However, teachers cannot assume that their sense of caring creates good discipline habits in children. Some children have had habits of inappropriate behavior for years before entering a particular classroom, many children misbehave at times, and most children today test the sincerity and consistency of teachers until they develop trust in their methods of discipline. Teachers must anticipate the need for a carefully planned and implemented approach to discipline and behavior. Children are well served by adults who insist on appropriate behaviors that enable students to work hard, learn a great deal, and function at a competent level in school and elsewhere. Children function best with adults who are competent and disciplined. Teachers must create a coordinated system of discipline in their classroom management that becomes part of the structure of their daily planning of curriculum.

Discipline That Prevents, Supports, and Corrects

Other chapters focus on planning appropriate and interesting curricula as a major component in developing appropriate behaviors in children. This section examines the specific planning of discipline. In order to plan for discipline teachers should divide their thinking about it into three areas: prevention, or the avoidance of situations producing misbehavior; support; and correction (Charles 1992).

In terms of prevention teachers can and should anticipate problems based on prior experience and careful observation of students. For example, if a mathematics class directly after lunch seems to produce an unusual level of misbehavior, a preventive teacher might move mathematics to an earlier time and save a quiet independent activity for the period after students return from lunch. If two students are constantly getting into arguments, their seats might simply be changed. If the class is going on a trip to the symphony, the teacher must spend considerable time beforehand preparing the students for the behavior expected there. Orderly and predictable classroom routines prevent discipline problems, as do consistent and fair responses to misbehavior in the classroom.

Supportive responses to discipline might be referred to as "heading problems off at the pass." Students need help in knowing when their behavior is beginning to cause a problem and guidance in changing their behavior. Reorientation of behavior often requires a brief discussion that helps students reflect on what they are doing and to choose a new direction. Teachers who want to support positive behavior should attempt to quickly reorient students at the first sign of misbehavior. This avoids a more punitive or negative confrontation if the behavior is allowed to escalate and gives students the opportunity to redirect their own behavior before real problems develop.

One example of quick avoidance of a serious problem might be when the teacher observes two students whispering at the beginning of an independent activity. The teacher might say, "I know it is difficult to change from our exciting math lab to a quiet activity, but please move back into your seat and begin your work. I am very interested in seeing how you develop that essay." Likewise, if a class is becoming increasingly restless and inattentive, the teacher might say, "I'd really hate to see such a great day for this class become difficult right at the end. Thank you for being so attentive in your lessons, and let's try hard to finish this social studies project today with cooperative behavior." A child who has been the focus of specific behavioral interventions might need a whisper, a quiet but serious glance, or a brief reminder such as, "I know you are going to start painting right away, because you have been improving so much this week."

Small errors, mishaps, or lapses in behavior should be expected from children. Patient and vigilant teachers support appropriate behavior by catching problems and reorienting behavior before it escalates to a level of class disruption. The supportive teacher focuses more on redirecting the behavior than on threatening punishment if the problem escalates. Unnecessary antagonism has no place in the student-centered classroom.

No matter how skilled and cooperative the teacher and students are in managing discipline in the classroom, problems and misbehavior will occur. Students have bad days, developmental changes create new problems, and the stresses of society will be evidenced in the behavior of children in the classroom. Some children present persistent challenges, perhaps on a daily basis. A few children are so difficult to manage that supportive school services are required. Corrective responses of the teacher should focus on suppressing negative and unacceptable behaviors and remediating behavioral problems. Verbal corrections of behavior should be effective communications with several important components:

1. Stopping the activity long enough to gain the attention of the student(s)

2. Telling the student(s) exactly what they are doing wrong

3. Telling the student(s) exactly what you want them to do in order to change their behavior

4. Encouraging the student(s) or expressing belief in their ability to improve (Fennimore 1992)

For example, three students are talking and laughing during library circle time. The teacher might say, "I need your attention. You are talking and laughing and disrupting other students. I expect you to stop now and read your books quietly as I asked you to at the beginning of the class. I am sure that you will be able to follow my directions and enjoy your books." If behavior problems are more severe, teachers have to decide whether to address them immediately or wait until they can meet with the student(s) privately. Corrective responses are not necessarily confrontational. In fact, open confrontation with students should be avoided. Children often have less to lose than teachers in a confrontation, because a teacher who is intimidated or is forced to back down risks losing the respect of other students in the class. Neither students nor teachers should be forced into situations that result in humiliation or personal defeat. Correction is most positive when it actively reorients toward specific schoolwork or instruction (Kameenui and Darch 1994).

Consider the student who throws all her books on the floor in frustration because she cannot find her history assignment. Her teacher might say, "Throwing your books on the floor is not appropriate and does not solve your problem. I do not want you to do this again, because it has disrupted our class and created extra work for you. If you do not find your assignment as you put your books neatly back in your desk, I will give you extra paper for now. After school we can make a plan about what else to do." The place of punishment in correction of behavior is discussed in the next chapter. However, it is important to remember that a central goal of correction is improving the level of communication and cooperation between teacher and child. From an interpersonal standpoint discipline should be as positive as possible.

Much of this material may seem like common sense. However, in the busy and demanding climate of the classroom the teacher must coordinate these discipline strategies with all other learning activities. A good way to think about discipline as you teach is this: "My own planning can prevent many problems, I try to catch problems early and solve them with positive intervention, and I correct or suppress misbehavior with the goal of redirecting my students toward meaningful and interesting classroom work." It is also important for teachers to remember that affectionate, caring, and dedicated commitment to children is a critical structural element of student-centered classroom discipline.

THE REALITY OF SERIOUS BEHAVIOR PROBLEMS

Chapter 1 focuses on the realities in the lives of modern American children. Poverty, abuse, neglect, violence, and a host of other family and community factors do indeed take their toll on the well-being of the children they affect. On the one hand, teachers must avoid focusing on these problems when doing so circumvents the responsibility of the school to successfully build and enhance the competencies of all children. On the other hand, physical danger, emotional pain, hunger, neglect, and other problems do affect the daily behavior of children in school. Students who do not have consistent discipline at home, or whose lives are difficult and chaotic *may* require more patience and understanding at school. It is as wrong to assume that all disadvantaged children present problems as it is to assume that *only* disadvantaged children are difficult to manage and discipline in school. Children from all socioeconomic groups experience abuse, addiction, neglect, divorce, and other problems in their homes. Some family problems are obvious (poverty, for example), whereas others may be carefully hidden (addiction or abuse in more advantaged families, for example). Children from all socioeconomic groups may experience serious emotional or psychiatric problems. Teachers should know that the causes of many problems of children are difficult or impossible to establish. Rather than assume that teachers are always aware of the bases of behavior problems—they often are not—teachers should focus on understanding how best to deal with the problem in the classroom.

The home or community is not always the source of difficulty. Although some children come to school with serious behavior problems, others develop serious behavior problems once they get to school. Schools that fail to respect the culture and experience of the children and instead embody a negative climate and low expectations are inadvertently encouraging negative feelings and bad behavior. Likewise, schools with inflexible programs of discipline that assume that children will be problems and that do not consider the emotional and developmental experiences of children can create negative behaviors. Teachers need to be aware of their own bias ("I know that I tend to assume that children who are on public assistance will be behavior problems, although I know that habit is unfair") and work hard to overcome it ("I make sure I pair less and more advantaged children in my seating arrangement and try hard to treat both equally in all regards") (Borich 1992). Teachers must anticipate behavior problems but should not stereotype that anticipation. Only when a serious behavioral difficulty is observed and documented in a specific child over a period of time, during which other interventions have been consistently applied, should teachers assume that the problem requires special attention and assistance.

Teachers in general are not trained to handle problems that seem to involve serious emotional problems and need the support of those with more expertise, but teachers may find themselves dealing with such problems in their classrooms. They need to know the best ways to use their skills in student-centered management to help these children to get the most from schools.

QUESTIONS TO CONSIDER

1. Why do you think the problems of less advantaged children might be more obvious than those of more advantaged children?

2. Can you think of any ways that the educational institutions you attended as a child and adolescent actually caused behavior problems in students? Can you recall any teachers whose behavior in school might have caused classroom problems? How might you describe that behavior?

Thinking About Difficult Behavior

Many children with difficult behaviors reflect the serious problems facing schools and communities. It is not productive to focus on the perceived failings of individual students when their behaviors reflect acknowledged family, community, or social trends. For example, many educators openly acknowledge the failure of American schools to successfully meet the needs of all children. This is perhaps most strongly evidenced in the many students who are not sufficiently motivated by their educational environments to finish high school. In many states up to one-third of all students fall into this category (Bellon, Bellon, and Blank 1992). Clearly, these students have not, for a variety of reasons, discovered a strong sense of their personal promise and capabilities in the school setting. The loss of their motivation to become educated is a sad and potentially expensive loss to themselves and all of society. It may be easier to blame the students and their families for failure, but in fact a goal of every good school can and should be to motivate all to succeed. Perseverance should make sense to students because of the encouragement, support, and interesting curricula provided by their schools (Bellon, Bellon and Blank 1992).

Serious behavior problems exist when teachers are faced with disruptions in discipline serious enough to upset them, distract other students, or interrupt the flow of daily activities. These problems can range from mild to severe and include the following manifestations:

Getting out of seats

Making disruptive noises

Refusing to listen

Hitting, kicking, or shoving

Stealing

Defiance

Throwing materials

Cursing

Refusing to share

Speaking out of turn

Giggling

Crying over small matters

Arguing

Repeatedly asking the same question

Making fun of the teacher or other students

Forcing others to do things

Destroying materials (Horne and Sayger 1990)

Each problem is different. Correction and support are often intertwined, and patterns in student behavior should be taken into consideration. The student who occasionally makes fun of others or scribbles on other students' papers must be treated differently from the student with frequent violent temper tantrums involving destruction of furniture. The first case requires clear communication of disapproval, whereas the second may require outside help and intervention. Escalating problems are different from those that are stable but annoying. For example, the student who is becoming increasingly defiant and insulting presents a more serious problem than the student who curses every now and then.

Teachers must become skilled at matching corrective responses to the level of difficulty presented by the misbehavior. A brief glance, a warning, or a clear correction is often sufficient. Teachers who overreact to annoyances may unwittingly fuel confrontations and cause small problems to escalate. On the other hand, teachers should not overlook potentially serious misbehavior. By the time teachers seek help from school support staff or administration for a child whose

misbehavior seems severe, they should have tried progressively intensive interventions and still feel that neither they nor the student(s)
involved are in control of the problems.

Avoiding Bias in Classroom Discipline

It should be clear by now that the relationship between student
behavior and institutional practice is strong. However, many other
discussions in schools or publications might reflect a "school-neutral"
approach. The stated or unstated assumption therein might be that
schools do provide an opportunity for all children to be successful
and that children who fail in school are responding to problems in
their homes or communities. Is this true? Educators must acknowledge the statements of the National Coalition of Advocates for
Students (NCAS; 1991), along with many other groups concerned
about equity in education, that bias and discrimination remain an
active component of many public schools in the United States.
Active exclusion through tracking or neglect through differentials in
funding and services can destroy dreams of success and build anger
and resistance.

Differences in the application of school discipline policies
can also be found between different groups of students. The
National Coalition of Advocates for Students cites, for example, a
study done by the U. S. Department of Education in 1988 indicating that African American students were suspended at twice the
rate of their White peers (NCAS, 1991). Teachers should be aware
of the danger of bias and prejudice in the treatment of behavior
problems in the classroom. They, like many Americans, may be
affected by violent images of certain groups. The images may
cause fear and resentment that are reflected later in biased treatment of children who belong to those groups. Sleeter and Grant
(1994) state that marginalized children become alienated in
school, particularly when they are the target of more reprimands
than other children with similar behaviors. Teachers do not want
to think of themselves as prejudiced, but the evidence suggests
that they must actively acknowledge the danger of bias and
resolve to be continually reflective in order to avoid it.

ACTIVITY AND DISCUSSION

James, a ten year old, comes from a less advantaged community. He was given a readiness test before he entered elementary school and was labeled "transitional and at risk." He spent kindergarten in a special classroom and was then placed in first grade with a teacher who referred to her class as "the problem kids." James became a behavior problem in second grade and was placed in "in-house suspension" six times for engaging in angry verbal exchanges with his teachers. Since second grade James has been a poor student with a negative attitude toward school.

Some educators would argue that James's poverty and family life have been the main contributors to the problems he has experienced in school. Others would argue that he never really got a chance to be successful in school. Formulate a brief position statement that incorporates both points of view. With which do you agree more and why?

Disorders That Require Support

Some behavioral problems are beyond the intervention of the classroom teacher alone. Although teachers are not qualified to diagnose these disorders, they may encounter them in the classroom. The children who have these disorders are suffering from their effects and deserve the support of all adults responsible for their care. Irresponsible or insensitive labeling or disclosure of confidential information about children must be stringently avoided by professionals in the classroom.

One such behavior is attention deficit disorder (ADD), which is also sometimes called attention deficit hyperactivity disorder (ADHD). This is the most widely studied behavior problem, the subject of almost three hundred articles or books between 1976 and 1984. The children who have this disorder may internalize, or become overcontrolled, inhibited, anxious, or withdrawn. They may also externalize, or become defiant, noncompliant, disruptive, or aggressive. The cause of attention deficit disorder remains a point of speculation, but suggested causes are genes, neurobiological or neurochemical conditions, diet, toxic factors in the environment, depression, or ineffective parenting. One to 20 percent of American children are assumed to be suffering from some form of this disorder, which results in inappropriate behavior such as inattention, impulsivity, and hyperactivity (Breen and Altepeter 1990).

Teachers of children with this diagnosis need to know whether they are taking medication, and they need to solicit suggestions from parents and professionals involved in the student's treatment.

Another serious behavior problem has been identified as conduct disorder. This difficulty may involve aggressive behavior such as theft or physical violence, or nonaggressive behavior such as violation of rules, running away from home, lying, and stealing. Children with conduct disorder may also demonstrate no concern for others, blame others for their problem, or indicate complete inability to make friends and get along with others (Breen and Altepeter 1990). Clearly, some of these behaviors can be observed in all children but they are far more serious and resistant to intervention in some than in others. Again, teachers should consult with parents and related professionals to obtain relevant information and to design effective interventions. Warm and caring professional concern in the classroom enhances other interventions that may be available to the child.

Oppositional disorders involve the violation of minor rules, temper tantrums, provocation, stubbornness, or argumentative behavior. Oppositional defiant disorders may involve temper, argument, defiance, and spitefulness stemming from anger and resentment (Breen and Altepeter 1990). Again, these behaviors can often be observed in "normal" and mainly well-behaved young students. Disorders become more apparent when they are persistent, resistant to change, and when they present an interruption in the daily process of classroom discipline and management. Teachers dealing with these problems need support and information from parents and other professionals who are working to assist the child in therapeutic situations.

Teachers Have Feelings Too

It is true that teaching is a human service profession and that teachers are responsible for meeting the needs of their students as much as possible. However, teachers have feelings and problems of their own. Children who are continually disruptive and difficult to teach take their toll on the enthusiasm of teachers trying to manage thirty other children at the same time. It is hard to care, plan, work hard, and yet feel that your best efforts are being undermined by difficult children. This is even more true when teachers do not think they are receiving appropriate support from parents, guidance specialists, or school administrators. Certainly it is not ethical to strand teachers in classrooms with problems beyond their control and somehow expect them to retain undaunted enthusiasm for their work. However, teachers and students alike must work productively in schools where conditions are not always optimal. The focus must always be on the progress and growth of all children. Simply put, great teachers persevere.

Chapter 7 further develops the concepts of discipline and management by suggesting more specific strategies that are helpful in solving the interesting challenges of helping students to learn appropriate behavior that supports their growth and learning in the classroom.

PROFESSIONAL DECISION

At a Crossroad

Min Lee has just begun her third year of teaching in the fifth grade of a new elementary school. Three months into the school year she realizes that her classroom has some serious problems. Several other teachers have complained about the noise in her classroom and in the hall when her class uses the bathrooms. At least half the children are not consistently attentive during lessons, and several children are disruptive. One boy has ripped the library books of some children who sit near him. Min Lee feels that the quality of homework is only adequate and is concerned in general that her class does not enjoy the school day as much as it should.

Min Lee has learned that most of her students attend the before-school program that begins at 6 A.M. and that most also either attend the after-school program or let themselves into empty homes (some with younger siblings). Her students are talking about television shows that are on late at night. Only one-third of the parents attended the last parent-teacher meeting.

Min Lee wants to avoid focusing on home or community problems. She decides to analyze her situation and identify some immediate and long-term solutions to her problems.

1. What do you think is Min Lee's most critical management problem?

2. What do you think is Min Lee's most critical discipline problem?

3. What are the first three things you think she should do to begin to address the problems in her classroom?

4. What long-term discipline and management goals would you suggest to Min Lee?

CHAPTER SUMMARY

This chapter began with a focus on the importance of discipline habits in the classrooms of individual teachers. It established a focus on school discipline as an interesting (rather than negative) problem and stressed analysis and categorization of problems. The chapter suggested that teachers must know and articulate exactly what they expect from their students and then teach and reinforce the behaviors expected. The concept of misbehavior was explored, and discipline was described as a plan to handle positive as well as negative behaviors throughout the school day. This chapter suggested that classroom management was the overall approach to organized and positive learning environments for which teachers are responsible and that discipline is an important component of management that focuses more on the behaviors and misbehavior of the students. The idea of guidance was explained in the context of student-centered management and discipline, and the contrasting ideas of compliance and competence were also explored. The role of teachers in preventing misbehavior, supporting positive behavior, and correcting misbehavior when it occurs was explained. The chapter ended with a discussion of the serious behavior problems and related stress that teachers may face.

CHAPTER REFERENCES

Banks, J. (1994). *Introduction to multicultural education*. Boston: Allyn & Bacon.

Bellon, J. J., Bellon, E. C., & Blank, M. A. (1992). *Teaching from a research knowledge base: A development and renewal process*. New York: Merrill.

Borich, G. D. (1992). *Effective teaching methods* (2nd ed.). New York: Merrill.

Breen, M. J., & Altepeter, T. S. (1990). *Disruptive behavior disorders in children*. New York: Guilford Press.

Charles, C. M. (1992). *Building classroom discipline* (4th ed.). New York: Longman.

Dangel, R. F., & Polster, R. A. (1988). *Teaching child management skills*. New York: Pergamon.

Fennimore, B. S. (1992). The multicultural classroom climate. In E. B. Vold (Ed.), *Multicultural education in early childhood classrooms.* Washington, DC: National Education Association.

Gartrell, D. (1994). *A guidance approach to discipline.* New York: Delmar.

Horne, R. N., & Sayger, T. V. (1990). *Treating conflict and oppositional defiant disorders in children.* New York: Pergamon.

Jones, V. F., & Jones, L. S. (1990). *Comprehensive classroom management* (3rd ed.). Boston: Allyn & Bacon.

Kameenui, E. J., & Darch, C. B. (1994). *Instructional classroom management: A proactive approach to behavior management.* New York: Longman.

National Coalition of Advocates for Students. (1991). *The good common school: Making the vision work for all students.* Boston: Author.

Sleeter, C. E., & Grant, C. A. (1994). *Making choices for multicultural education.* New York: Merrill.

7 STRATEGIES FOR MANAGEMENT AND DISCIPLINE

The behavior of students in school is always related to the context of all that is taking place in the process of education. It is always productive to conceptualize positive discipline and management as part of the curriculum and the overall mission of the school rather than as a separate problem of some children or teachers. It is also important to realize that positive discipline is necessarily a long-term goal in the process of modeling and shaping student behavior rather than a quick fix when problems occur. The goal of establishing positive discipline is more easily met when concerned and caring teachers are well prepared and skilled in preventing problems whenever possible. And however skilled and concerned teachers may be, they will undoubtedly be called upon to solve discipline and behavior problems on a regular basis in their classrooms. They must also be familiar with several models of discipline and behavior management and should have a repertoire of interventions appropriate for addressing student misbehavior ranging from mild to severe. Teachers must also be able and willing to address the often uncomfortable possibility that their own behaviors or misdirected goals may be causing avoidable problems in their students. The ultimate goal of strategies for management and discipline is the empowerment of students to develop self-direction and self-control in school and in the totality of their lives. Teachers who model humane and caring personal behaviors help students to strengthen their own self-control and to make good choices about their actions in the classroom. This chapter discusses the following topics:

- Behavior problems occur within a context
- Guidelines for effective management
- Models of thinking about behavior
- Ideas for positive management
- Starting the school year
- Behavior must be taught on a continual basis
- Learning to observe and analyze problems
- The challenge of communication
- Misbehavior in the classroom
- Avoiding "teacher misbehavior"
- Looking at student misbehavior
- Looking at punishment
- Rewarding appropriate behavior

BEHAVIOR PROBLEMS OCCUR WITHIN A CONTEXT

This chapter focuses on specific suggestions to help teachers to manage classrooms while maintaining a focus on the developmental needs of their students. Like Chapter 6, this chapter discusses discipline and management as separate issues that require teacher strategies interwoven in the basic order of daily classroom life. Problems in the behavior of students usually have some logical pattern. Teachers who have developed skills in management look for reasons that the problems might have occurred in each specific instance. Chapter 6 suggests that discipline be viewed as an interesting rather than a negative problem. Teachers who develop the habit of looking for connections between all the events in their classrooms, including incidents of misbehavior, can make logical decisions about how to react. However, it is not realistic to expect that it will always be easy to make the right decisions about behavior in busy classrooms. Consider this example:

Ms. Roberts is a first-year teacher in a sixth-grade classroom. During her college training her professors stressed the importance of responding to classroom misbehavior in consistent and predictable ways. Ms. Roberts graduated from college confident that she was prepared to develop an effective program of student-centered classroom management. However, she has become less confident during her first months of teaching.

On one day, for example, three students forgot their homework. One student had never before forgotten homework, one had consistently forgotten homework all year, and the third had a parent in the hospital following a serious car accident. Should each student be treated in the same manner? On another day two students were reported as having misbehaved in the lunchroom. The discipline report said both had talked back to the lunchroom aide. One student explained that he had been arguing to call his mother because he felt sick, and indeed Ms. Roberts later learned that the student had a high fever. The other student explained that he had been detained from going out to play after lunch because he did not have a coat, but his aunt had not sent him with a coat that day. Had these students actually misbehaved? On yet another day Ms. Roberts had planned a game for her class that turned out to give unfair advantage to one team. Students from the other team were angry, and several got into inappropriate verbal exchanges. Should Ms. Roberts punish students for inappropriate argument or use her error in designing the game to lead a group discussion on positive ways to deal with mistakes and disappointments?

Another thing Ms. Roberts noticed was that her students always misbehaved after returning from gym. She consistently heard other teachers report the same problem and began to wonder whether the gym teacher was frustrating the students in some way. The problem of responding to misbehavior is more personalized and confusing than Ms. Roberts had ever anticipated.

Ms. Roberts is developing more mature professional concepts that will serve her well during her entire teaching career. Teachers must approach discipline and management as ongoing challenges requiring constant evaluation and decision making. All behavior (and misbehavior) occurs within a context (Bellon, Bellon, and Blank 1992). No "fail safe" methods can be developed because such methods cannot be adapted for every event in all classrooms. Compassionate teachers decide to respond to student behavior in a responsible manner that takes the needs of students, conditions of the classroom, and unanticipated events into account. However, it is important that they avoid bias as they try to individualize their responses to student behavior. In truth, competent professional interaction with a group of students is an exacting task. Teachers should expect to make some errors, reflect on them, and rectify them. They will also experience success and refine the skills that promote a pleasant and organized classroom environment.

Many experts have worked hard to develop interesting and exciting approaches to classroom discipline. The models and suggestions of these experts can help classroom teachers to maintain order and make positive decisions about student behavior. However, many teachers never have the opportunity for intensive training in any one model. Also, most teachers work in isolation and deal with complex realities that call for immediate thoughts and solutions. There is often no substitute for intelligent decisions and humane responses of committed teachers within the daily context of classroom life. Great teaching never occurs without caring and respect for the children in the classroom. Teachers who dislike their students and feel uncomfortable with the requirements of their jobs cannot bring a suitable level of caring to their classrooms. In the absence of interpersonal care discipline becomes a negative and potentially counterproductive educational endeavor. On the other hand, teachers who are determined to understand their students and who are fulfilled by their work with young people have the potential to become lifelong learners of effective management and discipline strategies.

GUIDELINES FOR EFFECTIVE MANAGEMENT

There is no recipe for effective management in classrooms. However, educational research shows that certain teacher characteristics and behaviors build strong and stable classroom environments. Every teacher should try to implement suggestions made by researchers who have studied discipline and management in depth. Bellon, Bellon, and Blank (1992) have identified four assumptions of effective classroom management:

- The teacher is the final authority.

- Good management is related to sound instruction.

- Prevention of problems is basic to good discipline.

- The teacher must have a comprehensive prevention response system for sound management and discipline.

All these assumptions recognize that management of classroom behavior is a complex task that requires ongoing self-questioning and careful reflection on the part of the teacher. The function of classroom management is control, but how much control is necessary and what means of establishing it are legitimate in an educational institution? Effective classroom managers find a balance of control that supports students and assists the learning process while also maintaining a productive group environment (Kauffman, Hallahan, Mostert, Trent, and Nuttycombe 1993).

Teachers who manage classrooms effectively recognize that planning that structures lessons and daily activities in meaningful ways is a major factor in preventing behavior problems. Their managerial skills take social needs into account by maintaining a positive classroom climate and creating rules adjusted to the realities of students (Bellon, Bellon, and Blank 1992). Effective teachers who plan comprehensive management are also willing to accept personal responsibility for student learning and behavior. They continuously examine their instruction to be sure students understand and find meaning in learning material. Effective teachers also believe that inappropriate behavior can be redirected and retrained and that they can help their students find alternatives (Jones and Jones 1990).

Instruction is the primary function of the school and the basis of a great deal of classroom management. Teachers who are sensitive to the academic needs and interests of students use methods that facilitate optimal learning. They use organizational strategies that help students work with one another within a structure of diverse activities and approaches to learning (Jones and Jones 1990). Teachers who are effective managers demonstrate what Kounin (1970) identifies as four competencies in the classroom:

"*Withitness,*" or the ability to scan the room at all times, intervene in situations promptly, and avoid timing and target errors

Overlapping, or the ability to do more than one thing at a time while dealing with both the group and individuals as necessary

Momentum during lessons, which enables students to overcome potential distractions and reflects solid preparation and a brisk teaching pace

Challenge and variety in assignments, which maintain the interest and task orientation of students in the classroom

Good and Brophy (1987) suggest that consistent classroom feedback, complex teaching of increasingly challenging material, and provision of more opportunities for students to respond and ask questions are also effective ways to maximize student potential and thus avoid classroom problems.

All these classroom management skills are connected to long-term instructional approaches. They are not to be mistaken for isolated or abbreviated responses to misbehavior. Management skills are part of comprehensive teacher competencies that prevent a great deal of misbehavior. Weber (1984) suggests that all teachers use a systematic, long-term approach to management by:

1. Identifying reasonable class conditions

2. Identifying reasonable student behaviors

3. Analyzing current conditions through observation and accurate description

4. Describing current conditions

5. Targeting and prioritizing specific behaviors for change

6. Selecting and applying intervention strategies

7. Evaluating and adjusting interventions

Again, these techniques help teachers to continually reflect and plan for better management by mapping long-term goals. For most teachers the process of building and maintaining classroom management requires keen insight and an abundance of patience.

QUESTIONS TO CONSIDER

1. How do you think new teachers can establish control while attempting to be sensitive to the personal and social needs of students? What are some mistakes that you think new teachers may make in the area of control?

2. How do you think new teachers can evaluate problem situations and decide whether their instruction or their management is escalating behavior problems? What steps might they take in deciding on the most probable source of difficulty and the most effective intervention?

MODELS OF THINKING ABOUT BEHAVIOR

Management and discipline are critical challenges for every teacher. Effective instruction absolutely depends on reasonable order and attention to tasks in the classroom. Because so many teachers continue to have serious difficulty in this area, much attention has been given to the development of specific approaches to discipline and management in the classroom. None of these approaches can replace the intelligence, patience, and reflection required to deal with behavior problems. Nor can any approach eliminate the frustration or anger that is sometimes part of the school experience for students and teachers alike. No single approach to discipline can incorporate the compassion needed to teach children who reflect the serious ramifications of poverty, violence, abuse, neglect, or loss in their family or community lives. Nor can any approach solve the problem of sadness in teachers who realize that their best efforts cannot alleviate suffering in the lives of their students. However, every approach can better inform teachers about productive ways to approach the daily challenge of managing the behavior of young students.

Some school districts have adopted one formal approach to classroom discipline, whereas others have offered teachers in-service training in various techniques. All teachers, whatever the philosophy of their school districts, benefit from a variety of perspectives on behavior and an eclectic approach to classroom interventions. Effective classroom management always requires complex decision making, personal caring, and sensible application of meaningful theory in the context of specific events.

ACTIVITY AND DISCUSSION

Although you have not yet read about the different methods of approaching classroom behavior, you already have some definite ideas about the best ways to approach discipline in the classroom. Take a few minutes now to jot down what you would consider your basic beliefs about the best ways to promote positive classroom behavior.

After you have read the section entitled Models of Thinking About Behavior, review the techniques you described. Which models do you seem to have included in your ideas? Why do you think you included them? Would you add more ideas from other models now? Why or why not? Discuss your opinions in a small group.

Looking at Models of Classroom Intervention

This section is an overview of specific models that have been created to help teachers approach behavior difficulties in a systematic and effective way. It is not intended to provide enough information on any one specific model to enable you to become competent in direct implementation. Such competence requires in-depth study and comprehensive training. Rather, this chapter discusses five specific models that have a great deal of information to offer teachers who take an eclectic approach to applying models in their classrooms. Such teachers can use a combination of information from models, knowledge gained from their experiences, advice from respected peers, and training provided through their school districts to support a positive philosophy of classroom management and discipline.

Careful reflection on the five models can inform the perspectives of teachers who are working hard to balance all the knowledge, skills, and sensitivities that are required for successful management of groups of children. Teachers who want to know more about specific models should read the theorists who created them and review texts that discuss them in greater detail.

Behaviorism, Skinner, and Neo-Skinnerians

A great deal of school practice is based on the reinforcement theory most commonly associated with work of psychologist B. F. Skinner (see Chapter 4). Reinforcement theories continue to be developed by "neo-Skinnerians," who have refined methods of applying behavior theory to classroom practice (Charles and Senter 1995). Whenever teachers respond to student behavior with reward or punishment, they are applying Skinner's theory that all behavior is reinforced and shaped by consequences. Such punishments as school suspension, paddling, detention, and loss of privileges are widely used in schools. Also widely evident are reward systems such as special privileges, trips and parties, edibles, good report cards, praise, stickers, and tokens.

Every teacher uses reward and punishment at times. However, all teachers must be aware that both rewards and punishments have drawbacks. There is no substitute for the genuine reinforcements inherent in an active and interesting curriculum that fosters feelings of personal competence. Aside from curriculum, the strongest reinforcement for positive behavior in many children is the presence, proximity, and personal attention of a dedicated caring teacher (see Exhibit 7-1). The effectiveness of all consequences depends on the quality of human relationships that govern them.

Assertive Discipline

The concept of assertive discipline was developed to strengthen the power of teachers to request and gain appropriate behaviors from students (Canter and Canter 1992). Assertive discipline also suggests a way to construct logical and consistent consequences for misbehavior. Teachers are encouraged to exercise their power of authority by insisting on cooperation and following through with a well-organized system of behavioral consequences. The continuing work of Lee Canter and Marlene Canter, creators of the concept of assertive discipline, has sparked attention and controversy. Although not all educators agree with assertive discipline techniques, their widespread adoption in school districts is an indication of the need of American teachers for practical skills in organized behavior management (Charles 1992).

EXHIBIT 7-1   ### Reinforcement Theory in the Classroom

Mr. Matthews is in his second year of teaching fifth grade in a large elementary school. During his first year he experienced several serious problems with classroom behavior. Although he received a satisfactory rating at the end of his first year, his principal expressed some concerns about his ability to control his class. Mr. Matthews plans this year to apply systematic thinking and planning to a design of classroom management.

Mr. Matthews has selected the five theories discussed in this chapter for his focus. First he intends to implement the reinforcement theories of B. F. Skinner and the neo-Skinnerians. This is what Mr. Matthews intends to do:

- He will try to build as many positive reinforcements as possible into his regular classroom environment. He will concentrate on providing:

  1. Consistent praise for following directions

  2. Private "motivational moments" for as many students as possible during independent seatwork

  3. One weekly behavior goal that will be rewarded on Fridays with pizza, movies, or free time

- Mr. Matthews believes that he actually reinforced negative behaviors last year by being overly attentive to them. He will avoid focusing inordinate time and attention on the few children who are consistently misbehaving this year by:

  1. Correcting this behavior privately when possible

  2. Circulating regularly to be close enough to students for quick, quiet corrections

  3. Ignoring small distractions caused by less serious misbehavior

Assertive discipline is based on the conceptualization of the teacher as final authority in the classroom. Many children in America today do not give automatic respect to adults who are authority figures. Teachers are encouraged to be clear in articulating their expectations, firm in setting behavioral limits, and organized in establishing an order of consequences. One specific implementation of assertive discipline is the posting of written rules and a graduated schedule of consequences in the classroom (Charles 1992). Canter and Canter (1992) suggest that teachers stress positive discipline at the beginning of the year by designating and articulating appropriate student behaviors, informing students of expectations and consequences, informing parents of rules and consequences, and implementing rules and consequences immediately. They further suggest appropriate rewards and methods of dealing with persistent and serious behavior problems.

Assertive discipline is based on reinforcement theory and has helped many educators to think more clearly about their communication of expectations to their students. Questions about assertive discipline center on the value of contrived reinforcement to long-range intrinsic development of self-control and responsible personal behavior (Charles 1992). The relationship of student behavior to the quality of the real learning environment, and the quality of interpersonal relationships between students and teachers, must be considered, along with the value of structured rules and consequences (see Exhibit 7-2).

Haim Ginott

The model posed by psychologist Haim Ginott (1972) continues to influence classroom teachers. Ginott focuses on the emotions of children and moves the focus of behavioral control from overt contingency to quality of human interaction. Ginott encourages teachers to accept and acknowledge the feelings of children in difficult situations and to avoid negative (and often unfounded) diagnoses and labeling of underlying problems. Ginott discourages inappropriate teacher behaviors such as rudeness, overreaction, cruelty, and intimidation of children. He further suggests that self-discipline in teachers, who can model the best behaviors for children, is the most important ingredient in classroom control. Teachers who implement the Ginott model use clear communication—sane messages that they expect change—to invite cooperation as they confront unacceptable behavior.

Ginott presents educators with a vision of humane interactions that depends on the maturity, self-control, and encouraging

EXHIBIT 7-2   ***Assertive Discipline in the Classroom***

Mr. Matthews has seen improvements in his class through his application of reinforcement theory. However, he has encountered continuing problems in two areas. His students are running in the halls when they go to lunch, and they are pushing one another in the bus line. There have been two injuries serious enough to involve the school nurse this year.

Mr. Matthews has decided to use the technique of assertive discipline in the following ways:

1. He has posted a Do and Don't list in his classroom. (*Do* walk quietly down the hall, *don't* run down the hall, *do* wait quietly for the bus in order of arrival at the line, *don't* push and shove each other.)

2. He has explained the rules about running and shoving to his students several times and has established a sequence of consequences:

   • Warning.

   • Stay in at lunch.

   • Lose one Friday pizza, movie, or free time.

   • Meeting with parents.

3. He has sent a letter to the homes of each student explaining the rules and consequences and asking families to speak with their children in support of the rules.

dispositions of teachers. He encourages teachers to remember that the child is immature and to focus on the situation more than on potential character deficiencies in students. Ginott views the teacher's ability to guide and redirect behavior as central to the protection of the self-esteem of children (see Exhibit 7-3). He wisely counsels teachers to focus on "little victories" rather than on counterproductive negative thinking about ongoing behavior challenges in the classroom (Ginott 1972; Charles 1992).

Rudolph Dreikurs

Dreikurs (1968) theorizes that children deserve democratic consideration in the classroom. He suggests that teachers build democratic environments by giving children freedom of choice, making sure that they understand consequences, and helping them to see the ways in which poor behavioral choices limit their freedom (see Exhibit 7-4, page 183). Dreikurs encourages teachers to set limits in a positive accepting atmosphere. Although teachers have the responsibility to set limits until children acquire sufficient discipline, they also have to

---

EXHIBIT 7-3   ***Ginott's Theory in the Classroom***

Mr. Matthews has seen real improvement in his classroom management. The principal and bus monitors have complimented his class on positive changes in behavior. However, Mr. Matthews wants to protect the warmth of the interpersonal relationships he has tried to build with his students. He has noticed that some children have responded to the posted rules and consequences with resentment or more withdrawn behavior. Mr. Matthews has decided to implement the following ideas from Ginott:

- Rather than simply give the warning listed on his posted rules, he gives a sane message ("Jane, I really think you can concentrate on remembering to walk the rest of the way down the hall. Just think of trying to slow those feet down—why not look at the pictures on the wall as you pass by? This is a warning, but I know you'll improve.")

- He monitors his tendency to get angry quickly and raise his voice. To do this Mr. Matthews makes a real effort to relax and to demonstrate understanding when he corrects behavior. ("It is hot in here, isn't it? You are tired and you want to get home. But I saw the beginning of a push, and I do not want to see any more. Let's all relax and be patient.")

- He actively reminds himself to focus on situations rather than assumptions based on background or past behavior. To do this he makes a habit of never referring to past misbehavior when giving a warning and of maintaining an even tone when speaking to every student in the class.

---

create an environment in which children become more self-sufficient and responsible for their behavior. To this end Dreikurs suggests that children participate in setting class rules and consequences.

Dreikurs also provides insights into why children misbehave. He theorizes that children have mistaken goals or beliefs that attention is best gained through disruption or disobedience. The four kinds of mistaken goals Dreikurs identifies are:

Attention getting, sought because adequate recognition of self is not perceived

Power seeking, stemming from a belief that disruption is the only way to get attention from adults

Revenge seeking, or making up for personal hurts and seeking personal significance by hurting others

Displaying inadequacy, or exhibiting helpless withdrawal from meaningful effort in the classroom (Charles 1992).

Dreikurs suggests that teachers attempt to discern the mistaken goal and question the student about it ("You felt hurt when you were not chosen for the spelling team this morning. Is that why you wanted to hurt Kim by calling her a fool?"). Then the teacher can help to

---

EXHIBIT 7-4   ***Dreikurs' Theory in the Classroom***

Helping Children Learn

Mr. Matthews has definitely achieved better class discipline this year. However, some students in his class have engaged in persistent misbehavior. Mr. Matthews wants to help those children to improve, and he wants all the students to develop a greater sense of responsibility for themselves and others. He recognizes that Dreikurs viewed discipline as an ongoing process during which students continually gain skills in self-direction, and has thus taken the initiative to implement the following:

- When a child in his class demonstrates a disruptive behavior, Mr. Matthews tries to articulate the misguided belief that may be causing the problem. For example, a boy who has had difficulty in math all year persistently antagonizes the girl next to him during math period each day. The next time he does so, Mr. Matthews says, "Maybe you are trying to annoy her because she enjoys doing math and you have been having some problems with math this year? I'd like to give you special help today. Please begin your problems now, and I will come back in a few minutes to work with you."

- Some children who have been more difficult to handle have also been children who are not well accepted by the rest of the class. Mr. Matthews has noticed that these children are sometimes excluded from games and activities. He tells the class that he wants everyone to help him identify one class rule about including all students in activities. The class decides the rule should be, Everyone who wants to play a game should be allowed to join the group. Mr. Matthews has also been monitoring his efforts to give equal opportunities to all the children.

- He has included more "self-checking" in his learning activities. At the end of the week students rate their behavior for the week and write a small reflection to place in their weekly work folders.

---

redirect the behavior so the student can gain greater proximity to the real goal ("Why not go back over to the spelling area and practice the words in Section Four. You have another chance to make the team next week.") Dreikurs suggests that consequences be matched to misbehavior (students who do not finish work in a reasonable amount of time come in early from lunch recess). He firmly believes that teachers should be required to display all behaviors requested of their students (Charles 1992).

William Glasser

Psychiatrist William Glasser is a theorist who changed his mind in the course of his work. He describes his original theory in the book *Reality Therapy: A New Approach to Psychiatry* (1965). Glasser suggests that significant personal and behavioral change can be created by dealing with current realities rather than past experiences. He extends this concept of therapy to students in schools by suggesting that personal circumstances do not excuse students from meeting behavioral standards. Rather than focus on disadvantaged or disabling circumstances in the lives of their students, teachers should hold all students accountable for appropriate behavior and successful learning in schools.

Intrinsic to Glasser's original theory is the belief that schools offer a substantial opportunity to any student with sufficient self-control. However, by 1985 he had shifted from a focus on student behavior to a critical look at the instructional practices of the school. Glasser contends that students need the opportunity to engage in meaningful and interesting learning activities that sustain their sense of motivation. He decided that a school-based focus on fragments of learning to be retained for standardized tests causes frustration and resistance in students. Furthermore, Glasser now believes that teachers who use their power and authority to impose this fragmented standardized curriculum fall into a trap of adversarial relationships with students. He argues that discipline programs must be connected to satisfying schoolwork of appropriate depth and quality for individual students (see Exhibit 7-5). Glasser contends that students who

---

EXHIBIT 7-5   ### Implementing Glasser's Theory in the Classroom

Mr. Matthews is pleased with the success his students have had in taking more responsibility for their behavior. However, he has become increasingly aware of the frustrating nature of some of the standardized curriculum in the classroom. There is no doubt in his mind that some of the restlessness and disruptiveness during the day is related to the dissatisfaction of his students with the work they are required to do. In setting his goals for the rest of this year, and looking ahead to next year, Mr. Matthews is turning his attention to his curriculum as the driving force in his classroom. He plans to implement Glasser's theory in the following ways:

- He is designing a choice of monthly projects. Students can choose a project at the beginning of the month and will have time each week to connect daily learning activities to project design. In one month, for example, Mr. Matthews will be covering condensation in science, measurements in mathematics, and biographies of inventors in language arts. Each student can choose one of the following projects: writing a fictional account of an inventor who figures out a way to keep soil from becoming too dry in a season of drought, designing a model of a laboratory in which condensation experiments are being conducted, or designing a game that requires accurate measurement of at least ten items in the classroom using creative units of measure.

- He plans to ask students to maintain learning journals, in which they note the most interesting things they did before leaving school each day. By reviewing the journals Mr. Matthews hopes to better meet the students' need for satisfying school activities by incorporating in his lessons the areas of interest they mention in their journals.

meet their personal needs by completing quality classroom work do not require coercion in the form of punishment (Charles 1992).

Summing Up the Models

Each model explained in this chapter helped the hypothetical Mr. Matthews to build comprehensive improvements into the structure of his classroom management. When used concurrently in different ways, the models add multiple points of focus and depth of teacher reflection and self-improvement. These five models provide teachers with methods for structuring their classroom-learning environments (Skinner), clarifying important rules and consequences for themselves and their students (Canter), building a humane focus on the feelings of students in specific problem situations (Ginott), forming a more democratic environment in which students begin to take more responsibility for their own actions (Dreikurs), and creating more avenues for students to engage in meaningful and satisfying classroom-learning activities (Glasser). All teachers can continue to think about and implement these ideas in the careerlong process of building positive opportunities for growth in student-centered classrooms.

QUESTIONS TO CONSIDER

1. Experienced classroom teachers sometimes express the feeling that so-called expert advice is not relevant or practical in real classrooms. Why do you think this is the case? How do you plan to continually apply the methods of theorists to your classroom practice?

2. Do you think any of the five models were used in the schools you attended as a child? Which ones do you remember? Did you like or dislike the models as they were implemented by your teachers?

3. Remember to think about the question posed before you read about the models. Which models were part of your original ideas? Which would you add now, and why?

IDEAS FOR POSITIVE MANAGEMENT

The models offer specific suggestions for approaches to classroom discipline and management. There are other practical ideas that are useful to teachers as they plan their approach to each school year. Note that most of these ideas require planning as intensive as that connected to instruction. Management and discipline need to be carefully conceptualized and effectively built into every aspect of classroom life.

Prevention Is the Key

Chapter 6 stresses that prevention of problems is crucial in the classroom. How is prevention best conceptualized? Some of you may be old enough to recall the early days of television, when cowboy shows were prevalent and popular. Viewers would watch riders gallop after one another in a chase scene. At one point in the chase a group of cowboys (usually the good guys) would rein in their horses and stop to think. The leader would try to analyze the route of the riders they were chasing and then would say, "Let's head 'em off at the pass." By reaching the intersection first, they gained the advantage over their opponents.

Although teachers should not view students as their opponents, they can benefit a great deal from the "head them off at the pass" philosophy of management. Most decisions about prevention must be based on experience. All problems cannot be prevented, but once they occur they provide a rich opportunity for teacher reflection. Every problem should be analyzed to determine whether it was caused by the design of the room, placement of students, daily routine, or method of instruction. Even more important, however, is a carefully designed approach to the various ways a teacher will be required to manage the classroom during the school year.

Savage (1991) identifies an entire domain of planning for management and discipline (see Exhibit 7-6). Teachers who want to prevent a wide range of problems can plan their approach to each dimension of classroom interaction:

Leadership and authority

Motivation of students

Physical environment of the classroom

Daily time management

Daily lesson management

Group dynamics and patterns of cooperation

Responses (unobtrusive) promoting self-control

Responses (obtrusive) that restructure the learning environment

Plans to deal with persistent misbehavior

Plans to deal with serious misbehavior

By reviewing Savage's list, teachers can make a comprehensive preventative plan. How do they view their authority, and how will they present it to their students? How will they motivate their students to engage in meaningful learning activities? How will the day be designed and lessons structured? When will students work in groups, and how will the responsibilities of groups be articulated? What consistent responses of a less obtrusive nature will be made to small distractions or disturbances? What decisions of a more obtrusive nature will be made when behavior problems seem to be related to the classroom environment? How will persistent misbehavior be approached? What methods will be used to work with students exhibiting serious misbehavior? Making preliminary decisions ahead of time helps teachers approach the challenges of daily life with more confidence.

Keep in mind that persistent and serious misbehavior is a relatively small part of the total preventative plan of the efficient teacher. In many cases effective prevention can help the teacher to avoid the occurrence of misbehavior. Charles writes, "In classroom discipline, an ounce of prevention is worth much more than a pound of cure, for once misbehavior has occurred even the best corrective techniques (despite what the various proponent-experts might say) disrupt teaching and take their toll on feelings and relationships" (1992: 29).

Bellon, Bellon, and Blank (1992) point out that a lack of prevention can result in behavior problems that consume large amounts of teaching and learning time. Every disruption or interruption has the potential to get the entire group off track, to inspire other students to experiment with the misbehavior gaining all the attention, and to interrupt students' work and trains of thought. Disruptions, warnings, and assignments of punishment can also result in open confrontation. Once a student becomes openly defiant, the teacher has inevitably lost a considerable amount of control. The student who loses face in front of peers will remain humiliated and angry; the teacher who loses face in front of students is going to face more challenges to her or his authority. Every act of planning and prevention that helps the teacher avoid angry confrontation is worth all the time and trouble involved.

EXHIBIT 7-6   **Planning Management and Discipline**

Ms. Valeria has recently transferred to a new school where she will be teaching sixth grade for the first time. She plans to use this opportunity to design a comprehensive approach to management. Using the domains identified by Savage (1991), Ms. Valeria plans to implement the following:

Leadership and authority	She is going to be firm, direct, and consistent in building the confidence of students in her competence as the classroom authority.
Motivation of students	Ms. Valeria will focus on developmentally appropriate practice and motivate her students through intrinsically interesting activities and projects. She will balance her authority against the many personal choices her students will be able to make during classwork.
Physical environment of the classroom	Ms. Valeria is going to arrange desks into groups of four and place materials in different centers around the room. She will post the four most important rules in the front of the room and place a small handbook of class expectations in the personal "mailbox" of each student.
Daily time management	Ms. Valeria has familiarized herself with the daily schedule and has identified several potentially distracting events in the day. Some of her students are in the band, several are in a special tutoring program, and the bus-riding children leave twenty minutes early three times a week. Ms. Valeria has decided on a routine that includes an orderly opening each day and a message system for students who have been absent for all or part of the day.
Daily lesson management	Ms. Valeria will focus on a balance of active and quiet lessons, as well as on independent projects. She will do most of her direct instruction at the beginning of lessons.
Group dynamics and patterns of cooperation	Ms. Valeria will assign her students to working groups throughout the year and promote cooperative group work on projects as well. She will emphasize for students democratic participation and responsibility to themselves and others throughout the year.
Responses (unobtrusive) promoting self-control	Ms. Valeria has developed stern glances that are effective in helping distracted students to regain their focus during lessons. She has decided to develop a method of briefly reminding students to stay on task as she teaches.
Responses (obtrusive) that restructure the learning environment	Ms. Valeria knows that she has been too easily frustrated by misbehavior in the past. She has decided to think about difficulties this year in the following ways: What is the most important problem? Can I control it by changing the environment? Can I make my lessons more interesting or active? Can I talk this problem over with the student later?

(continued)

EXHIBIT 7-6   ***Planning Management and Discipline*** (*continued*)

Plans to deal with persistent misbehavior	At the beginning of the year Ms. Valeria is going to identify consequences for specific misbehavior with which she has had difficulty in the past. She is also going to do the following when specific children persistently misbehave: (1) meet with the child individually to discuss the problem, (2) make a plan for improvement, (3) create a timeline for improvement, (4) involve the family if necessary and possible, and (5) involve school support staff if necessary and possible.
Plans to deal with serious misbehavior	Ms. Valeria has already spoken to the principal and part-time guidance counselor about services available for children and families. She has prepared a system for observing and documenting serious problems and has identified several methods of working with children and families on specific behavior modification programs.

STARTING THE SCHOOL YEAR

Many experts agree that the start of every school year is critical (Canter and Canter 1992; Wong and Wong 1991; Bellon, Bellon, and Blank 1992). Children form lasting impressions and are highly attentive to the initial talk and actions of teachers. Teachers must greet students warmly and set the stage for satisfying projects and strong interpersonal relationships in the classroom. They should also explain their rules and why they exist. Other than the non-negotiable rules that are central to order and safety, the students can participate legitimately and meaningfully creating rules, routines, and relationships in the classroom at the beginning of the year.

Structure and Routine Are Critical

Warm and caring teachers also need to create reasonable structure in the classroom. Children appreciate a sense of order and consistency. Some students have experienced only authoritarian classrooms and test new teachers to see what they can get away with. Teachers need to anticipate testing behavior with structure and routines, even when they are determined to create a democratic classroom environment. When children believe that they can trust their teacher to help them become disciplined and competent, they are more able to take responsibility for their behavior as the year progresses (see Exhibit 7-7).

EXHIBIT 7-7

The Gerbil Ate My Homework

Ms. Williams has taught in a child care program for several years and is beginning her first year as a third-grade teacher in a public school. She wants to demonstrate her flexibility to students at the beginning of the year, so she tells them, "Try to do your homework if you can. If it is not completed for a good reason, just give me an explanation when you come in to school." To Ms. Williams's dismay, more and more students begin to ignore homework assignments. Much of the beginning of the school day is taken up with excuses about why the work was not done. She realizes that the students are not really prepared to handle the freedom she has given them.

Now, although she is still determined to be sensitive to her students and to help them develop personal responsibility, Ms. Williams has changed the way she structures homework. The students know that it is due each day. They may have two "excused homeworks" a year, but the assignment is due the next day. Children who do not make up missed assignments must stay in from lunch on Friday to complete their work for the week. Ms. Williams has made more flexible arrangements with two children who missed long periods of school because of illness and with one child who is responsible for two younger siblings from the time he gets home from school until each evening.

Rules and Emotions

When teachers prepare and post rules at the beginning of the school year, they should attend to the emotional as well as the disciplinary aspects of what they write. The tone of those rules communicates a great deal about the climate and relationships in the classroom. Teachers should be sure that posted rules are not demeaning or unnecessarily threatening. Any visitor to the classroom should get the sense that students are respected, that the rules are democratic whenever possible, and that rules emphasize positive relationships. (Commonly used statements like "Keep your hands and feet to yourself" might better be expressed as "Be kind to one another" and "Respect your belongings and those of your classmates.")

   Most adults can remember times during childhood when adults dared them to misbehave ("Don't even try to talk without raising your hand in my classroom!") Threats can either antagonize and upset children or actually create an interest in misbehaving just to meet a challenge. Children have a right to respect and basic consideration in school. Allowances should be made for the fact that many school rules exist only to enhance the functioning of the institution or to assist the adults who work within it. Children should be told when the rules exist to help them work and to enhance their relationships ("Silence is required at the beginning of group work so I can help each group get off to a good start and have fun during the session") and should be thanked when their cooperation is necessary to help adults do their jobs well ("Thank you for waiting so patiently when Mr. Thompson came to the door to tell me about the change in the bell schedule. It is complicated to run a school this big, and I know it is sometimes hard for you to wait for the adults to complete their work").

Children should understand at the beginning of the year that the rules can be relaxed, changed, or dropped as they take more responsibility for their own learning and behavior. Dreikurs (1968) suggests that students be encouraged to take responsibility for helping each other to behave in appropriate ways. Savage (1991) suggests that one of the most important outcomes of education in a democratic society is the formation of self-control. Teachers should not be seeking the submission of children; they should be constructing an environment in which appropriate structure frees children to develop competence and self-direction.

ACTIVITY AND DISCUSSION

Mr. Nguyen has accepted a substitute-teaching position in an elementary school. His class has had three other substitutes this year, all of whom had so much difficulty that they requested other assignments. There was so much chaos during his first day that Mr. Nguyen thought carefully about whether he would return. Various children had talked, laughed, or thrown things during his lessons. One student had called him insulting names. Most children had messy desks and no organized method of writing down or completing homework. A few children were withdrawn or sullen, and one boy cried for most of the day. The teacher next door told Mr. Nguyen that the child had just been removed from the shelter where he had lived with his addicted mother and placed in foster care. Mr. Nguyen felt sad that the children had experienced so much obvious disruption and neglect in their classroom. He decided to accept the challenge and see whether he can develop and maintain an orderly learning environment for the rest of the year.

In small groups, discuss the following questions:

What should Mr. Nguyen do first?

What should his focus be during the first week?

What rules should he establish right away?

How can he win the cooperation of this class?

BEHAVIOR MUST BE TAUGHT ON A CONTINUAL BASIS

In America many adults persist in strongly discouraged habits such as cigarette smoking or speeding in cars. These negative adult behaviors take place despite intensive public policy initiatives. It is neither fair nor realistic to expect children to be able to change the way they act on a moment's notice when adults rarely have the capacity to do so. Children need teachers to support them with time and attention as they engage in the long-term process of improving their behavior. They also need to be taught alternatives to their misbehavior. Many children enter the classroom with habits or dispositions in place (last year's teacher allowed them to call out answers to questions, parents allow them to stay up late and watch TV while doing homework, care givers allow them to "talk back"). Teachers are going to have to be patient as they instruct their students in how to act in school.

The most effective ways for teachers to approach behavior are to plan behavioral instruction as part of the overall curriculum design. Assumptions like "They should know this by now" or "I shouldn't have to tell them again" are not productive. The best approach is to think through behaviors that will be necessary for the day's activities, anticipate problems that might occur, and provide explicit instruction so children know exactly what they are expected to do.

LEARNING TO OBSERVE AND ANALYZE PROBLEMS

One effective way to counteract feelings of defeat and frustration when misbehavior occurs is to develop the mindset of a researcher. Teachers who learn how to observe and analyze problems can manage their classrooms more effectively. They often also uncover facts that surprise them and help them to resolve difficulties. A "bad class" may turn out to be twenty-five reasonably cooperative children, and five students who represent five different behavioral problems. A "disruptive child" may be an excellent language arts student who becomes restless and anxious when he has to sit for long periods without the opportunity to speak. A "withdrawn student" may be shy and seated next to an antagonistic classmate. Teachers who observe and ask meaningful questions instead of making unfounded assumptions gain important insight that helps to center their classrooms on the needs of students.

Teachers who act as researchers can gather important data. Methods of data collection are anecdotal descriptions of behavior, tallies of observed behaviors that fall outside of classroom norms, time sampling of daily behaviors, and other recordings of targeted behaviors occurring on a daily basis (Jones and Jones 1990). Many teachers rightfully argue that data collection is difficult during the regular school day. However, most problems cannot be addressed until their frequency and intensity are understood.

Teachers can designate and maintain a notebook with a section for group observations, individual observations, and general anecdotal notes. If a class or individual problem emerges, teachers can designate a daily or weekly time to make notes about the problem. Teachers can keep check lists on their desks for quick tallying of behaviors during the day, and children can maintain check lists to help them to keep track of their behavior. (For example, one teacher might ask a certain child to mark a chart every time he notices himself talking to the children around him during reading period. Teacher and student could compare notes at the end of the day or week to reach a conclusion together about progress that is being made.)

Observation and systematic recording of classroom data help teachers to understand the depth of behavior problems and to identify the small victories taking place in the process of improvement (Ginott 1972). It also alerts teachers to problems that are escalating or becoming more serious. Teachers are better able to enlist the support of administrators and parents in solving problems when they have documented them in a reliable way. Children may be motivated to try to change and improve when confronted with evidence that they are causing serious problems in the classroom. Glasser (1969) suggests that teachers discuss the problems with the student, demonstrate warmth and willingness to get involved, help the student analyze the evidence and make a value judgment about the behavior, and with the student develop a plan for improvement.

Teachers who develop skills in routine observation of classroom problems should also take note of environmental conditions that may be contributing to the problem. Are problems associated with room temperature, weather, certain subjects, schedule changes, seating, group activities, or time of day? Sometimes solutions to difficulties are found after deciding to return to an original schedule, be more sensitive to student fatigue at certain times of the day, or be more flexible in assignments to groups. Once teachers have documented a problem, they can set realistic goals for individual students or the entire class. Their decisions about how to approach problems will be less subjective and strongly rooted in positive classroom interventions.

THE CHALLENGE OF COMMUNICATION

Meaningful communication is the key to successfully implementing many solutions to problems in student-centered classrooms. The emotionally charged area of school behavior is particularly dependent on verbal descriptions of existing problems and clarifying expectations for change. Teachers who realize that they will always be explaining their expectations and teaching their students specific behaviors are less likely to become frustrated and to be drawn into negative and angry verbal interactions. Teachers who yell at or continually berate their students appear insensitive and incompetent to administrators, parents, and peers. They also create tensions that are likely to continue to cause negative interactions in their classrooms.

Good Directions Are Important

Teachers often are surprised when many students have misunderstood or misinterpreted what they thought were clear directions. It is important to realize that directions need to be given several times, restated in different ways, and modeled for students. Even then, at least some students will have questions about directions as the lesson or activity continues. Teachers who make unfounded assumptions about students' level of understanding, or who refuse to repeat directions, can create or escalate behavior problems. Students (of all ages) need constant reminders of exactly what they are expected to do at any given time. Jones and Jones (1990) give the following advice:

- Give precise directions.
- Describe the quality of work desired.
- Vary the approach to directions.
- Have students paraphrase instructions.
- Be positive in accepting questions about instructions.
- Place instructions where they can be seen and referred to.

- Have students write out instructions.
- Model instructions whenever possible.

Teachers who take a friendly approach to constantly clarifying directions will avoid many communication problems in student-centered classrooms.

Class Meetings

All social groups have some interpersonal problems, and classrooms are no exception. Teachers and children together can meet at designated times to talk over difficulties or confusion about classroom expectations. Glasser (1969) suggests group discussion for problem solving and identifies three formats for meetings in the classroom:

Social problem solving—This meeting helps students discuss problems caused by living together in the school environment.

Educational diagnostic—This meeting is directly related to challenges in the process of teaching and learning in the classroom.

Open ended—This meeting enables the teacher and students to pose and discuss thought-provoking questions in examining behavior and promoting positive change.

Student-centered classrooms need to have many avenues for creative and productive dialogue. The environment of the classroom is more relaxed and inviting when teachers and students routinely converse about problems and solutions.

QUESTIONS TO CONSIDER

Think of an activity, (paper folding, dancing, writing) that requires five or more specific directions. In a small group give the directions once, and observe how many members are able to complete the activity successfully without further clarification or assistance. Then discuss the following questions: Why did some confusion exist? What tensions are created in the process of giving directions? What would be the best way to handle directions for that activity?

MISBEHAVIOR IN THE CLASSROOM

Misbehavior makes the classroom lives of teachers more stressful. The teacher who is realistic about expectations and genuinely enjoys working with students will most often overcome the natural frustration and anger that misbehavior can inspire. When students misbehave, teachers must deal with their own emotions and try to use effective discipline techniques. However, they must also reflect on whether teacher "misbehaviors" are contributing to the problem. When punishment of the student appears necessary, it should always be part of a comprehensive effort to teach or help students to impose limits on themselves (Charles 1992). It is hard to link punishment and positive intervention when misbehavior has thwarted the teaching process and upset the feelings of the teacher. However, in controlling their negative responses and directing their efforts toward the positive, teachers are the best role models for students experiencing problems in controlling angry or frustrated emotions in the classroom.

A teacher faced with misbehavior must analyze the situation as comprehensively as possible. Kauffman and colleagues (1993) suggest that the following questions can provide the basis for a fair and helpful analysis:

- What is the most positive place to begin to address the problem?

- What are my assumptions about this student?

- How would I define this misbehavior?

- What are the cognitive aspects of the problem?

- What are the emotional and interpersonal aspects of the problem?

- How can the problem be measured?

- How can changes in the behavior be measured?

- What is a reasonable goal at this time?

Naturally, a teacher cannot do all this analysis on the spot. But the well-planned preventative structure of classroom discipline should guide the teacher's immediate response. In the long run, however, more comprehensive thought and planning are of great assistance in addressing serious misbehavior.

AVOIDING "TEACHER MISBEHAVIOR"

Teachers are well justified in the natural emotional responses they have to misbehavior that interrupts their teaching, disrupts other students, thwarts their best efforts, and brings them face to face with the limitations of their high hopes for their students. It is entirely appropriate for teachers to insist on reasonable behavior and to maintain the control necessary for teaching and learning to occur (see Exhibit 7-8). However, inappropriate teacher responses to misbehavior include shouting, belittling, intentionally hurting, destroying self-esteem, and discouraging students from believing they can change and improve. Teachers who lack self-control cannot teach

EXHIBIT 7-8   ***Staying Centered***

Ms. Janus has been warned by several teachers that her third-grade class this year has a few children who constantly misbehave. She has heard comments in the teachers' lounge like, "The whole family is out of control," or "He used to be on medication, but the mother took him off," or "I think he needs to be placed somewhere else with people who can deal with problems like that." Ms. Janus has decided to make a list of three things she is *not* going to do and three things she *is* going to do.

She is not going to   1. Act toward the children as though she is anticipating problems

2. Discuss problems with other teachers in negative or unprofessional ways that would reinforce low expectations or circulate confidential information

3. Blame family background for classroom problems or make unwarranted and unqualified assumptions about personal problems or situations

She is going to   1. Explain her expectations clearly, reinforce them consistently, solve problems as quickly as possible, and act as though every day is a new day in terms of high behavioral expectations

2. Select one or two colleagues with whom she can share her problems and frustrations in professional ways. She will shape her conversations with these colleagues to solve difficulties with children rather than blame or criticize children

3. Focus on shaping the classroom environment and preparing curriculum and strategies rather than on looking outside the classroom for reasons that misbehavior exists

Ms. Janus is determined not to increase the negativity toward the students in the school and to protect her sense of responsibility for helping students to improve.

self-control, and they pose serious problems to the quality and reputation of their profession.

Teachers do not exhibit appropriate professional behavior when they refuse to reflect on their actions or when they resist preventative approaches that might help difficult students to improve. Professional educators sometimes resist their responsibility for implementing changes in environment or practice that could help students to improve their behavior. Some excuses given by teachers might be

- Nothing really works anyhow.
- Home background of students is the problem.
- Some children are emotionally disturbed.
- Individuals cannot be helped in a large group.
- Problem children should be removed.
- Behavior intervention is too much work.
- Districts are just saving money by asking regular classroom teachers to deal with difficult behavior problems. (Mongon and Hart 1989)

Sylwester (1971) identifies four ways in which teachers can actually *cause* misbehavior:

- Inadequate preparation
- Special relationships with students (positive or negative)
- Verbal abuse of children
- Unfair punishment

In addition, massive time wasting in poorly managed classrooms encourages unruly or unproductive student behavior (Charles 1992). Teachers who want to actively avoid creating or enhancing behavior problems in the classroom can reflect on the following questions:

1. Is there an inappropriate aspect of my teaching method or curriculum at this time?

2. What are my reasons for demanding or prohibiting certain student behaviors?

3. Why do certain behaviors bother me more than others?

4. Is the behavior bothering me developmentally significant (does it really matter in terms of students' growth?)

5. Should I really focus on this problem more than other problems at this time?

6. Will resolving this problem solve any other difficulty I am experiencing at this time? (Kauffman et al. 1993)

If teachers view professional development as a lifelong process and accept their own need for growth and understanding, they will approach their problems with an open mind. It is true that almost nothing of real value "works" easily or right away, but the small victories accomplished through honest effort and good intention can add up to strong solutions in the long run.

Labeling Raises Ethical Questions

A serious impediment to teacher attitude and effort is the widespread labeling of difficult students. Once a student is stigmatized by a "reputation," particularly when it is accompanied by deficit terminology in the school, change is more difficult to accomplish. Ginott (1972) states that labeling is disabling because so many teacher behaviors and responses are shaped by beliefs about the intrinsic qualities of students. Mongon and Hart (1989) suggest that, although problems would not evaporate if the use of labels ceased, the climate of human relationships in schools would improve. They further state that labels are usually inappropriate because they lack a substantive basis and collectively have no clear point of differentiation. When teachers say students are "maladjusted" or "disruptive," there is an implicit problem in the teacher's relationship with the child (Page 1991). The best way for teachers to avoid labeling is to either ask a question instead of simply labeling ("Why is Sally so disruptive in school this week?"), or start a discussion about a student from a point of strength ("Because Joe is so generous with his classmates, I am not sure why he gets into fights on the playground").

Teachers as well as students face behavioral choices in the classroom. They can choose to exhibit high standards and excellent professional behavior or to allow their frustrations to lower the quality of their interactions with students. It is possible for teachers to "misbehave" through labeling, resistance to learning and growth, or belittling and hurtful behavior toward their students. The first step toward handling misbehavior in children is to be sure that the teacher, as the responsible adult, knows how to apply skillful and ethical personal standards of professional interaction in the classroom.

ACTIVITY AND DISCUSSION

In a small group examine each of the following statements about children that might be overheard inside a school. Reword each statement by using the label to ask a question about how intervention might alleviate the problem.

1. Charles is just so difficult. His mother was an addict, and he was born a crack baby. By the end of the day he just cannot sit still.

2. Bonita is an at-risk child in my kindergarten. She cries for an hour after she gets to school and then becomes increasingly disruptive.

3. Juan is SED (socially and emotionally disturbed). He has been placed in a regular class this year and is causing that teacher so many problems that he is going to be reassigned at the end of the year.

LOOKING AT STUDENT MISBEHAVIOR

All interpersonal relationships involve some conflict, miscommunication, or misunderstanding. This is certainly going to be true in the relationships between teachers and students in the classroom. A realistic approach helps teachers to anticipate the inevitable difficulties which will arise at times, and to build and maintain a sense of positive equilibrium in their classrooms.

Misbehavior Must Be Expected

It is reasonable to expect some misbehavior or mistaken behavior from every child at one time or another. Children are in rapidly changing developmental stages; as their perceptions develop, they naturally test the world and the adults around them. Most young students have not had a great deal of experience in decision making, and they may live with adults who do not always make mature decisions. Many children are exposed to undesirable examples of behavior in the media or in real life that are beyond the control of their teachers and sometimes their parents as well.

Misbehavior Must Be Addressed

Teachers certainly must be concerned about misbehavior when it disrupts academic success, damages relationships, and underscores poor work habits and negative dispositions and feelings. However, teachers must be careful not to overreact to misbehavior, unfairly blaming themselves, parents, or the children. Misbehavior is a reality, and some approaches to it are going to be far more effective, student centered, and developmentally appropriate than others.

The first step in responding to misbehavior is to try the simplest and most obvious intervention (Kauffman et al. 1993). It can be effective to simply suggest the appropriate positive behavior, even when the student is a persistent problem. (A teacher's failure to give this a try is often an indication of a negative "special relationship." It is difficult for students to change for the better in an atmosphere charged with expectation of failure.) Every teacher should have a repertoire of simple correctives, which are always the first step in dealing with student misbehavior:

Eye contact

Nonverbal communication

Redirection of behavior

Calling on student to desist behavior

Change of activity

Teachers using simple correctives must be firm and direct but can also be warm and encouraging or use humor. They must evaluate each situation and decide the first point of intervention most likely to work without escalating the negative emotion or behavior. The atmosphere of management should not be so structured with consequences that there is no room for a more casual response to occasional student misbehavior.

When the misbehavior of an individual or group does not respond to the first line of fire, the teacher needs to maintain a level of active intervention short of punishment. Teachers can move seats, rearrange groups, or quietly contact and reprimand the student(s) involved. If the situation is tense, students can be separated to cool down, or an individual can be isolated until he or she can reestablish control (Jones and Jones 1990). If the situation has been escalating, the teacher can give a specific warning ("If I have to come over here again to break up a fight, you both will need to stay in from the playground so we can solve this problem"). Dangel and Polster (1988) suggest that teachers seeking compliance from students

- Make one request at a time.
- Be specific.
- State the request clearly.
- State the request once and then wait for compliance.
- Slowly increase the number of requests.

Considering the natural tensions and conflicts experienced by all people who try to live together, the system of classroom management should have room for resolution of problems short of overtly negative or overly controlling teacher responses. So long as a timely and reasonably smooth solution can be implemented, it is often in the best interest of teachers and students to avoid some potential conflicts and hostilities created by punitive school situations.

QUESTIONS TO CONSIDER

1. How would you respond to an experienced teacher who says, "No matter what they tell you in college, once you get into the schools you will see that the one and only thing kids really respond to is the threat of punishment"?

2. What steps do you think a teacher can take to shape a classroom environment in which punishment does not play a central role in behavior management?

LOOKING AT PUNISHMENT

Punishment is certainly an option in the overall design of classroom management, and punishment sometimes appears to be the most sensible and meaningful intervention. However, basic common sense requires all educators to reflect on the limitations of punishment. Although punishment is routinely practiced in American schools, misbehavior has continued to be a major and increasing challenge for teachers (Charles and Senter 1995). Why does widespread practice of punishment continue if the results are not convincing? Punishment is a historical response to misbehavior and is very much a part of the

American childrearing culture. Children (like their teachers before them) are most often accustomed to some forms of punishment at home and therefore expect punishment when they break rules or misbehave. Many adults believe that punishment enhances students' awareness that all actions have consequences and that inappropriate behavior can bring negative outcomes.

The use of punishment in schools is so widespread that some estimate it is used 80 percent of the time as a response to misbehavior (Bellon, Bellon, and Blank 1992). Punishment does satisfy the emotional responses of teachers to misbehavior, and it often does reestablish temporary control in the child and classroom. Good and Brophy (1987) state that punishment may be used as a last resort, because it can provide a necessary control, but also suggest that the teacher first threaten, then relate the punishment to the offense, explain the punishment to the child, remediate the behavioral problem as much as possible, and seek to be fair in all cases.

Why the suggestion that punishment be a last resort rather than a standard management technique? B. F. Skinner, the famed expert in reinforcement techniques, expressed reservations about punishment because its effectiveness also creates implicit drawbacks. Skinner theorized that any form of suppression can bring unanticipated negative repercussions and warned that malicious or unwarranted punishment caused bad feelings and desire for retaliation. It is difficult for busy teachers in demanding classroom situations to be certain that they are fair and that the appropriate punishment is always levied against the most deserving student. Punishment also carries the message that "might makes right," perhaps inadvertently communicating the message that students need to be stronger and more clever rather than cooperative and more sensible.

Other drawbacks to punishment include reduction of self-esteem or an unanticipated rise in the status of the offender in the eyes of peers. Students who have been making consistent efforts to improve but make isolated or inadvertent errors can lose heart when punished, and students who believe they have been treated unfairly can become hostile. Many violent episodes in schools began as minor incidents and were aggravated by the complications of punishment and retaliation. Another problem is that teachers who are punitive and confrontational are not the most desirable role models for students who need help in finding positive outlets for negative emotions.

Children who experience many of the difficult circumstances discussed in Chapter 2 may have already suffered so much that school-designed punishments are not deterrents to inappropriate behaviors connected to negative feelings. (In such cases genuine caring and helpful guidance are the most effective deterrents.) Perhaps most important, the interruption of the flow of instruction for the entire class and the negative energy created in punitive circumstances almost always have some adverse effect on the learning process. Students may develop increasingly negative attitudes toward schoolwork and project the blame for their failures on the punitive and negative adults around them (Englander 1986).

Making Consequences Meaningful

Although controversy over punishment continues, it remains standard practice in schools. Indeed, punishment sometimes seems appropriate and necessary to the most student centered of teachers. Children who are hurting themselves and others with repetitive behavior that is inappropriate need help in changing their damaging actions. The word *help* should guide all behavioral consequences designed to improve ways in which children act in school. But how do teachers really focus on helping the children when they need to regain control of their class (and sometimes themselves)? Teachers who experience serious problems with disruption or insubordination while in charge of large groups of children are indeed stressed. They need more than superficial advice or simple prescriptions in order to feel in control of the serious challenges they face (Tattum 1986).

The first step to creating meaningful consequences is to recognize the powerful emotions that can arise when children misbehave. Teachers may be angry—indeed, *furious*—when thwarted or defied in the classroom. It is difficult to remain calm when lessons dissolve, but it is important to try to do so. Teachers should respond decisively to misbehavior and exert control over the time and place that they deal with it. Consequences should relate directly to the building of student competencies ("You need to listen to my directions so you can complete assignments with success") rather than to character building ("You need to develop politeness and good manners in my classroom") (Cangelosi 1993). Consequences should be reasonable and should be based on the meaningful use of authority ("I am your teacher, and I must require you to listen when it is important to do so") rather than power ("You are going to listen to me, or you are going to regret it") (Froyen 1993). Students need assistance in understanding that behavior is a choice with consequences. Savage

(1991) suggests that teachers find the time to meet privately with students to discuss their behavior and take the following steps:

- Ask the student to describe the behavior.
- Accept no excuses for the misbehavior.
- Ask the student to make a value judgment about the behavior.
- Ask the student to identify consequences of the behavior.
- Work with the student to develop a plan.
- Implement the consequences.
- Be persistent in supporting the student in behavioral improvement.

Consequences do not have to be punishments. However, if punishment appears to be a meaningful consequence, the teacher can decide to assign extra homework, require completion of work during lunch or recess, temporarily remove classroom privileges, deny the opportunity to engage in special activities, detain after school, or telephone parents to report the circumstances of the misbehavior. However, the teacher must decide what the ultimate consequences of imposing punishment will be, both for the child and the relationship of the child to the teacher—will it be more negative than positive?

Avoiding Negative Consequences

Punishment effectively administered should make it more likely that students will choose more appropriate behavior in the future (see Exhibit 7-9). Any punishment that interferes significantly with the ability of the student to function successfully in school is questionable, if for no other reason than it does not achieve positive outcomes. Punitive teachers have more aggressive students who are less interested in learning (Bellon, Bellon, and Blank 1992). Students who become more angry and aggressive are not only less likely to progress in school but are more likely to become increasingly disruptive or violent.

Teachers should not make themselves targets for hostility by imposing punishments that allow students to blame teachers for negative events. The best interventions are those that help students reflect on their behavior and connect self-improvement to clear goals and outcomes. However, teachers who have designated class

---

EXHIBIT 7-9   *Laying Down the Law*

As a college undergraduate, Ms. Garcia decides to avoid the use of punishment in her classrooms. After graduation she obtains a position in what is considered one of the most difficult schools in her large district. She encounters behavior problems she finds shocking. Although most children are generally cooperative, some refuse to listen to directions or to obey important rules. One child runs out of the playground and into the street during recess, and another hangs her feet out of a third-floor window. Several children who are capable of finishing assignments appear to be completely unwilling to do so. They talk, laugh, distract the children around them, and ignore Ms. Garcia's attempts to encourage and motivate them.

Ms. Garcia believes in a student-centered classroom, but she also decides that some of her college courses were not substantial enough to help her. She realizes that she lacks some basic skills in managing her students and that some of her students have problems far more serious than any her professors had discussed. Ms. Garcia decides to take a much stronger approach, gain a comfortable level of control, and then focus on more democratic behavioral goals in her classroom. She creates three non-negotiable rules and consequences for her class:

- No sitting on windows or putting any part of your body out the window

- No running into the street or outside the limits of the playground

- No talking until silent seatwork is completed and checked.

If children break a rule about window, street, or playground safety, they have to stay in from recess for one day. Also, Ms. Garcia calls homes to discuss the problem and ask parents for support. If children distract others instead of doing seatwork, they receive a verbal warning and their name is placed in the "warning zone" on the chalkboard. If they heed the warning and complete their work, there are no further consequences. If they ignore the warning and persist in the behavior, they have to stay in from recess the next day to complete their work.

Ms. Garcia does have mixed feelings about using punishment, but she felt an urgent need to establish more control. Her principal, who had been quite concerned about the playground incident, is pleased with the improved behavior she observes. Also, the serious child safety issues are resolved. Ms. Garcia would like to eliminate the need for punishment by the end of the year by positively reinforcing obedience when she observes it and by helping her students to monitor their behavioral choices. She has put a stronger emphasis on cooperation and the responsibility of all the children to the group.

---

punishments must be consistent in applying them. If reasonable warnings have been made by the teacher and ignored by the student, the designated punishment should be assigned. Brophy (1985) suggests that the teacher convey sadness instead of vengeance. This sadness results from the student's failure to make the best choice and the necessity of a temporary interruption to what the teacher views as a positive relationship.

Corporal Punishment

The most extreme negative consequence in school is corporal punishment. Although corporal punishment is legal in forty-three states (it is outlawed in the other seven), and it is widely used, many educators believe that it is ineffective and leads to more misbehavior. Questions of abuse arise in regard to any violence toward children authorized by schools, particularly when corporal punishment is no longer sanctioned in prisons or institutions where young people are incarcerated (Bellon, Bellon, and Blank 1992). All teachers who are concerned about violence in school and society must recognize that corporal punishment is poor modeling of adult aggression, particularly when we know that aggression begets aggression. They must also question the ethics of punishment that satisfies the adult need for vengeance while not necessarily meeting any developmental needs of the children involved. Educators cannot justify demeaning and hurting students while failing to provide healthy alternatives to their misbehaviors (Jones and Jones 1990). Instead of using corporal punishment, Cangelosi (1993) suggests that educators think of alternatives, act on alternatives, and teach as many alternative behaviors to their students as possible. Teachers who work in districts where corporal punishment is an option can be school leaders in modeling alternatives and articulating their success.

Suspension from School

Suspension, much like corporal punishment, can satisfy the adult need for punishing students while actually failing to meet the developmental needs of children. Young students who are so out of control that they are making it impossible for their teachers and classmates to function, or who are posing real danger to themselves or others, must be restrained from causing serious harm. One effective way for many schools to deal with behavioral extremes in students is to require that they do not return until school administrators, teachers, parents, and other support professionals have had an opportunity to assess the situation and improve it.

However, children must attend school to learn and to benefit from the opportunities it offers to grow and improve. The ethics of interrupting the school attendance of children without serious justification should be questioned. Such interruptions have negative consequences and carry no assurance that they will result in improved attitudes or behaviors. Routine suspensions for infractions that do not involve serious loss of control or danger to anyone in the school should be carefully examined. Active intervention and teaching of alternative behaviors are likely to be far more helpful to students— and in the long run to all the teachers who will be working with them in the classroom.

QUESTIONS TO CONSIDER

You are a teacher in an elementary school where teachers can send students to the office for paddling. Although you are completely opposed to corporal punishment and have never written a referral, you are concerned about the situation. In what ways do you think you could be an advocate for alternative approaches to punishment? How do you think you might be able to influence your principal or other school administrators in a positive and nonthreatening way?

REWARDING APPROPRIATE BEHAVIOR

Whenever children are asked to evaluate their teachers, children almost always focus on the teachers' affective qualities. Children (and adults who recall their early school experiences) express gratitude for teachers who are patient, caring, loving, empathetic, and humorous. They also appreciate teachers who are firm, responsible, good role models, and attentive listeners (Johnson and Johnson 1990). Note that children do not cite rewards as one of the things they like most about teachers. Rewards, like punishments, are often not as meaningful to children as general, sustained, positive interactions with teachers. Nor do rewards substitute for the power of teachers who are excellent role models. Rewards and punishments share some drawbacks: lack of home-school relevance, weak relation to real improvement in schoolwork or attitude, and lack of genuine or positive effect on school relationships. Many children (and adults) have specific unhappy memories about other children who received awards for reasons that seemed unclear or unfair. Favoritism, whether real or suspected, is a real possibility in any school reward system.

Teacher-constructed consequences, whether positive or negative, are never a sure thing in the overall management of a student-centered classroom. People often assume that rewards are more effective than punishment in the classroom, but more than seventy-five published studies indicate that rewards can reduce intrinsic motivation (Jones and Jones 1990). Teachers therefore should not confuse the intrinsic motivation supported through the developmentally appropriate practice discussed in this book with the extrinsic motivation of reward systems created by schools or teachers. Such reward systems are commonplace and can play an effective role in schools, but they also can have a negative effect when inappropriately designed or used. Children should behave because of their intrinsic interest in their work and their meaningful and supportive relationships with responsible adults.

Reinforcement theory, discussed in other sections of this book, remains central to consideration of reward as well as punishment. Many educators argue that the environmental "rewards" children desire most are caring, acceptance, encouragement, and success in developing competencies. Teachers who strive to create classrooms in which these desires of children are met are creating reinforcements of the strongest kind. Children may also enjoy food, trips, small gifts, and other tangible incentives that make their lives in school more pleasant. Teachers can try to modify student behaviors for the better by identifying rewards that the children truly enjoy (a class trip to the movies, for example) and then specifying clear goals to be met before those rewards are made available. Teachers and parents can work together to observe and document the behavior of a specific student and agree on rewards to be made at home or in school. (For example, a child who completes all assignments for a week is allowed to go shopping with friends on the weekend.) When rewards are used in this way, consistency is important. Also, rewards should be shaped to help the child internalize behavioral changes that are not dependent on intrinsic rewards in the future.

Praise as Social Reinforcement

Verbal communication in the classroom can be a powerful form of positive reinforcement. Teachers can congratulate children on jobs well done, encourage them to continue doing well, and praise commendable efforts or products in the classroom. However, praise is like other forms of reward—it can be counterproductive if not used appropriately. Children should learn to assess their work and efforts so they are not always dependent on the approval of adults. (Such dependency can lead to dispositions to do only the minimum of work required by adults and only when adults will assess and reward it. Such dispositions can be evident even in college-level learners if they focus more on minimum requirements for desired grades rather than on taking personal initiative to work as hard and learn as much as possible.)

Praise should focus on competence ("You have designed that building very effectively") rather than personal qualities ("It is so nice to have someone like you in my class"). Praise is often most effective when it is in the form of encouragement ("Nice going! You have completed three assignments and should have no trouble finishing the rest") (Gartrell 1994). The following suggestions about implementing praise in the classroom (Dangel and Polster 1988) should be helpful:

- Use praise during or after desired behaviors.

- Make praise simple and sincere.

- Be sure praise describes the competency.

- Use praise to encourage future efforts.

- Praise students who have been having difficulty when they complete parts or take steps toward larger goals.

- Make praise as individualized as possible.

- Use physical proximity and praise when appropriate.

- Vary praise in tone and content.

Other Rewards or Positive Reinforcements

Many different forms of rewards can be used successfully, depending on the interests of the students and the structure of the school. Grades are a form of positive reinforcement for students who meet their academic goals. (However, grades can also provoke considerable anxiety, be a negative reinforcement, or fail to indicate all the competencies students have actually achieved.) Froyen (1993) identifies four kinds of reinforcers that can be used in classrooms:

Social reinforcers, such as approval, praise, attention, or physical proximity

Activities and privileges, such as freedom to move around the room, use of special library books, or choice of activities at certain times

Tangible rewards, such as objects, edibles, or certificates

Tokens, to be used in a "classroom economy" to purchase rewards over time

It is important to communicate clearly the ways in which rewards are earned and to give all students an equal chance to gain them. Comments like "good reports from other teachers" or "no problems in the lunchroom" may not be the best basis for reward because they do not always include reliable or observable data. Children need to know exactly what they must do ("Please walk quietly from our door to the lunchroom, and sit down in your seat"), and they must feel that it is possible to meet goals set out by the teacher. (All children can aspire to improve in a subject, but improvement for some is a small struggling step. Such steps must be included in reward systems.)

Fairness must be achieved, or rewards will become a cause of anger and resentment in the classroom. Also, children may grow tired of meeting constant contingencies or may grow frustrated because their efforts are not recognized. Teachers must be sure that all students are rewarded at times.

Thus part of good management is spontaneous reward built into the regular school week. Such a reward can be a free period, permission to talk during library, an edible treat, or a walk outside. All children (even those who have been difficult) should be able to share in these rewards, and teachers should make it clear that they are rewarding the students because they are pleasant and competent daily company. A positive atmosphere that includes some fun and rest for students can go a long way toward eliminating the need for more structured behavioral consequences—negative or positive—in the student-centered classroom.

CHAPTER SUMMARY

This chapter focused on strategies for positive management and discipline in the classroom. Behavior was viewed within the context of daily events in school, and general guidelines for positive management were discussed. The theories of Skinner, Canter, Ginott, Dreikurs, and Glasser were reviewed in terms of their potential contribution to the management strategies of teachers who have not had specific training in any one model. Prevention of problems through systematic design of management and instruction was presented as a critical educational strategy, and the beginning of the school year was described as important to overall discipline.

This chapter discussed rules, structure, and routine as necessary features that should be student centered. It stressed that behavior must be taught and that teachers must observe carefully and communicate effectively. Misbehavior was discussed as inevitable and part of the developmental process for many children. Some significant drawbacks of punishment were explored, as were effective ways to develop meaningful consequences in the classroom. Rewards were also discussed in terms of strength and weakness, and some positive uses of rewards and praise were suggested. Readers are urged to continue to center their major focus as educators on the overall quality of human relationships in schools based on thorough preparation and developmentally appropriate instruction.

PROFESSIONAL DECISION

From Theory to Practice

You are being interviewed by a panel of principals and teachers for a teaching position in a large and diverse school district. From your advance preparation you know that the district has a high rate of school suspensions and dropouts. Several of your friends opted not to apply to the school district because it is reputed to have many difficult students. You were a student teacher in the same district, and your school principal at that time advised you to "talk tough about discipline" in interviews because "that college stuff" might make you seem naïve and unprepared. You feel that your own philosophy of student-centered management is well developed and effective.

Write down your answer to the following question as posed by the interview panel:

> *Assume that you have a class of thirty-eight students, one-quarter of whom have been retained in grade at least once. Of the ten children held back a year, two have been in special classes for emotional challenges, and five were suspended from school once or more in the last two years. How will you design your overall management and prevention approach, and what role will punishment and reward have in your classroom?*

CHAPTER REFERENCES

Bellon, J. J., Bellon, E. C., & Blank, M. A. (1992). *Teaching from a research knowledge base.* New York: Merrill.

Brophy, J. (1985, Autumn). Classroom management as instruction: Socializing self-guidance in schools. *Theory into Practice, 24,* 233–240.

Cangelosi, J. S. (1993). *Classroom management strategies: Gaining and maintaining students' cooperation.* New York: Longman.

Canter, L., & Canter, M. (1992). *Assertive discipline for today's classroom.* Santa Monica: Lee Canter.

Charles, C. M. (1992). *Building classroom discipline* (4th ed.). New York: Longman.

Charles, C. M., & Senter, G. W. (1995). *Elementary classroom management* (2nd ed.). New York: Longman.

Dangel, R. F., & Polster, R. A. (1988). *Teaching child management skills.* New York: Pergaman.

Dreikurs, R. (1968). *Psychology in the classroom* (2nd ed.). New York: Harper & Row.

Dreikurs, R., Grunwald, B., & Pepper, F. (1982). *Maintaining sanity in the classroom: Classroom management techniques* (3rd ed.). New York: Harper & Row.

Englander, M. (1982). *Strategies for classroom discipline.* New York: Praeger.

Froyen, L. A. (1993). *Classroom management: The reflective teacher-leader.* New York: Macmillan.

Gartrell, D. (1994). *A guidance approach to discipline.* New York: Delmar.

Ginott, H. (1972). *Teacher and child: A book for parents and teachers.* New York: Macmillan.

Glasser, W. (1965). *Reality therapy: A new approach to psychiatry.* New York: Harper & Row.

———. (1969). *Schools without failure.* New York: Harper & Row.

———. (1985). *Control theory in the classroom.* New York: Harper & Row.

Good, T. L., & Brophy, J. E. (1987). *Looking in classrooms* (4th ed.). New York: Harper & Row.

Johnson, S. O., & Johnson, V. J. (1990). *Better discipline: A practical approach.* Springfield, IL: Charles C. Thomas.

Jones, V. F., & Jones, L. S. (1990). *Comprehensive classroom management: Motivating and managing students* (3rd ed.). Boston: Allyn & Bacon.

Kauffman, J. M., Hallahan, D. P., Mostert, M. P., Trent, S. C., & Nuttycombe, D. G. (1993). *Managing classroom behavior: A reflective case-based approach.* Boston: Allyn & Bacon.

Kounin, J. (1970). *Discipline and management in classrooms.* New York: Holt, Rinehart, and Winston.

Mongon, D., & Hart, S., with Ace, C. and Rawlings, A. (1989). *Improving classroom behavior: New directions for teachers and pupils.* New York: Teachers College Press.

Page, R. N. (1991). *Lower-track classrooms: A curricular and cultural perspective.* New York: Teachers College Press.

Savage, T. V. (1991). *Discipline for self-control.* Englewood Cliffs, NJ: Prentice-Hall.

Sylwester, R. (1971). *The elementary teacher and pupil behavior.* West Nyack, NY: Parker.

Tattum, D. P. (1986). *Management of disruptive pupil behavior in schools.* New York: Wiley.

Weber, E. (1984). *Ideas influencing early childhood education.* New York: Teachers College Press.

Wong, H. K., & Wong, R. T. (1991). *The first days of school: How to be an effective teacher.* Sunnyvale, CA: Harry K. Wong Publications.

8 ISSUES OF EMPOWERMENT IN STUDENT-CENTERED CLASSROOM MANAGEMENT

Teachers must be prepared for the challenges they will encounter throughout their careers. The implementation of student-centered classroom management requires a determined effort to create responsive and humane institutions. Teachers should be aware of empowerment as a concept that can strengthen their efforts to support student-centered management in schools that successfully engage teachers, communities, and students in the process of education. This chapter discusses the following topics:

- Exploring the concept of empowerment
- Empowering schools, families and communities
- Empowering teachers
- Student empowerment and teacher advocacy

This book provides a comprehensive conceptual framework for student-centered classroom management. It has not been designed to assure teachers that they can count on step-by-step approaches to solve their classroom discipline problems. Such empty promises belie the importance of personal interpretation of problems and application of sensible decision making in the context of real classrooms. Overly simplistic classroom suggestions also lose sight of the important fact that teachers have *relationships* with the children whose behavior they wish to influence. This book is designed to help teachers apply concepts from theory, research, and developmentally appropriate practice to a creative approach to daily classroom life.

The goal of this chapter is to strengthen the total framework of student-centered classroom management with a sense of empowerment for teachers, students, and schools. It is a bridge from strategies in management and discipline in Chapter 7 to a "can do" approach characterized by constant reflection and willingness to seek out meaningful ways of changing and improving schools (Wasserman 1989). This chapter adds sections called Try These Ideas—suggestions for teachers in the real world who are determined to empower their professional lives and the opportunities of the children in their classrooms.

EXPLORING THE CONCEPT OF EMPOWERMENT

This book has encouraged teachers to prepare realistically for student-centered classroom management. Many schools in America fall short of the ideal in practice and design. The best-prepared teachers still face the challenges of tight budgets and structural upheaval in schools. They need to be creative and innovative to implement student-centered management in schools that are struggling with many demands for change. Teachers also face the complications of supporting an American child population widely acknowledged to be experiencing serious economic, family, and educational difficulties.

Responsible educators must recognize existing problems while holding themselves accountable for addressing the problems to the best of their ability. Teachers enter their profession not only to function within it but to change and improve it during their careers. Educators concerned with classroom management need to relate the behavior problems of their students to potential ramifications of inadequate resources, inappropriate curricula or insensitive expectations for children in schools. Teachers need to stand up for their students (even when they are difficult to manage) and be advocates for humane, properly funded, and developmentally appropriate schools. They can do this by continually seeking ways to empower themselves, their students, and their schools in the process of education.

Looking at Empowerment

The concept of *empowerment* implies constant change in self and others in the process of creating student-centered education in a democratic society (Shor 1992). The change created by empowerment is fueled by a sense of freedom to make decisions, to reflect on actions, and to envision a future better than the present. Empowerment is a form of energy that can help all who work in schools to be more productive. Chapter 3 stresses the responsibility and accountability of schools to children. Empowerment, in the truest sense, is a determined willingness to embrace responsibility and commitment to equitable and excellent opportunities for all children (see Exhibit 8-1). The *power* in empowerment comes from within all who share a commitment to the schools of America.

TRY THESE IDEAS

New teachers who begin to feel discouraged by the many barriers to student-centered management in schools can try some of these ideas:

- Remain in contact with former teachers or professors who are willing to serve as mentors. Ask them for ideas, and model the attitudes that made these people impressive teachers.

- Stay attuned to the *reasons* that your students seem to get into trouble. This will help you to remain sensitive to the problems they face within schools.

- Make mental or actual written notes of the biggest problem areas for your students—lunchroom? bathroom? silence in halls? running outside? Think of ways you can empathize with them, and help them to avoid difficulties.

- Analyze your day for moments of kindness and humanity. Greet every child with warmth in the morning, have a few silent rest periods, read one joke a day, play quiet music after lunch, or read aloud for ten minutes at the most stressful point in the day.

- Try not to waste energy on problems out of your direct control. Work on empowering yourself and your students to create a positive class environment and satisfying interpersonal relationships.

EXHIBIT 8-1   *Looking at Empowerment in Schools*

Mr. Martini is a new teacher who has recently completed a fellowship sponsored by a national foundation committed to improving education in American schools. He has had the opportunity to visit schools and meet prominent scholars around the United States. He has been encouraged to become a leader and an advocate as well as an excellent teacher. In exchange for his fellowship grants, Mr. Martini has committed to three years of teaching in a large urban elementary school in one of the most impoverished areas in the United States. He has been in his fourth-grade classroom for one month and is creating an environment of student-centered management. Mr. Martini has been surprised by the number of children in his class who already have in-school or out-of-school suspensions on their informal records. He has analyzed these records and noted that almost every behavior problem relates to the following circumstances in his school:

- Forty-five children are assigned to a fourth-grade classroom that was built at the turn of the century to accommodate 15 to 20 students. Space is a constant problem.

- Children must line up in a large cafeteria and wait with their lunch tickets for twenty minutes before obtaining their food.

- Children ride thirty to sixty minutes on crowded school buses that require them to sit three across on seats built for one or two passengers.

- Children must line up in the hall to go to the bathroom twice a day. Teachers must insist on absolute silence to avoid disruption of other classes on the floor.

- Children must sit in hot crowded lunchrooms on cold or rainy days when the principal has determined that they may not use the playground.

- Children are required to practice for months for standardized tests by doing multiple dittos and worksheets.

Mr. Martini knows that he is committed to teaching and that it will take several years for him to develop the excellence of which he is capable. Because of his confidence in himself and his profession, he is somewhat surprised at the feelings of frustration which have already surfaced. He remembers that his fellowship director warned him about some initial negative reactions he might develop when confronted with the realities of teaching in a large urban public school.

Mr. Martini calls his former director to discuss some of the institutional barriers he has encountered in trying to develop student-centered management. The director is sympathetic and reminds him that empowerment was emphasized throughout his preparation. "No one promised an ideal environment or even sufficient materials. Your job is to try as hard as you can to empower yourself and your students to grow and change in the circumstances you confront. I suggest you focus on the following areas of empowerment: school, community, teacher, and student. Please feel free to call again."

Mr. Martini decides that he will call his fellowship director in a few weeks to discuss the progress he is making with his class. He also decides on three initial steps he will take to empower his work:

- He will maintain an anecdotal record of "trouble spots" in the day to further analyze the institutional challenges to student-centered classroom management.

- He will start to talk with his students about those trouble spots and help them express their difficulties and frustrations.

- He will read for ten minutes a day to his class and play five minutes of quiet music before the last period of the day.

EMPOWERING SCHOOLS

Teachers have a great deal of autonomy in their classrooms, but their work is strongly influenced by the quality and climate of the schools in which they work. Group expectations always shape the work of individuals (Charles 1992). Chapter 3 discusses ways in which the restructuring of schools in the United States may be creating more opportunities for teachers to participate in the governance of their schools. All teachers should be aware of opportunities to influence school policy and collaborate with peers to improve and empower the process of education.

Working with Administrators

As school leaders, administrators depend on the cooperation and professional skills of teachers. It is part of the contractual responsibility of teachers to follow the directives of school administrators. However, many teachers may be able to take advantage of current trends toward shared decision making inside schools. They can also accept invitations extended by administrators to participate on committees and task forces designed to improve schools. Responsible teachers should share their insights and commitments in appropriate ways with their principals whenever possible. The concept of covenant can empower schools to build responsive discipline and management policies. Teachers who want to enhance school responsiveness should signal their willingness to participate on committees concerned with school climate, curriculum, home-school relationships, and many other issues. They can make an important contribution (see Exhibit 8-2).

TRY THESE IDEAS

- Do not become overly discouraged about negative features in the environment of the school. Focus on the control you do have over personal efforts to make the school a more positive experience for your students.

- Respond quickly to invitations from principals or administrators to participate on committees. Your contribution will make a difference and will make it more likely that you will be viewed as a committed teacher.

- Try to identify and join other teachers who seem to be interested in making meaningful changes in some relevant part of policy or procedure.

- Do not hesitate to make specific positive suggestions to administrators or peers when you have the opportunity to do so and when you share responsibility for work.

- Do not discount the importance of written policies in schools. They set an important tone and are well worth your professional attention in committees.

- Have confidence in the positive effects of any seemingly small effort to empower students and teachers to develop stronger relationships in improved learning environments.

EXHIBIT 8-2   *Empowerment and Participation on Committees*

Mr. Martini is enjoying his growing relationship with his students, and is more confident in his teaching skills. At times, however, he feels a bit overwhelmed by the daily requirements of his teaching schedule. While he has been successful in his attempts to begin to implement student-centered classroom management, he is also aware of the gap between the idealism of his fellowship experience and the reality of daily life for the children and teachers in his school. He has a growing appreciation for the encouragement he had received to develop an independent sense of accountability for improving school climate and relationships.

Mr. Martini's fellowship mentors frequently discussed the responsibility of teachers to participate in school governance when possible. He responds right away when his principal sends him a personal note informing him of openings on several schoolwide committees that are part of the district's restructuring efforts. Although a few teachers have dismissed it as a waste of time, Mr. Martini decides to join the School Discipline Committee. He is pleased to find that several other, more experienced teachers in the building have already initiated the task of rewriting the school mission and discipline statement.

Mr. Martini begins to meet with those teachers once a week after school to help revise the statement. The principal attends one meeting and asks for suggestions about the statement. Mr. Martini suggests that the revisions focus on three areas:

- Removing unnecessarily antagonistic language such as "will not tolerate insubordination" and "will be removed from the premises until such time as same student can demonstrate respect and self-control"

- Placing greater emphasis on the relationship of discipline to competencies implicit in developmentally appropriate curriculum

- Focusing on the quality of relationships between children and all the adults who work within the school.

His suggestions are well received by the principal and the group. Mr. Martini works with the group all year and agrees with most of the final revisions.

EMPOWERING FAMILIES AND COMMUNITIES

Chapter 2 discusses the economic and social stress experienced by many American families. One ramification of stress may be the inability of families to meet school expectations for participation in the educational interests of children. It is difficult for teachers to feel that parents are not supporting their efforts in school or to be disappointed in a lack of parent participation in open school nights or other school events. It is also frustrating when parents do not seem to be willing to reinforce the standards of appropriate behavior set by the school.

Although interest in greater parent participation in school is widespread, Weinstein and Mingano (1993) point out that parents and teachers can be adversaries. Teachers may not feel that they have time during the busy school day to devote to parents and may suspect that some parents view them as free babysitters. Some teachers fear that parents who become more involved will criticize them or interfere with their autonomy. Parents, on the other hand, may have bad memories of their school experiences. They may be unnerved by contact with the school, particularly if they fear criticism. Some parents are reluctant to disclose serious problems, and others believe that the education of their children should be left to the experts. The difficulties may be great, but teachers must fulfill a basic obligation of schools in two ways: by making consistent efforts to communicate with families, and by supporting efforts of parents to fulfill their basic obligations to their children (Weinstein and Mignano 1993).

Teachers can empower parents through positive communications that encourage them to show continual interest in the school experiences of their children. Letters from teachers or schools at the beginning of the year that ask families to be supportive in specific ways are effective. Parents should also know the rules or guidelines that their children are expected to follow. When behavior problems occur, teachers can help parents feel more confident about reinforcing school expectations at home. If severe recurring behavior problems exist, parents can be encouraged to work closely with the school to help the child develop alternative behaviors (Kameenui and Darch 1995). Student-centered management requires teachers to keep parents and families informed and to invite them to engage in cooperative efforts to support the education of their children (see Exhibit 8-3).

Chapter 3 discusses a national trend toward parent and community involvement that is related to restructuring efforts in schools. In many districts some form of elected or appointed community-school councils are being formed to engage all school "stakeholders" in productive dialogue. Some teachers may want to be members of these councils, and many others may choose to attend open meetings or submit recommendations when appropriate. Teachers can help to inform parents about opportunities to participate on boards or in councils and encourage them to do so. All teachers should view efforts to involve families and communities in schools as an empowering opportunity to improve education for all children.

EXHIBIT 8-3   ***Empowerment and Families***

Mr. Martini starts to suspect that most parents of children in his class feel alienated from the school. His first open school night was not well attended, and several parents who came seemed nervous or antagonistic. During his fellowship Mr. Martini had the opportunity to hear panels of parents around the country discuss their feelings about schools and teachers. Many parents, regardless of ethnic background or socioeconomic status, feel that schools are not as responsive to their needs as they would like them to be. They also report that the time constraints of employment and family responsibilities make it difficult to participate in school programs and activities. In some cases parents have negative impressions of the ways in which teachers treat them and their children.

Mr. Martini asks the principal and several other teachers for their general impressions of parent involvement in the school. Each person with whom he speaks feels that there is little or no real involvement. However, the district is in the process of designing elections for home-school-community councils in each school. Mr. Martini decides to attend an upcoming open forum for parents and teachers to discuss the new councils. He also decides to adopt the idea of another teacher and write "Let's Work Together" newsletters for parents each month. These newsletters connect the children's work in the classroom with interesting ideas for the parents. Mr. Martini recently planted seeds for his windowsills in the classroom, so the first newsletter informs parents about schools in the United States that have begun community gardens on the property. Mr. Martini also focuses on the cooperative behavior required of students during the planting activity and suggests specific ways for parents to promote cooperation at home.

Mr. Martini designs a check list with the names of at least two adults who live with or are related to each of his students. He plans to telephone one adult for each child in his class during the school year to express his interest in the school, the class, and the individual children.

TRY THESE IDEAS

- Think about the ways in which the parents and families of the children in your class seem to relate to the school. Assess the situation, and formulate reasonable goals for building stronger relationships during the school year.

- Talk to colleagues about parent and community involvement. Elicit their ideas about the current situation and the potential for improvement.

- Observe what your professional peers are doing, and adopt approaches to and ideas about positive role models that seem to be working. Suggest ways to collaborate on projects concerned with parents.

- Set up some form of systematic yearlong dialogue with parents. Do not be discouraged by a lack of response or the fact that some parents are hard to contact. Newsletters are an effective place to start.

- Have a list of parents and family members and phone numbers, and plan to make at least one yearly contact of a positive nature with one parent/guardian/relative of every student.

- Inform families about your methods of student-centered classroom management. Give them ideas for using those methods at home.

- Take some part in your district's efforts to engage families and communities in the process of education.

EMPOWERING TEACHERS

Modern society expects a great deal from its schools. Teachers react with understandable frustration to expectations set by those who do not seem to understand much about daily life in the classroom. Teachers may sense a general lack of support for or understanding of the importance of their work. At times teachers may be exhausted from the demands of management and discipline in schools. Gartrell (1994) reminds us that teachers are human, they do get angry, and they need ways to adjust overly negative feelings. School restructuring at any level requires sensitivity to the feelings of teachers and a willingness to empower their personal and professional vision of what it will take to truly improve schools in America.

Putnam and Burke (1992) suggest that school dysfunction can be created by isolating teachers in their classrooms. Teachers, like their students, benefit from positive communication within supportive interpersonal relationships. They must be able to cooperate with one another to collaborate on student-centered management and learning. The Holmes Group (Putnam and Burke 1992) promoted the idea of schools as learning communities in which teachers can participate in reflection and research on practice. Teachers serve as role models for one another as well as for their students, and as such they can inspire and strengthen their colleagues.

Restructuring efforts around the country have focused on the need for communication and collaboration as a form of teacher empowerment. Universities and colleges that educate future teachers have been encouraged to work closely with schools to share responsibility for best practice in education. Teachers can become leaders by guiding student teachers, and by collaborating with university supervisors and researchers. Indeed, teachers are co-authors of a growing number of books and articles that include the voices of teachers as well as those of academics and scholars. Teachers may also find increased opportunities for leadership in schools and for participating on committees of teachers that have a direct influence on district policy. Teachers who feel strong and supported are in a far better position to support management and discipline policies that are centered on the needs of students in schools (see Exhibit 8-4).

TRY THESE IDEAS

- Build and maintain friendships with colleagues who share your positive approach to the problems in the school. Find those who generate creative ideas and participate in school initiatives, and share your ideas with them.

- Take the initiative to tell your principal about your creative ideas and projects in the classroom. Share the solutions that have alleviated problems. Principals appreciate the opportunity to work with enthusiastic teachers and are likely to provide them with empowering opportunities as they emerge.

- Take the initiative to keep guidance and support personnel informed of your interests and concerns, even if their services appear less than adequate for the needs of the school. You can help them stay sensitive to the problems of students and empower them to better meet challenges in the school.

- Be aware of newly emerging opportunities to work with colleges and universities in collaborative projects. Your willingness to participate in one activity will probably lead to other opportunities. Collaboration will empower your interest in retaining a creative approach to problems.

- Expect most opportunities for teacher collaboration in research or university initiatives to involve extra work, some of which may not be remunerated. Think through the professional benefits of working with other dedicated educators to build empowered school environments for students and teachers. The rewards can be well worth the sacrifices you make.

EXHIBIT 8-4   ***Teacher Empowerment in Schools***

Mr. Martini becomes aware that some of his colleagues are cynical about participating on school or district committees. One teacher tells him, "First of all, any suggestions you make can be taken the wrong way by your principal. This can result in lower ratings during your next supervisory evaluation. It's not worth the risk when you don't even know if there will be any real outcomes from your work. I close the door of my classroom and teach my kids. That's it." However, Mr. Martini continues his friendship with the teachers with whom he revises the school discipline policy. One becomes an informal mentor with whom Mr. Martini can share problems and ideas in confidence. Mr. Martini also works to maintain a good professional relationship with his principal and makes a point of mentioning different projects as he implements them in his classroom. The school has a part-time guidance counselor, with whom Mr. Martini maintains steady communication about a few students in his class who seem to be experiencing serious problems at home.

In the spring of his first year of teaching, Mr. Martini has the opportunity to speak with the university supervisor of the student teacher in the next classroom. The supervisor asks whether Mr. Martini would agree to participate in a three-year study of new teachers. He agrees, although he is somewhat concerned about having to fill out a long yearly questionnaire, take part in three in-depth interviews, and submit a few pages of the final report. Mr. Martini is particularly drawn to the idea of participating in the study because it concerns management and discipline problems. He wants to be sure that the study reflects his focus on student-centered management and ways in which institutional inadequacies undermine some of his efforts to help his students improve their school behavior.

STUDENT EMPOWERMENT AND TEACHER ADVOCACY

Teachers need to look beyond the four walls of their classrooms to envision social changes which could build a better environment for their students. The children of America, more than ever before, need committed and caring adults in their lives. For some children, teachers are the most consistent and caring role models. If children sense the presence of courage and determination in the adults who lead them and share their problems in schools, they may have a greater sense of hope in the present and future. Schools that build a framework of concern and support for children as they develop relevant skills and competencies are schools that are empowering children. When students are continually engaged in appropriate curriculum activities and meaningful relationships with adults, they are also developing skills in self-discipline that will empower them in the future. Student-centered classroom management helps children become adults who are confident in their abilities and able to use them to construct a stronger society.

Teachers who want to empower their students and support a better society for them can develop a personal philosophy of child advocacy. Child advocates see themselves as strong and informed enough to become responsible change agents within their daily school and social lives. Advocacy is a personal commitment to active involvement in the lives of children beyond remunerated professional responsibilities. The goal is enhancing the opportunities of those children for optimal personal growth and development (Fennimore 1989). A sense of advocacy can give teachers confidence to express their commitments openly, take advantage of opportunities to influence policy, and take personal responsibility for shaping the environments of student-centered schools (see Exhibit 8-5).

Teachers who become advocates can be proud of their reputations as dedicated professionals, even when their commitments lead them to take a position in more controversial educational issues. They may well find that advocacy is an antidote to the burn out which can affect other teachers, because they never lose sight of their own ability to affect at least small changes for the good of children. Advocacy can lead teachers to join groups and work with a wider circle of professionals and citizens to address the needs of children for care, protection, and equitable educational opportunities.

EXHIBIT 8-5

Teacher as Advocate

Mr. Martini experiences many emotions during his first year of teaching. There are days when he questions the validity of the ideals promoted during his fellowship. He wonders how many people really know what life was like in schools. But on many other days he is renewed in his excitement about being a teacher. Mr. Martini is absolutely certain that committed teachers make a tremendous difference in schools.

The fellowship director mails Mr. Martini materials about teaching throughout his first year. He becomes particularly interested in a national coalition of advocacy groups concerned with the conditions of American schools. One group is located in his city, and he contacts it for further information. Mr. Martini decided to join the group and participates in a task force on discipline policies and procedures in public education. Mr. Martini also volunteers to take responsibility for writing a newsletter article on school discipline as part of the final task force report. He finds it helpful to work outside the school with citizens from a variety of professions and backgrounds who have a specific interest in advocacy for the children.

Mr. Martini's sense of advocacy for his own students, as well as the many other students around the United States who share their challenges, has strengthened his belief in his power as an educator. He has worked hard to develop the reputation as a serious professional in his school whose primary dedication is to his students. Mr. Martini has also become more outspoken about the needs and problems of American children in his larger family and social circles. He has become better able to absorb frustrations or setbacks in his school, and has a stronger vision of himself as an excellent teacher who is going to make a lasting contribution to his profession.

TRY THESE IDEAS

- Don't be surprised at the effort it takes to stay centered on the needs of students. It is easy to become negative after you have become aware of the many barriers to true student centeredness in schools. Find the best ways to keep motivated—reading professional journals, going to professional meetings, collecting inspirational quotations about teaching, or other strategies.

- A sense of advocacy can strengthen you as you face challenges to student-centered classroom management. An important role of an advocate in education is to address problems such as funding, equity, or discriminatory discipline policies that stand in the way of the progress of children.

- Join an advocacy group that bolsters your idealism about teaching and enables you to address issues as a citizen as well as a teacher.

Your efforts to build student-centered classroom management strengthen the contribution you make to the profession of teaching. Your work may be discouraging at times, but every year you will be more skilled and confident in the classroom. Over the years you will develop a reputation as an excellent teacher because of your commitment to excellence in the curriculum and the rapport you build with your students. Look to the future, when young adults may return to your classroom to say, "You were the one who made a difference. Thank you for caring so much. I really learned to take responsibility for myself and my work in your classroom." Great teaching reaps great rewards.

CHAPTER REFERENCES

Charles, C. M. (1992). *Building classroom discipline* (4th ed.). New York: Longman.

Fennimore, B. S. (1989). *Child advocacy for early childhood educators.* New York: Teachers College Press.

Gartrell, D. (1994). *A guidance approach to discipline.* New York: Delmar.

Kameenui, E. J., & Darch, C. B. (1995). *Instructional classroom management: A proactive approach to behavior management.* New York: Longman.

Putnam, J., & Burke, J. B. (1992). *Organizing and managing classroom learning communities.* New York: McGraw-Hill.

Shor, I. (1992). *Empowering education: Critical thinking for social change.* Chicago: University of Chicago Press.

Wasserman, S. (1989). *Serious players in the primary classroom.* New York: Teachers College Press.

Weinstein, C. S., & Mignano, A. J. (1993). *Elementary classroom management: Lessons from research and practice.* New York: McGraw-Hill.

I N D E X

A

Accountability
  definition of, 36
  see also School accountability;
    Teacher accountability
Administrators, and empowerment, 219
Allington, R. L., 58
Altpeter, T. S., 165, 166
American Educational Association, 57, 59
Assertive discipline
  approach used in, 179–180
  example of, 181
Association for Childhood and Education
    International Exchange, 9
Association for Childhood Education
    International (ACEI), 57
Association for Supervision and
    Curriculum Development (ASCD), 57
At-risk label
  children of promise approach and, 18
  deficit theory of children as basis for
    term, 26
  multicultural approaches and, 19–25
  social problems and use of, 11–12
  stereotypes encountered in using, 12
Attention-deficit disorder (ADD), 165
Authentic assessment, 58–59

B

Baldwin, A. L., 86
Banks, J. A., 13, 14, 20, 21, 22, 45, 46,
    51, 156, 157
Baruth, L. G., 20
Bastian, A., 63
Behaviorism, 178–179
Bellon, E. C., 7, 9, 10, 27, 39, 40, 46, 52,
    77, 149, 151, 153, 162, 173, 174,
    175, 188, 189, 203, 205, 207
Bellon, J. J., 7, 9, 10, 27, 39, 40, 46, 52,
    77, 149, 151, 153, 162, 173, 174,
    175, 188, 189, 203, 205, 207
Bernard, B., 28, 48
Blank, M. A., 7, 9, 10, 27, 39, 40, 46, 52,
    77, 173, 174, 175, 188, 189, 203,
    205, 207
Borich, G. D., 7, 25, 78, 161
Bredekamp, S., 10, 47, 52, 53, 113
Breen, M. J., 165, 166
Brooks, J. G., 108, 109, 120, 128
Brooks, M. G., 108, 109, 120, 128
Brophy, J. E., 22, 24, 41, 50, 176, 203,
    206
Brown v. Board of Education, 30
Brueckner, M. M., 47, 62
Bruner, J., 48, 73, 76, 78, 130
Burke, J. B., 18, 224